A D V A N C E   P R A I S E   F O R

No Trespassing!

"An extraordinary and ingenious work, looking at the heroic efforts of squatters all over the world who defy the laws of 'private property' where such laws deny the right of human beings to have a place to live. *No Trespassing!* is an invaluable resource for activists everywhere, at the same time instructive and inspiring."

—Howard Zinn, author of *A People's History of the United States*

"*No Trespassing!* is not only thoughtful and thoroughly researched, it's also an exhilarating read. I learned that there are solutions to the ever more dire housing shortage— at least for those who are bold and adventurous enough to try them!"

—Barbara Ehrenreich, author of *Blood Rites*

"*No Trespassing!* is fabulous. A masterful job of making seemingly disparate struggles part of an integral whole."

—Medea Benjamin, author of *Don't Be Afraid Gringo*

"*No Trespassing!* is an informed account of a worldwide challenge to property. A squatter's manifesto is at hand."

—Charles Geisler, Professor of Rural Sociology, Cornell University

"Squatters of the world, arise! This inspiring book tells the rarely-chronicled story of your struggles. From landless peasants in Brazil to rent strikers in the Bronx, communities have resisted eviction and repression. Anders Corr, an experienced participant as well as a scholar of such movements, tells how they are organized, what makes them just, and what lessons can be learned to make them more effective."

—Jeremy Brecher, author of *Strike!*

"Anders Corr's *No Trespassing!* convinces me that committed activism, smart radical scholarship, and perceptive social thought are alive and well. A boon to squatters everywhere and to the radical tradition of non-violent direct action. A gold mine of movement histories, brimming with tactical and strategic political insights."

—James C. Scott, director, Yale University Program in Agrarian Studies; author, *Weapons of the Weak: Everyday Forms of Peasant Resistance*

No Trespassing!

S O U T H   E N D   P R E S S
C A M B R I D G E ,   M A

No Trespassing!

Squatting, Rent Strikes, and Land Struggles Worldwide

Anders Corr

SOUTH END PRESS
CAMBRIDGE, MA

Cover design by Ellen P. Shapiro
Author photo by Karen Evenson
Page design and production by the South End Press collective
Printed in the U.S.A.
First edition

Library of Congress Cataloging-in-Publication Data
Corr, Anders.
No trespassing! : squatting, rent strikes, and land struggles worldwide /
Anders Corr.
    p. cm.
    Includes index.
    ISBN 0-89608-595-3 -- ISBN 0-89608-596-1
    1. Squatter settlements. 2. Poor--Housing. 3. Rent strikes. 4. Housing policy.
5. Land use--Government policy. 6. Squatter settlements--Case studies. 7. Poor--
Housing--Case studies. 8. Rent strikes--Case studies. I. Title.
    HD7287.95.C67 1999
    333.3--dc21   98-56182
                                                      CIP

South End Press, 7 Brookline Street #1, Cambridge, MA 02139-4146
www.lbbs.org/sep/sep.htm
05 04 03 02 01 00 99   1 2 3 4 5

Table of Contents

Acknowledgments

Thanks go first to family members who helped editorially and otherwise, including Barbara Riverwoman, Judith Hurley, Michael Corr, Frank Schwartz, Patty Mullins, and Betsy Walsh. Thanks also to the Corr Clan, including Virginia Brodine, Pam Mills, Bill, Anton, Michael, Voltaire, Richard, and Barbara.

I also want to thank and credit the many activists, Quakers, students, and professors who helped write this book. Bob Barnhardt prodded me with his arguments to research underdeveloped ideas. Alan Strain, Doug Rand, and Yo Kalisher encouraged the earliest drafts. Elizabeth Stark, Maile Pickett, Danielle Blum, Angela Davis, and Elizabeth Martínez gave the book sharp but friendly feminist pokes. Gene Sharp provided bibliographic suggestions. Ton van Naerssen gave helpful comments on several drafts. Cristian toured me through dozens of squats in San Francisco.

Ted Gullickson contributed substantially to writing the material on the McKinney Act in Chapter 1; and I relied in Chapter 5 on Tracy Lingo's analysis of peasant movement growth in Chiapas.

A very special thanks to Professor Charles Geisler and my editors at South End Press: Steve Chase, Sonia Shah, and Loie Hayes. Each took an unaffiliated young person under his or her wings and reread and commented on the manuscript over half a dozen times. The remaining shortcomings are my own.

Thanks also to the reference librarians at UC Santa Cruz, UC Berkeley, and Yale; and to Amanda Wilbur, Cory Drummond, Erika Troseth, Francis Wright, Frida Stein, Garance Burke, George Jarrett, Heather Eisthen, Ilana Umansky, Jill Nagle, Joe Owens, John Berlow, Kelina Lobo, Mason Gaffney, Michael Windfuhr, Nicholas Tideman, Pat Harmon, René Poitevin, Woody Widrow, and everyone at Homes Not Jails.

Introduction

On March 2, 1998, 3,800 landless families in Brazil simultaneously occupied vacant land totaling an area over twice the size of Manhattan.[1] Their land occupation movement is the largest and most successful in the world. Since it began in 1984, the Movement of Landless Rural Workers — known by its acronym: MST — has won land for some 150,000 families.[2]

Also in 1998, but across the world in Copenhagen, Denmark, a community known as Christiania celebrated its 27th anniversary. In 1971, squatters had occupied the site, then a closed military base, and built themselves temporary homes. They successfully resisted eviction attempts by the government and now number 800 adults and 250 children.[3]

Christiania faces completely different circumstances than the Brazilian occupations. Countercultural interests motivate the Christiania squatters, while debilitating poverty and a lack of opportunity bring MST squatters together. Nobody has ever assassinated a Christiania activist, while landlords and police repeatedly use assassination and other forms of lethal force to terrorize MST activists. Christiania is a small group compared with the nearly 200,000 families associated with the MST.

Despite these important differences, Christiania and the MST share fundamental similarities. Both radically critique, by word and action, the economic structure of their societies. Both choose nonviolent direct action as their *modus operandi*. Both operate outside the law. Both have created their own systems of community organization and local governance. Both have succeeded in achieving the permanent transfer of unused land to dispossessed sectors of their societies and have established permanent sites of resistance in their respective corners of the world, despite the increasing concentration of political power and wealth. Finally, both serve as positive examples that group effort and solidarity can reap major social justice rewards – not only for land and housing movements but for any social movement that struggles for a dignified economic existence or positive political change.

Squatting, land occupations, and rent strikes are a growing phenomenon on the cusp of the 21st century. Throughout Latin America, Africa, and Asia, landless agricultural workers are organizing in groups of up to tens of thousands to occupy and plant vacant lands. Indigenous and colonized nations in both the Northern and Southern hemispheres of the globe are orchestrating land takeovers,

road blockades, and government building occupations. The homeless in most of
the world's major cities, and many of the smaller ones, are squatting vacant
houses and building shacks on abandoned land. In just as many places, the urban
poor are organizing rent strikes.

It is tempting to examine in detail direct action that involves "squatting"
resources other than land, including footpaths, air waves, the television spectrum,
and even websites. Each resource has its direct action campaigns or political agitation: the "right to roam" movement in Britain that fights the closing of footpaths; the microbroadcasting movement, nurtured initially by activists in
Berkeley, California, which squats the airwaves with homemade radio transmit-
ters; the "squatting" of rich corporations' World Wide Web domain names; and
the struggles in Congress to make media conglomerates pay for the latest un-
tamed frontier, a new television spectrum that promises massive profits.[4] But
these exciting new subjects will have to wait for other books. Here we concentrate on the main forms of land and housing direct action: squatting, rent strikes,
resistance to eviction, and land occupations.

The impoverished engage in these struggles to better their living conditions, but they also have broader aims. An equitable distribution of land and
housing, security of tenure, cultural sovereignty, self-determination, and an end
to environmental racism and degradation have all served as goals for land and
housing struggles. More often than not, landowners and government officials
stand in direct conflict with these goals, which threaten the system of landed
property from which the few garner massive benefits. Like feudal lords in the
middle ages in Europe, landowners and governments would enforce a principle
of *nulle terre sans seigneur* (no land without a lord).

Current land and housing activists follow in the footsteps of predecessors
who struggled for similar causes throughout history. During the reign of the Roman Empire at the end of the 5th century in Armorica, peasant insurgents expropriated land and created a virtually independent state. During the early 16th
century in northern France, peasants successfully battled feudal landlords and
stopped widespread eviction attempts. In the mid-17th century, the Diggers and
Levellers in England made short work of fences that landlords erected to enclose
the commons. During the Mexican Revolution of 1910, thousands of peasants
raised the cry of *Tierra y Libertad* (Land and Liberty) and gained land through
occupation. In every period of known history and in nearly every society touched
by forms of inequitable property, people have struggled for a more equitable distribution of land and shelter.

Grounds for Radical Action

Land and housing struggles form the cutting edge of an idea that seeks to transform the concept of real estate and land ownership. This book counters mainstream claims that the current distribution of land and housing is historically just and economically efficient, and points to land and housing occupations as an important facet of the decentralized yet worldwide struggle to redistribute economic resources according to a more egalitarian and efficient pattern.

To ground the central ideas of the book, the first two chapters deal with particular successful movements in particular time periods. During the summer of 1997, I acted as an observer in the San Francisco squatter organization Homes Not Jails, the subject of chapter one. I interviewed past and present participants in San Francisco, Santa Cruz, and Boston; attended meetings; and participated in late-night reconnaissance trips throughout San Francisco in search of squattable vacant buildings. Homes Not Jails allowed me full access to its files and press clippings. From these various sources, I have presented an unvarnished account of the organization and its history, both its positive and negative aspects. Homes Not Jails has succeeded in covertly housing from a dozen to 50 homeless people every night since the organization began in November 1992. Through public actions, Homes Not Jails helped to create sizeable electoral campaigns in San Francisco that garnered $100 million in city funds for affordable housing in 1996. In coalition with another group, Religious Witness with Homeless People, Homes Not Jails saved 466 units of abandoned military housing from demolition in 1998.

Concurrently with Homes Not Jails, a Honduran land and housing struggle (profiled in chapter two) faced different challenges and used different tactics, but similarly succeeded in gaining impressive concessions. In the mid-1990s, Chiquita Brands International closed several of its Honduran banana plantations and fired employees who had staged a strike. The former Chiquita workers on one plantation, Tacamiche, had no source of work or income during the strike, so they began planting food crops among the neglected and dying banana trees. In response, Chiquita thugs and police evicted the community in 1996. They beat and tear-gassed residents and bulldozed the entire Tacamiche community, including a school, a health center, three churches, and 127 houses. Through an internationally recognized struggle against Chiquita to regain homes and employment, the Tacamiches, as the residents are called, forced Chiquita and the Honduran government to allot alternate land; rebuild homes; provide funds for fish and concrete industries; and rebuild the town's infrastructure of schools, churches, and a health center.

Of Punks and Peasants

This book examines and compares the histories, tactics, and successes of land and housing movements worldwide. Many have raised eyebrows at the inclusion of diverse land and housing movements of both poor and wealthy nations under the same cover. In what way, people ask, are unemployed plantation workers in Honduras similar to punk and homeless youth in San Francisco? How can one compare the movements of middle-class rent strikers in London to the struggle of traditional farmers resisting airport expansion in Sanrizuka, Japan? What similarity exists between indigenous movements to save forest land in Brazil and urban squatters in South Africa?

Although students of social movements must remain cognizant of the various conditions and goals of campaigns in different regions of the world, potential coalition also makes an understanding of cross-cultural similarities essential. Renters, the landless and homeless, and the indigenous dispossessed have no real property and are divested of spatial control (whether they are prohibited from using a sidewalk, home, agricultural land, forest, etc.) by a society that accepts not only an unequal but an inefficient distribution of wealth. These dispossessed strata struggle against landlords, corporations, governments, and police that claim the right to decimate community, raise rents, and wage campaigns of eviction, thereby destroying neighborhoods and cultures. In their struggle for a decent standard of living, campaigns by the spatially dispossessed share deep-seated philosophies, tactics, and goals that create an international meeting of the minds.

Land and housing movements address issues beyond class and the distribution of wealth. They fight for culture and neighborhood, and their challenge to property law portends a *recuperación*, or recovery movement, to take back home and employment from the governments and corporations that are quickly monopolizing these most essential resources. Land and housing movements are infinitely diverse, yet enjoy exciting trans-global coalitions and mutual aid. The successful campaign by farmers in Larzac, France, against the expansion of an army base, for example, drew moral and material aid from the United States, Japan, Southeast Asia, and nations throughout Europe. Many more such coalitions are possible and practical. By bringing diverse movements under one cover we can more easily envision the coalition of these campaigns and their support for each other, a crucial ingredient for their individual success and potential proliferation.

Theory and Practice

Chapter three begins a comparison of land and housing struggles by detailing the theoretical and ethical arguments used by diverse movements in favor of squatting and land occupations. The chapter starts by examining the most common arguments based on need and equality. It then challenges the conservative arguments usually used to support absentee landowners against squatters. Arguments in favor of squatting provide the philosophical ammunition that squatters and rent strikers have found crucial for, and complementary to, their tactical considerations.

Chapter four, "Direct Action and the Law," explores and categorizes the legal and nonviolent steps leading to land and housing civil disobedience. It concentrates on the importance of power, detailing those movements whose attempts at legal methods of change, such as voting, litigation, or petition-signing, were frustrated and those movements that chose direct action as a way to continue building their campaigns. The chapter shows how legal inaccessibility for the poor, undemocratic political systems, and stalled legislative campaigns spark direct action, and how even laws that mandate land reform or rent control need enforcement by people power and autonomous social movements.

Unfortunately, direct action has a high price. Chapter five, "Repression, Violent Resistance, and Reform," explores the alarming repression used by governments and landlords against land and housing activists. This chapter continues tracing the trajectory of campaigns, including the ways in which squatters begin or contribute to revolutions and the attitude of revolutionary governments toward their squatter supporters. Finally, chapter five examines the tension between selling out, or cooptation, and realpolitik bargaining for reformist measures. It shows how small reforms do make positive improvements in the lives of activists and the dispossessed. The histories of various movements around the world serve to develop these themes, with special attention to Native Americans; the People's Park demonstrations in Berkeley; squatters in Mexico, Portugal, and Nicaragua in the 1970s and 1980s; and the largest rent strike in U.S. history, at the Co-op City housing development in the Bronx, 1975-76.

Chapter six brings the good news. "Tactics and Mobilization" examines successful movements to determine what made them succeed. Most importantly, it delineates the ways in which movements expand from small to mass struggles through recognizing their interconnections to, and creating coalitions with, other supportive sectors of society: ethnic groups, labor unions, academia, religious groups, anti-militarists, radical political groups, and even children. Finally, chapter six examines the psychological and propaganda effects of direct action, the tendency of successful action to proliferate (not only externally but internally), and the process of *conscientización*, or empowerment.

When I Squatted

I've never squatted an urban building for more than a few hours at a public takeover, and I've avoided the rigors of other types of outdoor squatting for the last seven years, but I began writing this book as a squatter, and I hope that squatter spirit permeates its pages.

My earliest memory of housing struggle is from the perspective of a five-year-old. My mother and I survived on welfare, and the two of us lived in a low-rent district of St. Louis. I remember my mother hurrying me down the stairs of our small apartment building to a meeting with our neighbors. The landlord, named Mr. Shady, ironically enough, wanted to evict us all on January 1 so he could remodel the building and raise the rent beyond our means.

The only memory I have of the meeting is an image of my downstairs neighbor. A Black man with an afro and a cigarette, he gestured with his fist and threatened something to the effect of, "If he tries to evict me, he'll be shady all right." Even now, I can feel my eyes widening. I felt scared at the allusion to violence, but at the same time safe. Ensconced within a group of angry neighbors packed into a small room, I felt protected, and indeed I was. On Christmas Eve, a week before the eviction, my mother threatened to break the story to the press, and the landlord surrendered. We lived in that apartment for several more years, so from early in life I witnessed the efficacy of solidarity against landlords.

The next strong influence on my understanding of land and housing movements occurred a dozen years later, at 17, when I spent a year in Nairobi as an American Field Service exchange student and met Third World squatters for the first time. Living with Kenyan families and attending a Kenyan high school exposed me to poverty and hunger more intense than I had ever witnessed or even imagined. A night watchman across the street in my wealthy neighborhood had to prepare himself daily for the cries of his four-year-old daughter, who wanted milk he could not afford. A landscape gardener in the neighborhood ate only one small sandwich a day. The little store I tended in a Kenyan mining settlement contrasted sharply with the expensive health-food stores to which I had grown accustomed in my hometown of Santa Cruz, California.

Midway through my year in Nairobi, I began searching for a way to understand these problems of hunger and poverty and my place within their structure. I read Mohandas Gandhi and the political writings of Leo Tolstoy, both of whom highlighted violence as the root problem. I saw that violence in the form of police who enforced landed property and kept my friend the landscape gardener from planting maize and beans where huge fields lay vacant and unproductive on the outskirts of Nairobi. Instead, he tried to get work as an ornamental gardener in my upscale neighborhood. I saw that violence in the form of border guards who perpetuated the poverty of my Kenyan friends by keeping them from emigrating. I began to wish for a world that did not order its agricultural land or political states through police and military force, lines of property, and international boundaries drawn on maps.

I could not, however, isolate the cause of violence outside of myself. I saw that, by using a United States passport, I tacitly participated in what I considered an injustice. In Kenya at the time, every day newspapers featured outraged headlines about apartheid in South Africa. It occurred to me that passports create a hierarchy, just as in apartheid South Africa, where whites carried passes that allowed them free access to and employment in the wealthy townships. Africans and other people of color carried passes that restricted them to the least productive, most overpopulated areas. Did the rest of the world, with its rich and poor nations and its passports, differ so much? Wealthy Europeans and North Americans could travel the world with impunity. The impoverished of the Third World, confined to their own countries and earning starvation wages, had no such luxury. I saw the world as South Africa writ large, with millions of illegal immigrants still imprisoned along with Nelson Mandela.

Driven by these sentiments and the compelling arguments of Gandhi and Tolstoy on the need for personal direct action, I wrote a letter renouncing my U.S. citizenship and returned my passport to the U.S. embassy. The American Field Service terminated my stay in Kenya a month early and expelled me from their program and the country.

Over the next several years, I embraced individual forms of activism, what the Quaker faith I practiced would call "witness." I chose acts that I felt challenged the division of land by international boundaries and landed property. I rode my bicycle from Santa Cruz to the interior of Mexico, convincing the guards at two checkpoints to allow my passage without a passport and visa. The third set of guards in Mazatlán deported me.

When I returned to Santa Cruz, I squatted in a tent on city and state lands, first for two months, then again three years later for nine months. Although I can't claim to have been in official residency at the University of California while I researched this book, the UC Santa Cruz library was a short walk from my tent, which was hidden on the outskirts of university property. Because security guards and police often caught me during my first two months of squatting, I spent a total of about 30 nights in jail.

In July 1992, I helped found the Santa Cruz Union of the Homeless, which organized a collective action that succeeded in gaining access to land. I marched with over 100 activists, homeless people, and squatters to a small plot of land owned by the state of California. With curious onlookers from a nearby mall and the media surrounding us, we unfolded tents, pounded placards for homeless rights into the ground, ate a hot meal, and, after much discussion, climbed into our sleeping bags. The occupation lasted four days, after which dozens of police arrived without notice, trampled the flowers and vegetables we had planted, loaded our political placards on a big garbage truck, and sent me and six others to jail for a couple of days.

The police abandoned the land in less than an hour, however, and in more than one way we succeeded. For five years, Food Not Bombs (a homeless activist group with chapters nationwide) served two free meals a week on the land. Where only a few trampled flowers struggled to take root in 1992, a large and flourishing guerrilla garden was developed to provide fresh vegetables for soup kitchens, welfare recipients, and food giveaways. In 1997, the brief flowering of the garden was destroyed and the land was fenced to clear a path for the chain stores Toys R Us and Circuit City.

Many in my Quaker community, as well as some friends and family, supported the takeover. But others questioned illegal takeovers on an ethical level. How could one justify taking the property of another? I found myself unable to change their minds, so I began researching the question and writing a pamphlet. I searched for political philosophers who wrote that all have an equal right to the earth and that therefore the private ownership of land is unjust. I found them, from the Gracchi in ancient Rome to Rigoberta Menchú in modern Guatemala.[5] I loved Gerard Winstanley's dedication, Thomas Spence's insolence, Herbert Spencer's logic, Leo Tolstoy's anarchist morality, Mark Twain's humor, Vinoba Bhave's insightful aphorisms, and Pablo Neruda's understated metaphors. All denounced unequal landed property, and many justified land takeovers. Finally, my research revealed to me that the actions of squatters in Kenya and homeless activists in Santa Cruz accounted for just a few of thousands of modern and inspiring land struggles and housing movements worldwide.

As the pamphlet grew into a book, my research shifted focus from the philosophical justification of squatting and occupations to the question of power. My readings provided a multitude of confusing and provisional answers to the question "How do social movements succeed?" Had I read this book before writing it and heard the many stories of powerful coalitions between grass-roots and more established groups, the Santa Cruz Union of the Homeless might have scored a more permanent success. The California Department of Transportation (Caltrans) owned the land at River and Josephine. They planned a freeway off-ramp, but it never materialized, and the land sat vacant for over a dozen years. State law SB-120 mandates that vacant Caltrans land be used to house homeless people. Had we known, we might have interested homeless service agencies in using our activism as a media springboard to lobby for the law's implementation.

Definitions

This book focuses on squatting, land occupations, and rent strikes worldwide. Each by definition raises the ire of law, for each entails the unauthorized and illegal use of land or housing. The term "land occupation" usually describes the takeover of agricultural land, a tactic widely used in Latin America, Africa, and Asia. Where I lived in Nairobi, nearly every five-foot-square piece of unused land in the city, whether construction site or road median, had a guerrilla garden growing on it.

Agricultural land occupations are sometimes called "squatting," but usually this term refers to the illegal takeover of vacant housing or urban land. As a form of shorthand, I sometimes use the word "squatting" to refer to both land occupations and urban squatting, but technically the two are separate. Because a lack of housing in the Third World has made existing houses so valuable that landlords leave very few vacant and available, urban squatting in the South usually means the illegal takeover of land, upon which squatters build shantytowns. In North America and Europe, on the other hand, squatting usually means the illegal takeover of *existing* housing, as landlords often leave a significant percentage of a city's housing stock vacant and deteriorating.

Rent strikes refer to tenants' refusal to pay rents, whether for houses or agricultural land. Unlike squatting, rent strikes can gain mass appeal in areas with few vacant houses. Squatting in the North lacks feasibility for most households since it risks too much and because enough good housing exists to shelter most people. Housing campaigns in the North struggle not so much for land as for good terms for rental agreements: how much to pay for what standard of shelter. Tenants withhold rent as a bargaining chip to force landlords to make repairs, provide services, and lower rent. Rent strikes form an important component in the repertoire of land and housing direct action since they provide a means of struggle to the already housed. Squatters generally have to accept severely damaged houses or peripheral land, but rent strikers struggle for better homes and land than they already use. Squatters and rent strikers have often supported each other because both resist eviction and because many of their arguments, tactics, and movement trajectories have similarities.

Though the categories of rent strike, squatting, and land occupation distinguish themselves relatively clearly, many land and housing movements resist easy compartmentalization. To call the Navajo and Hopi struggle against energy companies a squatter movement or land occupation would twist history. If anyone, it is the energy companies that deserve the title of "squatter," since they illegally take land owned by Native Americans. The fact that the mainstream media never refers to corporations as "squatters" or even "occupiers" reveals that the definition of the word "squatter" goes beyond the description of a strict legal or illegal status. More often than not, landless occupiers, rent strikers, and especially indigenous activists have solid legal claims to their land and housing through treaties, land reform, or rent control. They are called "squatters" more because of their supposed power-lessness than because of their legal status.

This book addresses not necessarily those who break the law, then, but those insurgent communities that resist eviction and eminent domain, such as the ongoing, now 33-year, struggle of Japanese farmers in Sanrizuka against the expansion of an airport. Indigenous takeovers and community resistance to eminent domain complete this study because they use tactics and arguments similar to other land and housing direct action, because they offer a rich history useful to current struggles, and because they are an important source of potential coalition.

Hidden Histories of Housing

The English word "squat" literally means to sit or hunch down in a temporary manner. In the former Yugoslavia, squatted housing is termed *crne gradnje*, which literally means "black housing."[6] Like "black market," the term indicates activity that must be hidden, in some sense, from authority.

The fact that governments have made squatting illegal, and that squatters take every precaution to maintain secrecy, makes any estimate of their numbers very difficult. To further compound this counting difficulty, some of those in the best position to know the extent of squatting (census counters, government aid agencies, and police) have reasons to hide the facts. Squatter settlements embarrass governments, which want to project an image of lucrative and secure investment possibilities. Large populations bent on the illegal takeover of productive assets mar this image of economic stability. Governments also cloak the existence of squatter communities from their own landless poor, who might be encouraged by squatter successes to begin additional campaigns, and from the liberals in their own government, who might use the often substandard housing conditions squatters endure as grist for social reform.

The number of rent strikes each year is also difficult to gauge. Mainstream newspapers rarely report them, and the alternative press only reports those whose participants they can contact and that last long enough to reach the next issue. In San Francisco, I almost never hear of rent strikes from the newspapers, radio, or television. With about 400,000 tenants, however, landlords evict 17,000 San Franciscans each year, according to Ted Gullickson, an organizer at the San Francisco Tenants Union. Gullickson says probably 70% of San Francisco tenants facing eviction "are making a conscious attempt to withhold rent in order to influence the landlord, usually to make repairs."[7] Despite underreporting, some of the most massive rent strike movements have gained the attention needed to register permanently in history books, including ones in Rhodesia in the 19th century, England during World War I, New York City in the 1960s, South Africa in the '80s, and Panama after the 1989 U.S. invasion.

Rural Rebels

Like the estimation of rent strike frequency, estimating the extent of land occupations for agricultural use is difficult. Nevertheless, the number of land occupations in agricultural economies is known to be extremely large. European and U.S. history include plenty of agricultural land occupations, from the Diggers in 1649 in England to dustbowl movements in depression-era America, but agricultural land occupation movements in the North declined dramatically somewhere in the middle of the 20th century with mechanized farming and the rising standard of living. Agriculture currently employs only 7% of the labor force in industrialized countries[8] and has thereby rendered production-oriented land occupations relatively uncommon. More common is resistance to eviction by foreclosure and eminent domain.

In the Third World, by contrast, agriculture employs 61% of the labor force, so that land occupations acquire the importance of Northern industrial strikes. In these instances, it is not the boss who demands profit but the landlord who demands rent who is the adversary. Latin America probably has the world's highest number of agricultural land occupations, both per capita and on an absolute basis. In the countries for which information is available (Brazil, Chile, Colombia, Honduras, Mexico, Nicaragua, Panama, Paraguay, Uruguay, and Venezuela), an astounding total of 1,175,552 separate land squats existed at one time in the 1960s, or 14% of the total holdings (individual parcels).[9] Many more land occupations take place every year that governments succeed in repressing. In his *Agrarian Revolution*, Jeffery Paige counted 463 land occupations by indigenous small farmers and agrarian wage laborers in Peru from 1955-70.[10] Probably many more squatters during that period, if they had it their way, escaped official notice. In a capitalist Nicaragua under dictator Anastasio Somoza Debayle, official statistics showed 240 land occupations from 1964-73 in the provinces of León and Chinandega alone, an average of two a month.[11]

Socialist governments face land occupations as well, especially when these governments economically stress the rural population. Regardless of their political philosophy, governments face land occupations when hungry and unemployed people have no land on which to grow crops. In 1988 and 1989, the Sandinistas in Nicaragua instituted harsh austerity measures that put 5,000 agricultural workers in León and Chinandega out of work. These workers joined 2,000 landless peasants in the area and organized some 20 land takeovers.[12]

Similarly, agricultural land occupations in the West occur most frequently in rural regions that suffer from poverty. The 1974 left-wing coup in Portugal sparked the largest popular land occupations in European history. Over 1.1 million hectares, more than 23% of Portugal's agricultural land, were occupied as part of the Carnation Revolution. Collectives farmed each occupied hectare, and the new farms provided employment for approximately 71,900 people.[13]

While not necessarily for agricultural purposes, indigenous communities in the United States, Australia, and New Zealand have used the tactic of land occupation extensively. In the United States, Native Americans have occupied land and buildings, sabotaged invasive construction, and asserted fishing rights in dozens of armed or nonviolent struggles since the 1960s. Early locations of these struggles include the Nisqually River in Washington State in 1964 and 1968 and Alcatraz Island in California in 1964 and from 1969-71.

The widely publicized second occupation of Alcatraz sparked dozens of additional occupations in the early '70s. In the most famous of these, the American Indian Movement staged an armed takeover of Wounded Knee on the Pine Ridge Reservation in South Dakota for three months in 1973. The media spectacle of firefights between U.S. marshals and a small cluster of Native Americans made the government more cautious in later confrontations, allowing the duration and success rate of occupations to grow. One Black Hills occupation in South Dakota lasted from 1973 to 1976 and another, which began in 1981, continues today. Ganienkeh in New York lasted from 1974 to 1978, and resistance at the Western Shoshone Dann Ranch in Nevada has continued unabated since 1974. Also in 1974, 10,000 Navajos and Hopis at Big Mountain began resistance to relocation, and their fight continues today. In addition to continuing resistance from the '70s and '80s, Native American activists in the '90s have resisted incursions on their land at Kanehsatake and Kahnawake in Quebec, Ipperwash Beach in Ontario,[14] and on the Golden Hill Paugussett Indian Reservation in Connecticut.

Urban Squatting

Urban squatter settlements are called "marginal housing" by many academics and government officials. But these settlements have grown profusely throughout the world to become central to the housing needs of many cities. The United Nations' *World Housing Survey 1974* summarizes a portion of its data:

> Current statistics show that squatter settlements already constitute a large proportion of the urban populations in developing countries. In Africa, squatter settlements constitute 90% of Addis Ababa, 61% of Accra, 33% of Nairobi and 50% of Monrovia. In Asia, squatter settlements form 29% of Seoul, 31% of Pusan, 67% of Calcutta, 45% of Bombay, 60% of

Ankara and 35% of Manila. In Latin America, squatter settlements form 30% of Rio de Janeiro, 50% of Recife, 60% of Bogotá, 72% of Santo Domingo, 46% of Mexico City, 40% of Lima and 42% of Caracas. Existing migration rates, especially in the less developed regions of Africa and Asia, indicate that these percentages will increase substantially.[15]

As the writers of the UN report expected, massive rural-to-urban migration in the '80s and '90s did increase the percentage of urban inhabitants that rely on illegal housing. Of the world's 5.8 billion people in 1996, the United Nations estimated 100 million were homeless and 1 billion lived in inadequate housing. These figures indicate an increase of 100 million inadequately sheltered people in the six years since the previous UN survey in 1990.[16] By the year 2010, according to the World Bank, 1.4 billion people will live without safe water and sanitation.[17] The urbanization trend continues unabated, even in Eastern Europe and the former Soviet Union. In non-aligned Yugoslavia, a major housing deficit (507,000 dwellings in 1971) forced an increasing number to choose the option of squatting. By 1972, more than 1 million of Yugoslavia's 22 million inhabitants lived in squatted houses.[18] With the break-up of that nation into small republics, the destruction of housing due to war, and the creation of massive numbers of refugees, urbanization has increased and with it the likelihood of higher squatting rates.

In other socialist countries, as well, urbanization is stimulating the growth of squatter settlements. In Cuba, rural migrants are swarming into the Havana area, where press accounts estimate that up to one in every five residents is a squatter. In a city of 2.2 million, that makes over 400,000 squatters. Fidel Castro has taken stringent measures against squatting. One thousand, six hundred squatters left Havana after regulations went into effect in 1997 that gave local authorities "the power to evict, fine and expel any 'internal migrant' not formally registered to live in the capital." Any new migrants to the capital must first obtain permission from authorities.[19]

Although on a much smaller scale than their counterparts in the Third World or former Soviet bloc, sizable populations in most large cities of North America and Europe squat in dispersed vacant housing. The largest squatter communities in Europe established themselves during the '80s in London, Amsterdam, and Berlin. But squatting pervades cities both large and small in Europe, including Hamburg, Freiburg, Zurich, Bern, Barcelona, Pamplona, Madrid, Milan, Rome, Prague, Athens, and Thessaloniki. In the United States, the largest squatter populations live in New York City and Philadelphia, with incipient squatter movements in San Francisco, Seattle, New Orleans, and Chicago.

Like their counterparts elsewhere, very few census takers in the Northern rich countries count squatted buildings, making it difficult to measure the squatter population. One exceptional study of the Netherlands in 1988, however, found 3,500 houses, 10,000 houseboats, and 21,000 barracks and caravans occupied and inhabited without permission of the authorities.[20] Caravans are groups of people who travel together in vehicles, similar to Grateful Dead followers in the United States or "new-age travelers" in England. The Dutch figures confirm the Nether-lands as having one of the highest rates of squatting per capita in Europe, along with England and Germany. London had approximately 31,000 squatters in 1987,[21] West Berlin had about 5,000 squatters occupying 180 buildings at a peak in 1982, and East Berlin had about 4,000 occupying 120 buildings in 1989.[22]

While urban areas undoubtedly offer the largest squatter populations overall, some people squat in even the smallest and least hospitable towns. In 1992, my own small corner of the world, Santa Cruz, California, had a population of only 50,000 and very few vacant houses. Even in this small, admittedly countercultural town, I personally knew more than two dozen people who were self-conscious squatters. I hear stories about squatters in the strangest of places: one guy up the road from a winery in Sonoma, California, who, to the distress of the landowner, built himself a teepee. One friend had to evict a squatter from her mother's cabin in a small New Mexico town. When I was three years old, even my mother and I squatted for a sum-mer. We lived in an abandoned farmhouse in the middle of Missouri. If my anecdotal experiences are any indication, most communities in the Northern wealthy nations probably host at the very least a few squatters per thousand residents.

As a three-year-old squatter in Missouri and a nineteen-year-old squatter in Santa Cruz, I was an archetypal isolated activist. But individuals and campaigns have succeeded in wrangling substantial gains from society even by working in relative isolation. The following pages include struggles that enforced land reform or rent control and gained land or homes without extensive connections to other groups. But at the same time, these isolated campaigns continually fall prey to re-pression, guaranteed by local and international economic systems that value in-vestment over the bare essentials of living. In the highly competitive international economic storm (otherwise known as "globalization") that is wreaking havoc at the dawn of the 21st century, governments are quickly and ruthlessly repressing land and housing movements to please international businesses all too ready to di-vert investments elsewhere.

To counter this repression, movements are building themselves ever larger. In Larzac, France, during the struggle against military base expansion in the early '70s, disparate movements joined the local farmers who faced loss of their lands. The closer that individual campaigns can come to a broad movement with exten-sive interconnections, the more they build a worldwide network of radical social movements. A well-organized worldwide coalition could make it increasingly dif-ficult for investors and international bankers to pressure local governments to take repressive measures. The goal of any worldwide coalition must be to start and strengthen local campaigns and thereby make international investment contingent on organizers' demands. Only through a strong sense of mutual aid and solidarity can movements hope to defend themselves against what may now seem like inevitable repression. Only by mobilizing and bridging differences between every possible community, both within and outside of their countries, do movements have a chance to change not only the system of land and housing but the social and economic systems more generally.

This book promotes squatting, occupations, and rent strikes as an important form of access to desperately needed land and housing. It shows that communities that struggle for better conditions, often get better conditions. Although research in Brazil by the UN Food and Agriculture Organization found that "squatters had an income almost double that of other small rural producers,"[23] squatting and rent strikes almost always provide inadequate housing with little or no security of tenure. Land occupations do not solve hunger on a long-term basis. The people who occupy land are the most desperate of the poor, people who hope that by choosing relatively unproductive land they might lessen the daily danger of eviction.

Long-term solutions to the land and housing crisis require a more permanent redistribution of wealth. Owner-occupied housing and land-to-the-tiller reforms, not squatting, are the long-term answer. Squatting is only a short-term strategy. "I always told tenants that a rent strike is only one tool and one organizing tactic in fighting against your landlord and should be viewed in that light," said Woody Widrow, a tenant organizer since the early '70s. "Too many tenants saw rent strikes as the goal. Rent strikes, squatting, and land occupations are all tools to be used in fighting for land and housing reform."[24]

For land and housing campaigns to succeed on more than a sporadic level requires building a worldwide or at least national social project with a realistic program that benefits society as a whole, a synthesis of right and left idealism that has yet to be adequately outlined after the perceived collapse of socialism. We need egalitarian economic and social systems, compassion for the neediest, a redistribution of wealth that takes historical injustice into account, and workers' control in the workplace. But we cannot afford to remain a small island of dogmatic leftists in a sea of mainstream ideas. In addition to knowing what to reject from the mainstream, we must also remain open to the possibility that we can learn some things from the London School of Economics, the editorial page of the *New York Times*, and the classical philosophers. The land and housing movements within these pages prefigure ideals that do not necessarily cleave to the left party line. These movements can achieve their goals to the extent that they and future movements grow and develop strong ties and joint programs with not only other progressive social movements, but broad sectors of mainstream society.

This book attempts to set aside the partisan political loyalties and rigid academic disciplines that color and determine the analysis of much social movement history. Instead, it presents the story of property struggle as much as possible from the perspective of the homeless or landless participant. Rather than chastising campaigns that stop struggling and "sell out" for concessions, this book notes that they achieved important goals. Rather than try to fit living, breathing, and unique campaigns into the template of an academic discipline, this book allows participants to tell their own story — each movement has a new lesson. The book attempts to be useful for readers interested in how social change develops in history, how philosophical arguments work against an inequitable distribution of land, and how squatters and rent strikers act under the pressures of repression. Perhaps most importantly, it attempts to hone the knowledge necessary for direct action by the reader.

The lessons derived from studying the movements detailed in this book relate not only to land and housing campaigns, but to movements for social justice in general. If you are thinking about organizing a campaign yourself, or if you already have, consider the following questions as you read. These questions apply even if the campaign you are considering has nothing to do with land and housing. Who will help organize the movement? How can you use the media to further your goals? Are there any laws in your favor? Which laws will be used against you, and what are the possible penalties? What existing groups will support your campaign and provide participants? What history is relevant to your goals, and is it useful to broadcast this history during the campaign?

After thinking through these questions (which are unanswerable in any definitive way, so don't think too long), plunge into the struggle and learn by doing. Direct action is admittedly a frightening process due to its unconventional nature, and there will always be those who call it counterproductive. They may be correct in particular situations, and prudence requires careful consideration of naysayer viewpoints. But when landowners and other adversaries refuse to act upon petitions, letters, demonstrations, and other mild measures; when they insist on exploitation to the point of starvation or exposure; when they repress the fair and just requests of individuals; then direct action in the form of land occupation, sqatting, and rent strikes is often the only viable choice to further social development.

"Peopleness manifests itself most dramatically when people risk their lives in struggle," writes veteran Japanese activist Muto Ichiyo.

> When the people take to the streets, fight the police, expose themselves to danger, and help each other, the people's spirit becomes visible. We have seen this in Rangoon, Seoul, Kwangju, Manila, Beijing, Bangkok, and even Tokyo. Men and women, young and old, many meeting for the first time and by chance in the tear gas fog, find each other comrades.[25]

In these instances, the most outrageous, radical, and unexpected tactics usually have the best chance of success.

CHAPTER 1

Homes Not Jails

The Secret Success of a Squatting Movement to House the Homeless

Two strangers arrived early at the Homes Not Jails meeting. One had been beaten by his spouse and was looking for a place to stay. The police had found and destroyed the other's campsite in Golden Gate Park on several occasions recently, and he was exploring alternative living arrangements. They needed housing and asked Homes Not Jails to help them squat.

Benjamin volunteered to open a vacant building on Shotwell and 22nd Street, and said I could follow. He had squatted it before, but the landlord had discovered and evicted him. Now Benjamin rented a sleazy downtown motel room, but he still had a sentimental attachment to the Shotwell place. About a week before, we had cased the building and found it still in relatively good shape: it had several sunny bedrooms, a kitchen, running water, and electricity. The building was dirty, trash-filled, and had a pink-and-white tiled dining room with matching pink walls, but a little elbow grease and paint would make it more than livable.

After a bus ride across town, we walked up to the alley door. Just as Benjamin produced his crowbar, a very large guy (smaller than Benjamin but much bigger than me) walked up to his own door just a few feet away. Benjamin thought quickly and pretended legitimacy by knocking. "Whatcha knockin for?" the neighbor asked. His eyes narrowed. "Nobody lives there."

Benjamin has broken into hundreds of buildings with Homes Not Jails and knew when to lead a tactical retreat. But he nevertheless circled the building and easily lifted his seven-foot frame over a fence and into the backyard. From my cowardly vantage point, I could see a weak flashlight beam flickering at us from a window in the second story of the flat next door. Was it the neighbor who confronted us? Did he have a gun? Undaunted, Benjamin climbed the back stairs, jimmied the door, walked out the alley, and welcomed the two homeless men into his former home. He promised to help change the lock if they stayed for a week.

Thus the vacant building on Shotwell became the most recent of half-a-dozen houses already occupied by squatters affiliated with Homes Not Jails. The building was no palace, but it served as a more safe and quiet alternative to the police harassment in Golden Gate Park and the uncomfortable, regimented conditions of the city's overburdened shelters.

Homelessness and the Growth of U.S. Squatting

Homes Not Jails began with the wave of other homeless activist groups that sprouted nationwide following the economic recession of the '80s. As a result of soaring rents, small-business failures, and massive corporate layoffs, landlords evicted thousands onto the streets. These new homeless, who were sometimes well-educated, drug- and alcohol-free, mentally stable, and, until recently, middle-class, joined the traditional homeless who more often suffered from addiction or mental problems. While the new homeless were more likely to get off the streets quickly, their proximity to homelessness (just one paycheck away, they reminded themselves) encouraged them to lend support to the homeless left behind.[1] In addition to traditional homeless advocacy, hundreds of homeless organizations that used squatting as a tactic sprouted across the nation. These included Community on the Move Homesteaders Association in the Bronx, Kensington Welfare Rights Union in Philadelphia, Mad Housers in Atlanta and Chicago, Drop-in Center in Cincinnati, Homes Not Jails in San Francisco, and similar groups in almost every major U.S. urban area. Groups in New York, Philadelphia, and Oakland successfully acquired titles to several squatted properties. In 1988, Operation Homestead in Seattle began occupying buildings and negotiating their sale to nonprofit low-income housing organizations. By 1993, it had successfully reclaimed 300 units.[2]

Like its counterparts, Homes Not Jails has enjoyed substantial victories. From its first public takeover of the building at 250 Taylor Street on Thanksgiving 1992 until the present, Homes Not Jails has fought City Hall and won, through extensive media coverage in support of affordable housing, through covertly housing homeless people in vacant buildings, and through the protection of buildings slated for demolition. This chapter details the history of Homes Not Jails (HNJ) in San Francisco and its fledgling offshoots in Santa Cruz and Boston. It asks what ethical, tactical, and visionary elements have made HNJ a success.

By opening vacant buildings like the one on Shotwell, Homes Not Jails hopes to provide at least some shelter for the growing number of San Francisco homeless. Between 1992 and 1998, available housing in San Francisco fell from a high of 6,500 vacant buildings (enough to house the city's entire homeless population) to less than 1% of the total housing stock. In 1994, estimates of San Francisco's homeless population were as high as 14,000; through 1996, the number grew by 300 per month. One hundred and fifty homeless people died on the streets of San Francisco that year. Between the last quarter of 1996 and the first quarter of 1997, the number of San Francisco homeless families doubled.[3]

Boston, where Homes Not Jails is also active, has thousands of vacant buildings that could solve the city's homeless problem. In December 1995, less than three weeks after the first HNJ Boston action, the Boston Emergency Shelter Commission counted 4,896 homeless people.[4] Many homeless advocates placed the number much higher. According to HNJ Boston, there are "thousands of residential units — largely derelict or foreclosed — which lie vacant and could be used for low-income housing or homesteading."[5]

The Power and Ethics of Media-Savvy Squatters

Homes Not Jails describes itself as an all-volunteer organization committed to housing homeless people through direct action. "It is clear to me that it is possible to house everybody in San Francisco," said Miguel Wooding, a member of HNJ and volunteer tenant counselor at the San Francisco Tenants Union. "It is clear that by pressing on the issues of abandoned, vacant, tax-default buildings, we can make housing a right to which everyone has access."[6]

With the power that public takeovers provide HNJ's media spokespeople, HNJ drives its message home to the general public. "Which Do You Believe?" questions one Homes Not Jails flyer:

1) People Who Are Homeless Should Fix Up & Live in Vacant Buildings.

2) Leave Buildings Boarded Up & Vacant; People Can Sleep Outside.

HNJ's tongue-in-cheek rhetorical question sums up its philosophy: common sense demands that vacant homes should house the homeless.

But common sense is not so common, wrote some big-name philosophers.[7] Even many homeless people, not to mention police, landlords, government figures, and members of the general public, consider squatting ethically or morally questionable. "People are scared to go open houses," said Connie Morgenstern, a

21-year-old who ran away from home in Israel at age 14 and started squatting with a gang of other Israeli kids. "Squatting is a violation of everyone's basic idea of society. Property is sacred. When you open a building, you are violating someone's property."

When I asked Jeremy Graham, who quit his office job to become a full-time homeless activist and squatter, how he would react to landlords calling him a thief, he flung the epithet right back. "For them to say that we steal their unused property, while they speculate on the rental market, is criminal. They steal when they charge us rent, as opposed to us stealing when we squat. We should not ask whether it is a crime to 'steal' a piece of property, but whether it is a crime to charge rent."

With or without government and landlord acquiescence, HNJ has three principles: nonviolence, no drugs, and consensus decision-making. These principles apply to both types of HNJ occupation: covert squats, like the one on Shotwell and 22nd, and public takeovers of symbolic buildings, when HNJ notifies the media and advocates for permanent homeless housing. This dual covert and public strategy allows HNJ to immediately provide housing for homeless people, while at the same time using the media to educate the public and pressure politicians.

In its first seven years of existence, HNJ has used covert squatting to house hundreds of homeless persons on a short-term basis in hundreds of vacant buildings, with some of the squats lasting for years at a time. "By opening squats every week, HNJ actively pursues the possibility of solving San Francisco's housing crisis," said Mara Raider, a member of Homes Not Jails who works with homeless people on a daily basis at the Coalition on Homelessness. "We are demonstrating that housing the homeless can be done cheaply, effectively, and in a more empowering manner than waiting in line at various government agencies."

While covert squatting affords HNJ members actual long-term housing, their public takeovers have come within a hair's breadth of convincing government officials to transfer legal title. Even though HNJ has thus far failed to gain title to any property, it has laid the groundwork. At every one of the 26 public takeovers that HNJ organized since 1992, members spoke to the media on homelessness, landlord neglect of vacant buildings, and the failure of government agencies to comply with laws that mandate the use of vacant government buildings as homeless shelters. This media coverage shaped public debate and gave HNJ tremendous political weight with local politicians relative to its small numbers. "We've been able to negotiate with the city in ways that other small groups can't approach," said Morgenstern. "Media coverage is good because it translates into political pull with city government. A group of ten people can make [Mayor] Willie Brown quake in his shoes."

HNJ used one of its occupations in 1995 as a media springboard for an anti-abandonment ordinance it had drafted and submitted to the San Francisco Board of Supervisors. "After the first couple of takeovers, we realized that we were not doing too well at articulating exactly what we wanted," said Ted Gullickson, who helped found HNJ and has worked with tenant groups around the country since 1973. "So we drafted the anti-abandonment ordinance as an example of what we wanted the city to do." That made HNJ one of the few groups, joked Gullickson, to write laws in the daytime and break them at night. Modeled on similar legislation in Seattle and Cleveland, the proposal would prohibit landlords from leaving buildings vacant and would allow the city to acquire vacant buildings owned by private landlords to house the homeless. The proposed law has 24 sections and covers everything from acquisition of buildings to the maximum amount of rent. Any landlord who failed to comply would face civil penalties.

Neighbors have varying attitudes towards HNJ. Some call the police when they see punks and obviously poor people move into a long-abandoned building. But others welcome squatters. At a public takeover on Labor Day in 1995, one neighbor told a reporter, "I'm glad Homes Not Jails came out. Something will be done now. The place is an eyesore. If they can clean it up and use it to house the homeless, okay. It's a hazard and it draws raccoons."[8]

Unlike most drug addicts, criminals, government agencies, and raccoons, HNJ enters a neighborhood with a sense of humility and respect. "Homes Not Jails is not some bureaucracy coming in and saying, x number of homeless people will live next door to you," said Graham, whose extensive covert squatting with HNJ afforded plenty of opportunities to talk with neighbors. "It's somebody coming up and saying, 'Hi. This is my name, this is me, I'm homeless, and I'm living here now. I'm putting my work and energy into this building and neighborhood. I want to be a good neighbor. I want your support.'"

The city and landlords oppose HNJ, even though it has actually improved San Francisco's housing stock. Homes Not Jails maintains a strict adherence to its policy of "sweat equity." In lieu of rent, HNJ expects all squatters to clean, paint, and even make structural improvements to their squats, both covert and public. The history of sweat equity stretches back to 19th century homesteaders, and more recently sweat equity has been advocated by groups such as Habitat for Humanity. Through sweat equity, homeless people live more comfortably, improve housing values, exchange construction skills, and emphasize the responsibilities attendant to any right to housing. Sweat equity works well for the many homeless people who are skilled workers but are unemployed, unfairly evicted, or victim to some other structural inequity. For the significant proportion of homeless people who struggle with substance abuse or mental illness, sweat equity offers additional benefits. "Sweat equity gives people the opportunity to participate in a common project and create an extended family in which homeless people have a place to heal," said HNJ member Whirlwind Dreamer. "That is what these people are really missing, a network of responsible friends they can count on."

HNJ is currently trying to interest a government housing agency in sponsoring a sweat equity project. "The sweat equity model," said Gullickson, "is formulated to address the problem that most affordable housing is unaffordable for people with no income or people on General Assistance [GA], Supplemental Security Income [SSI], or Aid to Families with Dependent Children [AFDC]. You need an alternative model for people who are destitute and need to do labor instead of pay rent." Sweat equity provides affordable housing not only for cash-strapped residents, but for cash-strapped governments, as well. The use of sweat equity decreases the amount of government funding needed to make affordable units available. For more complex building skills, like architectural or engineering work, HNJ has usually found volunteers. "The sweat equity idea," said Wooding, "is that you don't need to run nonprofit housing in as pricy a way as it is generally run. You can have people do the work on their own housing and cut costs significantly."

Since its crude beginnings, HNJ has refined the idea of sweat equity. HNJ held a number of all-day meetings on the issue when it almost gained legal title to a squat at 3250 17th Street from the U.S. Department of Housing and Urban Development (HUD). After drafting income and expense projections, HNJ members decided that every resident would pay 30% of her or his income as cash rent in addition to volunteering hours of labor on repair, maintenance, or other tasks. Projected residents were two families who received AFDC, two recipients of SSI, and four recipients of GA. A nonprofit land trust would actually own the land, and a limited equity co-op would own the house; individual residents would have membership within the co-op. Residents would accrue equity in an HNJ building at roughly 1% of the building's value for each year of occupancy. Residents would generally remain for one to three years as they gained job skills or completed drug or alcohol programs that would enable them to become independent. When a resident moved, the land trust would buy her or his share, and the next resident would begin the process anew. This would produce nest eggs for homeless people to move into their own rental housing on the open market.

First Squat: Serendipity on Golden Gate Avenue

Homes Not Jails emerged from two of San Francisco's most prominent activist organizations: Food Not Bombs and the San Francisco Tenants Union. Food Not Bombs cut its teeth serving free food to the homeless in front of San Francisco's City Hall. It has no permanent facilities and serves almost all its food on the street; it is, nevertheless, the city's fourth-largest soup kitchen. Since 1980, Food Not Bombs has sustained abuse by riot police and suffered over a thousand arrests for refusal to obtain food-service permits. The national media reported extensively on the arrests, and the group now has active chapters in over 40 cities across the United States. Established in 1971 and a bit more staid in its approach, the San Francisco Tenants Union organizes legislative campaigns to win stronger rent control laws and counsels tenants on their legal rights from an almost mansion-like Victorian home in the Mission District.

Both groups started squatting movements prior to HNJ, but both efforts failed. It took the catalyst of a Philadelphia homeless group, which called for nationwide takeovers on Thanksgiving 1992, to get the two San Francisco groups together and a long-lasting squatting movement established. Food Not Bombs had street smarts, extensive experience with local jails, and the courage needed for blazing new trails of civil disobedience through a thicket of real estate laws. The Tenants Union had an office, a database on vacant buildings, and lawyers who knew how to defend residents from the city's harshest landlords.

Foresight on the part of a participant visited success on the group at its very first meeting. A total stranger produced a key to a vacant building nearby in the Tenderloin district. He had posed as a potential purchaser and fooled the real estate agents into lending him the key long enough to make a copy. So, while everyone else at the meeting watched a video about squatting in Philadelphia, Ted Gullickson from the Tenants Union and Keith McHenry from Food Not Bombs walked a few blocks and let themselves into the building at 90 Golden Gate. They hadn't planned on squatting that night, but the surprise seemed auspicious and the building appropriate: it had two floors, showers, and was previously a homeless shelter.

After fetching the group, Gullickson and McHenry reconvened the meeting in the vacant building. They had just opened the first of hundreds of HNJ housing occupations. The 20 HNJ members who spent the first night soon grew to 30. Residents represented the diverse population of San Francisco, including Southeast Asian immigrants, gays and lesbians, three families, African Americans, and Vietnam War veterans. After moving in, the formerly homeless squatters pooled their food stamps, organized communal cooking, and worked long hours repairing the neglected building.

More than the building improved. "What most inspired me was the massive transformations in people," said Gullickson. "They got jobs by being able to finally stabilize their lives. People who moved in with shopping carts full of stuff, who had to get in line for shelter and scrounge around for food and General Assistance, finally found a place where they could take a shower, cook their own meal, leave their belongings, and go out and apply for jobs." The relatively long-term nature of the squat created a supportive atmosphere in which several members quit their substance abuse. A reporter from *SF Weekly* observed a scene in which E.T. Thomas, one of the squatters, announced that it had been five months since he last stuck a needle in his arm. "The room exploded in applause."[9]

The first HNJ squat at 90 Golden Gate lasted longer than expected — about two months. But when the landlord heard of the squatters he took immediate action. Police evicted seventeen adults and two children on January 1, 1993. The building remains vacant to this day.

Bolt Cutters and Bicycles: The Art of Covert Squatting

Beginning with 90 Golden Gate, HNJ's covert squatting campaign has provided the group with the majority of its buildings. Armed with bolt cutters and a list of addresses supplied by sympathizers, HNJ search teams break into vacant buildings on a weekly basis. They use bolt cutters on padlocks, tear plywood from windows, and pop door locks with credit cards.

Surprisingly, members of HNJ search teams rarely see police officers, and only three members, including Gullickson and Benjamin, have ever been arrested. But other dangers lurk. "We got jumped by a bunch of thugs in the Tenderloin," said one member who asked to remain anonymous. "We were trying to open the second floor of a building with an X-rated video parlor on the first floor. Our neighbors downstairs didn't like that too much, and actually grabbed one of us and pinned him against the wall. It freaked me out pretty bad."

For most, the positive aspects far outweigh the dangers of squatting. Eric, who at the time of his interview was expecting eviction from his run-down apartment any day, described his most satisfying search team. On a cold winter night, homeless people were sleeping in front of a boarded and padlocked building on South Van Ness and 18th Street. "We opened the building and housed three individuals instantaneously. It really touched me."

San Francisco has a small squatting movement compared with cities such as New York, Philadelphia, London, Amsterdam, and Berlin. But, given its hostile housing situation, San Francisco squatters can make a claim to being some of the most dedicated. Unlike other cities that have large blocks of vacant houses due to depopulation or redlining, high-rent units surround most of San Francisco's meager supply of single vacant buildings. This makes nervous neighbors and remodeling landlords much more common.

HNJ has organized at least one search team almost every week since 1992. On any given search, HNJ opens from one to a half-dozen buildings. Wooding estimates that in the past five years, over 250 search teams have opened between 700 and 800 buildings. If the building looks "squattable," as some HNJ members say, they replace the landlord's snapped padlock with their own or leave a window open, ready for any homeless person who might attend their next public meeting. From the weekly meeting, HNJ regulars then accompany the homeless person to the new squat, let them in, and provide repair, maintenance, and legal support during the months ahead.

HNJ has occupied hundreds of covert squats, most for under a month. But dozens have lasted between one month and a year; several have lasted over two years. From the beginning, the number of squatters in HNJ squats has never dipped below a half-dozen, and at times has reached almost 50, according to Gullickson. This is in addition to the five covert squats and a farm occupied by the Santa Cruz chapter in 1993.

The impact that HNJ has had on San Francisco squatting is much more significant than the numbers of current HNJ members would indicate. Many previously involved with HNJ met other squatters, formed support networks, and left the organization to squat on their own. "We teach people how to use a crowbar to pop open a door, how to get in different kinds of windows, how to use a bread knife to flip the lock latch on a window, how to re-key locks. The number of people who have learned the skills has to be in the hundreds, if not over a thousand people," said Jeremy Graham.

The overall number of San Francisco squatters at present, both affiliated and unaffiliated with HNJ, is impossible to know. By the nature of their endeavor, squatters attempt to remain hidden. But, if pushed, some squatters will venture a guess. Cristian, a 19-year-old punk who has squatted in Ohio, Southern California, Vancouver, and New Orleans, estimates 200 young punks were squatters in buildings in San Francisco in the summer of 1997, in addition to 200 non-punk squatters. Even more squatters reside in Oakland than San Francisco, he says, because of Oakland's higher vacancy rate. Connie Morgenstern estimates there are about 20 to 30 "crash pads," or short-term squats, in San Francisco that squatters rotate through on a regular basis, plus a few stable squats.

With the few exceptions of vacant buildings completely ignored by their landlords, frequent eviction is *de rigueur* for San Francisco squatting. "My experience in squatting was a lot of bouncing around, sometimes every few days," said Graham, who now lives in a cramped apartment with other homeless advocates. "You would come home and find that security guards had kicked your bedding around and pawed through all your stuff. You had to wonder whether it would be there the next day." More than once, guards busted in on Graham with guns drawn. "You don't want to think about that every time you go home, but you would go back because it was a great squat."

Although HNJ enjoys age and gender diversity, it is currently a largely white organization. In addition to HNJ squatters who appeared white, I met only one Native American, one African American, and one Argentinean during my seven weeks observing HNJ. Latinos, African Americans, and Native Americans sometimes squat with HNJ, but, according to HNJ members, homeless people of color usually prefer shelters or the outdoors, rather than squats. "African Americans have reluctance because of the police," said Whirlwind, a Native American squatter. "They have the experience that cops beat them and ask questions later."

Homes Not Jails has also had difficulty attracting non-white participants to public takeovers, where the risk of arrest is high and the immediate material benefits usually nonexistent. HNJ and other squatters have tried to form coalitions with non-white groups; but in most cases, non-white groups were generally uninterested in short-term rough squatting, with its risk of weekly eviction. This reflects the larger experience of urban squatting in the United States. Usually, longer-term poor people become interested when chances of success increase, when individual squats last long periods, as in New York City and Philadelphia, or when large movements gain permanent and legal rights to a building for a homeless shelter, as in Oakland. Otherwise, these groups have better options and no punk ascetic idealism that sees squatting as an esthetic in and of itself.

Homes Not Jails has had more success attracting non-white participants to its more stable squats. In its most long-standing squat, every resident was African American. HNJ squatted that building in the early '90s, when neighborhood cops had a more relaxed attitude toward covert squats. According to Graham, the message from particular cops on the beat was, "We won't act unless we get complaints from the property owners. We're not really going to try and prosecute people for trying to house themselves." This positive attitude from the police became clearest at HNJ's fourth covert squat at 850 Hayes in 1993. An eyesore in the neighborhood, the landlord had long abandoned it to drug addicts and the deterioration of San Francisco's saltwater fog and constant drizzle.

When HNJ squatted 850 Hayes, it held its first big workday, an urban barn-raising with over a dozen volunteers. They fixed the stove, installed window frames donated by a local free medical clinic that had just remodeled, and painted both the interior and exterior. During this very public process, many of the neighbors met the HNJ members. "Some realized we were squatters, and some didn't," said Graham. "All of them were really happy that this vacant, ugly building was being repainted and would have windows instead of plywood."

When the police finally arrived several weeks later, the squatters gave a tour of the house. The police remembered the former crack house and expressed shock to see people cooking dinner, watching television, and living a "normal life." The pair of cops remarked on what a positive transformation the squatters had engineered.

Because the landlord had not yet complained, the police took a soft approach. According to Graham, they told him and the other squatters, "We have to see somebody leave. Then we don't care what happens. If we get another call later on, we are not necessarily going to come back." Two of the squatters took a few things and walked around the block. When they returned, the police were gone.

Eventually, the landlord discovered and confronted the HNJ squatters. He wanted to demolish the building to build condominiums. When he came for the eviction, Tenants Union lawyers met him in front of the house. They informed the landlord that the squatters had lived at 850 Hayes long enough to obtain tenant status. It was now a civil, not a criminal, matter; the police could not legally evict without a proper eviction proceeding in civil court. To create further obstacles for the out-maneuvered landlord, squatters filed complaints at the Planning Department, which ruled against a demolition. Stymied at every turn, the landlord left town.

When the landlord returned a year and a half later, however, somebody lit the building on fire. Luckily, the squatters put the fire out in time, and nobody was hurt. They suspected the landlord had committed arson, but had no proof. Then, late another night, a second fire was set while everyone slept. The squatters escaped unhurt again, but, by the time firefighters extinguished the flames, 850 Hayes was gutted beyond repair.

The squat at 850 Hayes provided over a dozen homeless people with free housing for about two years. It lasted because the police originally turned a blind eye. But as HNJ continued both its covert and public campaigns, the police administration developed a much clearer policy of intolerance. The police began immediately and forcibly to evict squatters and re-evict if the squatters returned. Shortly after the evictions of 90 Golden Gate and two other covert HNJ squats, Mayor Frank Jordan, a former police chief who sailed into office on a law-and-order platform, addressed HNJ for the first time:

> We just cannot allow people to walk into any vacant building and just take it over as a homeless encampment. These are private buildings . . . and if the [owners] ask us to remove people, we try to do so. There are health hazards involved here. There are public safety issues if someone comes into a building and starts a fire.

Ironically, in the same January 4, 1993, speech, Jordan also apologized for not fulfilling his campaign promises to the homeless.[10]

Luckily, Jordan and the landlords could not keep track of all the vacant buildings. In the case of one building squatted by HNJ, neither the police nor the landlord discovered the squatters until five years after it had been taken over. HNJ had fiercely protected the anonymity of the building on Page Street because the length and continuity of the squat created the possibility of an adverse possession claim under California law (most states have a similar law). To get title, the squatters must "openly and notoriously" use and improve the property without consent

of the landlord for five continuous years and must pay the property taxes left un-
paid by the owner for those years. If the squatters meet all these conditions, they
can file a deed on the property and own it free and clear.

After the November 1998 eviction of the squatters, Homes Not Jails filed as
a nonprofit business and paid the $6,000 in property taxes owed to the city. On
January 1, 1999, HNJ held a press conference claiming ownership of the building
based on adverse possession and presented evidence of continuous occupation for
over five years. Included in this evidence was a *San Francisco Examiner* article on
one of the formerly homeless residents. Unaware that the Page Street building was
a squat, the reporter portrayed a man who pulled himself out of poverty and off the
streets to live in "legitimate" housing. Shortly after the January 1 press conference,
San Francisco police arrested the Homes Not Jails spokespeople for felony con-
spiracy to trespass. Whether the squatters will actually gain title in their battle with
the city and negligent owners is dependent on the vagaries of the legal system.

First Public Takeover: Sleazy Slumlord at 250 Taylor

For the first few months of its existence, HNJ squatted covertly. The group
planned its first public takeover for Thanksgiving 1992. A 40-unit apartment
building at 250 Taylor seemed perfect. The landlord, Robert Imhoff of Landmark
Realty, owned San Francisco properties valued at $20 million. He had escaped
prosecution for illegally evicting mostly low-income Filipino tenants from 250
Taylor in 1987 during a wave of gentrification. Many of the former tenants became homeless, and Imhoff then rented out all the units for high rates as luxury
apartments. The evicted tenants won a case and settlements in civil court, but Imhoff declared bankruptcy, and the judge allowed him to keep and continue renting his properties.

In addition to the building's caricature of a despicable landlord, HNJ chose
250 Taylor because the media would already be at the location. Every Thanksgiving, Glide Memorial Church serves thousands of homeless people a turkey
dinner across the street from 250 Taylor. The bedraggled homeless form a line
that stretches for blocks, and every year television cameras record interviews during the meal.

HNJ members expressed distaste for what they consider the media's con-
trived image of homeless people on Thanksgiving and Christmas. Jeremy Graham explained HNJ's perspective:

> By having actions on Thanksgiving and Christmas, we hope to change the
> way people view the homeless. The image of homeless people one sees in
> the media on almost every other day is of people who deserve what they
> get, people who have only themselves to blame, people who are dirty,

don't take care of themselves, and use drugs. You can't give them money because they'll just waste it all. On Thanksgiving and Christmas, you see families and the deserving poor, pathetic, helpless, passive, and grateful for their bowl of soup or toys for the kids.

HNJ wanted to depict an alternate picture of homelessness that bridged the dichotomy. "What we've tried to project is an image of people denied the resources needed to take care of themselves," said Graham, "people who are angry, competent, capable, and, if necessary, people willing to take extreme actions and be arrested and go to jail to get those resources."

HNJ's plan for 250 Taylor became its standard model for public takeovers. Members would secretly occupy the building the night before; then, on the advertised day of action, they would hold a public rally within walking distance of the squat. HNJ protesters would then march to the building and join the original occupiers inside. Banners would unfurl from the windows, and spokespeople would make statements to the media. Police would learn the site of the occupation only by following the march to its destination, at which point they would be too late to easily remove the barricaded occupiers.

On the night before Thanksgiving, HNJ activists converged on the Tenderloin according to plans. But reality rarely adheres to an ideal. "We were such amateurs, we overdid it," said Ted Gullickson. "We brought about 20 people to break in, but it only took one person to peel the loose plywood off by hand." HNJ positioned lookouts, connected by bike messengers two blocks away in every direction. Once inside the building, one of the HNJ members started to build a barricade. He did so much pounding with a hammer that somebody alerted the police. An officer bypassed the impressive barricade by simply entering through a side door and evicted everyone two hours before the rally.

Like HNJ, the police were new to housing takeovers: they left the building unprotected. So, the occupiers joined the 11 a.m. rally at City Hall and marched to the building with the whole group of protesters, which then numbered 75 people. In front of television cameras and hundreds of homeless people waiting in line for a free meal, the HNJ crowd once again tore plywood from windows and reoccupied 250 Taylor.

Cameras rolled, police chased the squatters up and down stairs, and HNJ spokespeople, leaning from windows bedecked by banners, used bullhorns to make demands to a mass audience for the first time. They wanted the San Francisco Board of Supervisors to take the building by eminent domain and transfer it to a nonprofit, affordable housing developer. It took only an hour for the police to find and re-evict everyone and make a couple of arrests. But that evening and the next day, several national television stations, including ABC, brought the event to millions of living rooms.

Public Takeovers: The Politics of Homeless Action

Since that first Thanksgiving in 1992, HNJ in San Francisco has organized 27 public takeovers, with a total of 242 arrests. The Boston chapter has organized four public takeovers in the two years since its beginning on Thanksgiving 1995, with 25 arrests. Each of these public takeovers costs municipal authorities large sums of money. On Thanksgiving 1993, a small group of about 60 people gathered in front of San Francisco City Hall, then peacefully marched to 250 Taylor. Two police vans, seven motorcycles, nine squad cars, and 53 visible police officers followed and made only four arrests. Over the next few years, the District Attorney spent nearly $100,000 on a failed attempt to prosecute the arrestees. The cost of controlling, jailing, and prosecuting HNJ members may seem a ridiculous waste of money on the part of authorities, who could have bought dozens of affordable housing units for the same price and possibly appeased HNJ activists in the process. However, if authorities overtly reward those who organize public takeovers, they may very well encourage more illegal action by others. Thus a classic government strategy in coopting movements is to make seemingly unrelated concessions to groups with the same base of support as the action group. These concealed concessions partially ameliorate the complaints causing the action, but provide less of an incentive for further protests. This point is further illustrated in this chapter and by many other cases in this book.

The arrests of the HNJ activists led to a court appearance. When brought to court, HNJ attempts a variety of legal defenses. The defense of necessity, for example, is intended to protect from burglary charges the defendant who breaks into a burning building to save a baby. Homeless activists have occasionally been allowed to use the defense of necessity in squatting trials by pointing to the number of homeless deaths. To save the lives of homeless people, one must value the necessity of breaking into a building to squat over the technical understanding of property law. In San Francisco, HNJ attorneys have prepared extensively for the necessity defense, including expert witnesses to testify to San Francisco's acute affordable housing shortage, the health and safety dangers that accompany homelessness, and the inadequate public provision of homeless services. The defense of necessity has worked best in San Francisco when utilized by actual homeless people, not housed homeless activists.

Other legal defenses apply to specific types of owners, like federal or state governments. In addition to vacant properties owned by negligent or rent-racking private landlords, HNJ targets vacant government property. In the case of state-owned property, HNJ can sometimes legally defend itself with California state law SB-120. This law makes any vacant property owned by the California Department of Transportation (Caltrans) subject to purchase for $1 by cities and municipalities who will use the property to benefit the homeless. HNJ has repeatedly occupied a vacant Caltrans building at 66 Berry Street to demand that the sale take place. The San Francisco Board of Supervisors subsequently passed a resolution urging the mayor to purchase the building. But Caltrans claims a legal technicality exempts the property, and successive mayors have failed to take even the first required step of requesting the purchase.

In the case of vacant federal building takeovers, Homes Not Jails cites the Stewart B. McKinney Homeless Assistance Act (1987). Title V of this little-known law stipulates that all "surplus, excess, under-utilized, and unutilized" federal property be used to "assist the homeless." The law says homeless use must take precedence over any other use. It specifies that vacant housing and other buildings can be provided to homeless people and nonprofit organizations through deeds or leases. To accommodate transfers, the law stipulates that each federal "landholding agency" must report to HUD any properties not being used. After a government agency makes notification, HUD determines the "suitability" of the building for homeless use and publishes available properties in the federal register. Homeless people or groups can then apply for deeds, leases, or "interim use permits."

Federal agencies, however, have adopted a self-serving and narrow interpretation of the McKinney Act. Those few that bother to report to HUD tend to do so incompletely. If they report anything, they typically report some remote vacant lot or unusable property. HUD lists only two available properties in all of San Francisco, one a remote "toxic waste" site at Hunters Point and the other designated a "landslide area."

Within the first year of the McKinney Act, the National Law Center on Homelessness and Poverty sued the federal government. One year later, in 1988, a federal judge in Washington, D.C., ruled that the government was violating McKinney and issued a nationwide injunction to begin its implementation. The government failed to do so, and other federal courts made similar rulings in 1989, twice in 1991, and in 1993.

Starting on President's Day in 1993, HNJ repeatedly squatted one unreported vacant building owned by the federal government at 1211 Polk Street. The government had seized it in a case that involved charges of tax fraud, racketeering, methamphetamine production, and the filming of child pornography. After its seizure, the building stood vacant for four years.

HNJ members occupied the building and barricaded doors and windows on June 13, 1993. Homeless street youth who frequently camped in front of the building joined the occupation. While the San Francisco Police Department (SFPD) waited for reinforcements, HNJ arranged an impromptu meeting with the

federal marshal who had responsibility for the building. The activists proposed to
the marshal that homeless people use sweat equity to create affordable housing at
the building.

To the surprise of both squatters and the SFPD, the marshal agreed to stall
any eviction while he forwarded the proposal to his superiors. He told the SFPD
that the building was federal property under federal jurisdiction, and that the SFPD
would have to leave the squatters alone. The thoughtful marshal gave his card to
the squatters and asked that HNJ call him if the SFPD returned. Twice during the
takeover the SFPD surrounded and tried to storm the building. Twice HNJ kept
them at bay with hastily reinforced barricades long enough to alert the marshal.

Midway through the takeover, HNJ realized that many of the homeless
kids survived by prostitution. Sarah Menafee, a member of HNJ, told the *San
Francisco Bay Guardian* that it would be divine justice if a building once used
for child pornography could be transformed into a home for teenagers who have
been "doing what they had to do" to survive on the street. The children's stories
and pictures were published in the media and increased public attention and sympathy. Practically every day, at least one member of the media arrived to snap
photos or write stories.

Meanwhile the federal government and the mayor's Office of Housing
took an open attitude toward the occupation. Federal attorneys jetted in from Nevada and negotiated directly with a Homes Not Jails team composed of homeless
people and political activists. After much discussion, the federal government and
activists came to an agreement. The government offered to sell the building to the
city for far less than market value. It asked only $77,000, the amount equal to
various liens on the building. It would then require about $210,000 worth of re-
pairs to bring it into use as a homeless shelter. Ted Dienstfry, the director of the
Mayor's Office of Housing, personally inspected the inside of the building, certi-
fied its habitability, and verified that purchase of the property would be a "prudent use of public funds."[11] Everybody anticipated that the city would agree to
buy the place; Mayor Jordan had only to write a letter of intent.

Earlier in the process, Mayor Jordan had stopped by the building in his
chauffeured town car. In what may have been a tragic misstep of hubris, young
squatters leaned out the windows and heckled this key player in the negotiations.
Whether or not this had an effect, it illustrates the uneasy relationship between
HNJ and the mayor. Contrary to the inclination of both the federal government
and his own Office of Housing, on July 4, Mayor Jordan refused to purchase the
building and the deal fell apart. Federal officials refused to lend the building directly to a nonprofit homeless advocacy group because, according to them, the
McKinney Act did not apply in the case of 1211 Polk. It was a seized asset,
rather than a property formerly used for federal purposes. At 6:30 a.m. on Sun-

day, July 11, the 27th day of the takeover, 36 federal marshals and San Francisco police evicted 12 residents and arrested two. The government eventually dropped all charges, probably to avoid facing the McKinney Act in court.

Over the next two years, HNJ attempted to retake the building seven times, but on each occasion the SFPD made quick arrests. Without benefit of an auction or open sale process, the federal government sold the property for $300,000 to a real estate developer in 1995. The developer flipped the investment on the same day and sold it for $340,000.

Wrestling the Big Boys and Winning: Homes Not Jails and Religious Witness vs. the U.S. Army

In 1989, the United States Congress passed the federal Base Conversion Act, which closed the Presidio Army Base in San Francisco and other military bases across the country. On the Presidio is Wherry Housing, originally 524 units of modern family housing used for enlisted personnel. Most of the units have hardwood floors and a "million dollar view of the Golden Gate Bridge," according to one columnist. An independent inspector valued the housing alone, not including the land, at $80 million.[12]

Homes Not Jails wanted to turn the Wherry complex into affordable housing for homeless people. HNJ members allied themselves with a group called Religious Witness with Homeless People. Led by Sister Bernice Galvin, a Catholic nun, Religious Witness includes leaders in its organizing structure from the Jewish, Buddhist, Native American, pagan, and Muslim communities.

But despite many people's desire to see the Wherry complex turned into affordable housing, President Bill Clinton appointed a board to decide the details without sufficient public input. Called the Presidio Trust, the board was filled with corporate luminaries who quickly slated the 524 units for demolition. In support of demolition were neighbors and developers who saw the proposed affordable housing as a potential source of crime. Likewise in support of demolition, the National Park Service considered affordable housing as being inconsistent with its mission to protect nature, conserve historic buildings, and provide large open parks for the public. Demolishing the Wherry complex would increase green space, they said. Yet the Park Service saw no contradiction in renting 900 units of officer housing on the base at market rates, from $1,500 to $4,000 monthly. Not only would the demolition of Wherry lose potential rental revenue for the Park Service, it would cost taxpayers $16 million. According to the National Park Service's own estimates, it would cost only $2 to $3 million to make the $80 million complex habitable.

According to Ted Gullickson, the Presidio Trust and the National Park Service violated the McKinney Act by failing to register the vacant Wherry complex with HUD. When military base closures began in 1989, amendments to the McKinney Act clarified that the law applies to base closures. Early in 1995, some of the Presidio housing was listed as available under McKinney, but the government quickly retracted it, calling the listing a "mistake."[13]

Once the National Park Service and Presidio Trust took control of the land, they demolished 58 of the 524 units. To protest the demolition, Religious Witness and Homes Not Jails occupied vacant buildings at the Presidio 11 times, with a total of 352 arrests. These actions put a media spotlight on the demolition plans and, after several years of repeated occupation, rallied the San Francisco public. Several environmental groups spoke in support of using the Wherry complex as affordable housing, and, by 1997, 250 organizations and 2,000 individuals had endorsed the Religious Witness campaign, including prominent local, national, and international religious figures. The San Francisco Board of Supervisors unanimously passed a resolution to preserve Wherry Housing, and Mayor Brown drafted several affordable housing plans for the Wherry complex.

With rising public pressure facilitated by Religious Witness and Homes Not Jails, the campaign to save Wherry Housing succeeded. Religious Witness set the keystone to success when it proposed a ballot measure to keep Wherry Housing and develop affordable housing at the Presidio. If the Presidio failed to follow the ballot measure, it would lose all city services, including trash collection, water, and street cleaning. The Presidio Trust finally relented in May 1998, when it became evident that the proposition to save Wherry Housing would pass, as indeed it did by 10,000 votes. The Presidio Trust promised to incorporate affordable housing into its master plan, repair Wherry Housing, rent it at market rates, and forego demolition for at least 30 years.

The Presidio Trust decision set a precedent as the first time that affordable housing would be included within the confines of a U.S. national park. In a city with as low a vacancy rate as San Francisco, saving 466 units from demolition was a significant success for Homes Not Jails, Religious Witness, and affordable housing advocates nationwide.

Quiet Victories: The Secret Success of Homes Not Jails

Since the late '80s, squatting groups across the United States have achieved spectacular victories. Dignity Housing West in Oakland staged public takeovers and gained funding to turn a vacant federal building into a homeless service center. Operation Homestead in Seattle used public takeovers to turn 400 vacant units into affordable housing. ACT-UP Philadelphia squatted and gained title to a vacant hospital, which it turned into an AIDS hospice. The Association of Community Organizations for Reform Now (ACORN) in New York gained title to several buildings through squatting.

With the exception of Wherry Housing, HNJ has claimed quieter victories. The group has not yet won title to any of its squatted housing. After almost 20 public takeovers and an equal number of public evictions in five years, the members continue a seemingly Sisyphean task of takeover, eviction, takeover, eviction. But Sisyphus has our sympathies, and HNJ our attention. In a masterful adaptation of Gandhian strategy, HNJ manages to squeeze moral success from each tactical defeat. Media venues regularly bring the ugly evictions of HNJ into the chic living rooms of otherwise comfortable voters, and politicians like Mayor Brown have begun to recognize the need for more affordable housing. On a purely cultural level, HNJ has succeeded through hundreds of television and newspaper stories in establishing a more empowering and accurate perception of the homeless.

Factors particular to San Francisco have frustrated the concrete success of acquiring a title deed by these squatters, among the most dedicated and active in the United States. Much higher vacancy rates in Seattle, New York, Philadelphia, and Oakland make it politically and economically easier for local and federal governments to acquiesce to activist demands for a title deed. The Bay Area's low vacancy rate and high cost of real estate make it more difficult both for covert squatting and for local and federal government donations of housing following a public takeover. During occupations of the HUD house and the Presidio in San Francisco, the federal government made this explicitly clear.

Housing activists in areas with tight housing markets, like San Francisco, face a more daunting task than in other places, but that greater difficulty makes their mandate particularly critical for homeless politics nationally. "The fact that you can squat in San Francisco at all," says Wooding, "means that squatting can be a remarkably powerful tool in most other places." If HNJ San Francisco can convince the federal government to change its rules, whether against the use of national parks for affordable housing or against a cap on HUD spending for a single affordable housing unit, that can set a precedent for the nation.

Even though HNJ has not yet won the war, it has won quite a few battles. Although the city government of San Francisco reneged on its promise to fund an HNJ pilot project, it has devoted more funding to homeless and housing services than it would have if HNJ had not raised public awareness and outrage by maintaining the intensity and frequency of its demonstrations and gaining national media attention.[14] Proposition A, a $100 million city bond measure for affordable housing, passed in 1996 with guidance from a coalition of affordable housing providers. But without five years of agitation by Homes Not Jails and other lower-profile housing groups, the sense of crisis that propelled Proposition A to passage would not have existed.

"Through educating people about the connection between the housing crisis and homelessness," said Gullickson, "we have definitely added to the overall atmosphere that the city needs to do more for affordable housing." Besides an occasional statistical study or quote from this or that nonprofit affordable housing provider, doubtless lacking in drama to television audiences, HNJ and Religious Witness are the only groups that have successfully created a hook, through arrests and militant demonstrations, on which the mass media can hang the issue of affordable housing. Only with this mass media attention did city voters in 1996 perceive a $100 million need for more affordable housing and, in 1998, vote to save Wherry Housing.

Although HNJ has not yet gained legal title to any property, it has still managed to provide a significant amount of long-term affordable housing to people who usually choose between the cold streets and impersonal, regimented homeless shelters. Since 1992, covert squats organized by HNJ have successfully housed thousands of homeless people in hundreds of buildings. Drugs, violence, and undemocratic decision-making have checkered some of these successes, but HNJ serves an important function by acting as arbitrator and by modeling the principles of nonviolence, sobriety, and the consensus process in the homeless community. HNJ also does a service to the broader community by creating a fair structure of dispute resolution to which homeless communities living on the streets, in parks, or in non-HNJ squats would otherwise have no access.

In retaining contact with drug-addicted squatters, HNJ provides compassion to a population that carries one of the worst of social stigmas. Said Chance Martin, a former HNJ squatter, "Substance abuse makes for some hairy times, but I finally got to the point where I had to say, if somebody sticks a needle in their arm, does that mean they have to live on the streets?" HNJ has attempted to create self-managed communities by entrusting homeless people with responsibility under the worst conditions. That trust has helped teach the responsibility and social skills needed to escape the forest of individual failures for a path of goals, work, and achievement, whether through political organizing or parting from HNJ and beginning a new life. "It takes people with a real commitment and vision to make a cooperative community work under adverse circumstances," said Jeremy Graham, "and HNJ has been very fortunate in the vast majority of our participants."

HNJ Boston has only existed since 1995, with a six-month hiatus due to a hurricane warning that sunk one occupation, but the group has weathered the storm and has a sunny optimism for future action. If it continues its rapid rate of public takeovers, which have increased community and media connections, it can expect its political power in Boston to grow in much the same way as in San Francisco. With a smaller vacancy rate, HNJ Boston can expect covert successes to match or exceed San Francisco's early covert squats; with lower real estate values, it could even gain legal title to a building sooner than its West Coast parent.

Homes Not Jails aims to set precedents, and it continues to attempt this at a courtroom level. Unfortunately, after Homes Not Jails and Religious Witness endured 483 arrests in Boston, San Francisco, and Santa Cruz, only one charge has gone to court. Caltrans and federal prosecutors have steadfastly declined to prosecute squatter defendants to avoid the embarrassing attention a trial would draw to SB-120 and the McKinney Act, or to the necessity defense, if it were allowed by an activist judge. The failure of the District Attorneys to prosecute raises questions as to the legality of the 483 arrests. Clearly much electoral and lobbying work needs to be done to strengthen enforcement of the McKinney Act and similar legislation.

Many tasks lay ahead. Rome was not built in a day, and neither will the legal victories and public opinion needed for practical answers to the problem of homelessness. "We had this naive attitude that people would just be supportive of what we were doing," said Graham. "If people were supportive, the politicians would have to endorse it, and that would put enough pressure on the building owners to negotiate a deal." Housing the homeless proved not so simple. But if public opinion flags and government funding thins at times, worse would befall society at a more rapid rate without groups like Homes Not Jails. Homes Not Jails has expanded media coverage of the need for affordable housing, provided tens of thousands of nights of squatted housing for homeless people, and helped save 466 units of beautiful housing at the Presidio. Like other squatter groups in the United States, Homes Not Jails provides a model of community action that works.

CHAPTER 2

Battling the Banana Baron

Rural Hondurans Bloody Chiquita Brands International

Third World squatting differs fundamentally from the practice of Homes Not Jails. Squatting in the United States revolves around political or social counterculture and the destitution of individual homeless persons in the midst of opulence. Squatting in the Third World is a logical reaction of whole classes of people to the concentration of land in the hands of the few.

Very few Third World nations have a significant number of vacant residential housing units, so urban squatters construct their own. Since much of the Third World poor rely on agriculture as employment, squatters occupy land as a means of subsistence. The large number of people in the Third World who cannot pay prevailing rents means large squatting movements that have significant political clout. They can squat land and hold it long enough to make the construction of shantytowns or the planting of crops a common and long-lasting endeavor.

Squatters in Tacamiche, Honduras, serve as a revealing counterpoint to squatting in the richer nations. Compared to Homes Not Jails, the Tacamiche community is larger, more tightly knit, and has more successfully built coalitions with other groups. The Tacamiche squat agricultural land instead of urban housing. Their origin and tactics are completely different from those of squatters in rich nations, and the government and landholder reaction has been much more violent and intense.

The Tacamiche land struggle originated in response to Chiquita Brands International's refusal to maintain wages for plantation workers, including those who worked and lived on their Tacamiche farm, on a par with the crushing 30%

Honduran inflation rate. Between 1987 and 1994, daily wages slid from US$8 to less than $3. Six thousand Chiquita workers from several of Chiquita's 22 Honduran farms called a labor strike in 1990.[1]

Honduran law specifically forbids the closure of a plantation to defeat a strike or unionization. Nevertheless, midway through the strike, in June 1994, Chiquita closed Tacamiche and three other farms totaling 1,200 hectares. These farms had provided much of the support for the strike and had a history of resistance to the company. Chiquita told 800 permanent workers to choose between relocation or $500 severance pay and laid off about 1,200 temporary workers. Residents in the villages who were not employees, including children and former employees, would receive nothing. Within one month, such tactics coerced the union into settling the strike for a 9% pay increase, which, considering Honduras' 30% inflation rate, meant a substantially lower real wage than that of the previous year.[2]

As for the possibility of future labor disputes, Chiquita had a plan. Most of the land in the decommissioned farms, according to Miguel Rodriguez, a vice-president of Chiquita involved with Honduras for years, will be sold at market rates as soon as the government grants permission.[3] For decades, United Fruit/United Brands, now known as Chiquita, has been selling its banana land in Central America, concentrating instead on the less controversial and more lucrative shipping and marketing end of the banana business. Smaller local producers grow the bananas more cheaply, Rodriguez admitted, because their labor expenses are lower than Chiquita's, whose work force is unionized. Rodriguez said these producers would find banana production on the abandoned lands more profitable because they pay lower wages, provide fewer benefits, and work on a smaller scale.

The Land Revolt

Many of the evicted Tacamiches were born in Tacamiche. Several of the families have lived in the area since the '20s, a decade before Chiquita's infamous corporate predecessor, United Fruit, gained title to the land for $1 as a railroad giveaway. Differing relationships to the land have driven the conflict, a battle between the visceral connection of locals and the profit-driven ledgers of Chiquita. "For the company, Tacamiche is just a former banana plantation that, after having the juice sucked from it, has been abandoned without a thought for the fate of those who lived here," Jorge Antonio told the *New York Times*. "But for those of us from Tacamiche, this is our life, these are the cabins that watched as we were born and grew up."[4]

Buoyed by such outrage and compelled by hunger, Antonio and others illegally planted corn and beans on part of the plantation when Chiquita closed it in June 1994. After Chiquita fired them, the former workers had few other sources of food. Their demand for land, if they could not have a job, had a precedent in the company's labor history. When United Brands (Chiquita's former name, which fell into disrepute) fired 3,000 workers at its Costa Rican plantation in 1983, 1,000 of them peacefully occupied 2,000 hectares of company land. Two months later, the Costa Rican government promised 300 parcels of land to the workers. A similar gesture from Chiquita would almost certainly have diffused the Tacamiche conflict. But Chiquita chose the stick over the carrot. Rodriguez said Chiquita insisted on eviction in the case of Tacamiche because the former workers, allegedly led and joined by "opportunistic" outsiders, had illegally occupied company land.

Chiquita first attempted to evict the Tacamiches on July 26, 1995, over one year after the initial occupation, when feelings of union solidarity had begun to subside and the remaining plantations had returned to normal. Four hundred police and soldiers arrested 26 plantation residents; injured about 75 more with tear gas, rubber bullets, and baseball bats; and destroyed 80 hectares of corn and beans planted two months before.[5]

But the Tacamiches beat the police back. Rocks thrown by the Tacamiches injured some of the troops, according to *La Nación*, and police retreated. Subsequently, the government agreed to give the Tacamiches until September 26, 1995, to vacate. The Tacamiches refused to retreat, instead expanding their occupation to 50 hectares on the Copén plantation in early January 1996.

A public outcry in Honduras delayed the second eviction attempt until February 1, 1996, when Chiquita finally had the approval of President Carlos Roberto Reina and the Honduran judiciary. This time, the police and military gave no advance notice. Caught by surprise, most Tacamiches lost everything except the clothes on their backs. An onslaught of 500 troops, a "field judge," and over 400 workers, hired by Chiquita especially for the task, made 100 arrests. Other Tacamiches hid in the town's three churches while the hired men bulldozed everything: subsistence crops, homes, the health post, and, after ousting the Tacamiches who had sought sanctuary there, the three churches as well. Kitchen utensils, books, bedding, tools, and radios were buried in the debris, carted away, or stolen by the hired men.[6]

Wilfredo Cabrera, a 34-year-old banana worker, told a *New York Times* reporter, "It was very painful to see all of our corn, peppers, tomatoes, carrots, and melons being plowed over by bulldozers, not to mention what they did to the churches. We have been peasants all of our lives, making the land produce, so we can never forgive that kind of destruction."[7]

Amidst the rubble and mud, Chiquita left only some ancient mango trees and the schoolhouse standing. The school served as a bunkhouse for the soldiers left to guard against workers returning to their land. The 50 or 60 dogs of Tacamiche ran away after the eviction, roamed the plantation during the day, and returned every night to the demolished village to howl. The soldiers eventually hunted and killed most of them.[8]

Asked why Chiquita gave no advance notice of the eviction, the surprisingly candid Rodriguez offered insight into the tactics of the Honduran police and military: "Whenever they announce that an operation is going to be undertaken, it is like going to war. You don't announce the moment you are going to strike, because at that moment the police were convinced that these outsiders would bring in five or six thousand people. It would probably have led to rock throwing, which is what happened on July 26, maybe even people killed."

Chiquita chose not to warn the Tacamiches because they feared a public outcry, but they received one nonetheless, both within Honduras and internationally. Due to this outcry, in a letter sent to thousands of concerned persons around the globe, Chiquita promised to re-house the Tacamiches. Yet Chiquita initially rebuilt only 46 ramshackle huts without electricity or water, mostly from lumber salvaged from the old Tacamiche houses. The Honduran government also attempted public relations damage control, promising to provide a school, health and sports centers, drinking water, and sewage systems. But after a year and a half, the government had built only the school and health center, and the 123 Tacamiche families never got compensation for their personal effects and crops.

In protest, the Tacamiches refused to move to the town partially constructed by Chiquita. They crammed into a one-room community center in the nearby city of La Lima and began a formidable public relations campaign while subsisting entirely on donations from friends, the surrounding banana plantation communities, and the local Catholic parish. But after almost a year, their sources of support were drying up, and they faced malnutrition, unhealthy close quarters, and an increasing epidemic of bronchitis.

Another Day, Another Dollar: Chiquita Evicts Again

Meanwhile, the three other plantation communities faced the unspoken threat of eviction. Of the four Honduran plantations "terminated," as Rodriguez described it, Chiquita evicted only Tacamiche. Communities at the plantations of San Juan, Copén, and La Curva still remained, and, in the case of these three, Rodriguez promised that Chiquita would not evict. "We know there are hundreds of people there who are no longer related to the company," Rodriguez said, "and yet we have decided to let them stay. Because these are just people who are out of a job, and they have no place to go. We don't want to exacerbate the social problem that Honduras has right now."

Chiquita's less magnanimous eviction of the Tacamiches dissuaded fired workers at the three farms from occupying land. They watched the events at Tacamiche closely and chose their course accordingly. Although Chiquita promised not to evict after the Tacamiche conflict, the former workers distrusted Chiquita's sincerity. Their offers to buy the land from Chiquita, like previous offers by the Tacamiches, were ignored. According to Joe Owens, a Jesuit priest and radio journalist in the area who adopted the cause of the Tacamiches, the independent producers who lease the defunct plantations from Chiquita put pressure on the former banana workers to leave. If evicted from their homes, the independent producers could then place their own workers in the company housing.

Community members at the three plantations organized militant protests against eviction in November 1996; in early 1997, they threatened to occupy Latin American and European embassies in the capital. "They say they are being made refugees in their own country, and their only option is to declare themselves political refugees and to escape into an embassy," said Owens.[9]

During this period, Chiquita acted as though the eviction of Tacamiche taught them nothing. In 1997, company security guards harassed 16 squatter communities in the San Alejo region in the hope of clearing about 650 hectares of land to produce palm oil. "These are very, very poor people, much poorer, in fact, than the banana workers," said Owens. Many of the squatters had lived on their tiny pieces of land since the '80s, when the agrarian reform law and organizers such as Elvia Alvarado helped peasants to occupy vacant lands.[10] But the government refused to legalize many of their occupations, and, in 1992, the agrarian reform law was repealed. Although Chiquita had delayed evictions, according to Owens, the company felt "emboldened by their [eviction of] Tacamiche, and the prostrate posture of the present government, [which] is not doing anything to defend *campesinos* against the company."

One teenager was found dead at a squatter camp; according to resident José Garcia, Chiquita security guards have assaulted and wounded various community members and killed domestic animals. In October 1996, Chiquita destroyed the homes and crops of three squatter communities near Urraco in the Sula Valley, uprooting 150 families, or about 1,000 people.

Chiquita's Criminal Conduct

According to local and international human rights groups, Chiquita had no legal right to evict the Tacamiches. The Tacamiches themselves cite Honduran land reform law, which mandates redistribution of defunct plantation land formerly used for export agriculture. That law mandates redistribution of any holding by a single owner of over 250 hectares. The law exempts land actively in use for export agriculture deemed essential to the Honduran economy. But, by

Chiquita's own admission, the Tacamiche land is no longer productive for large-scale banana production.

Michael Windfuhr, director of FIAN-International, a human rights organization, even questions whether Chiquita actually owns the land. On a visit to Honduras in August, Windfuhr viewed documents at the Honduran land registry indicating that Chiquita had sold the land three times since its original $1 "purchase" in 1936. "That is a problem not only relevant to Tacamiche; it is a problem for the ownership claims of Chiquita in Honduras generally," said Windfuhr.[11] But Chiquita's Rodriguez claims the title is air-tight.

"With respect to these lands, there is no question that we are the owners," said Rodriguez. He points to the fact that the land is in the public title registry under the name of the Tela Railroad Company, Chiquita's Honduran subsidiary, and that Chiquita has proven its ownership numerous times in Honduran courts. The president of the National Agrarian Reform Institute presented a certificate of ownership to Chiquita, and, as Rodriguez proudly notes, even the president of Honduras, Carlos Roberto Reina, appeared on television to affirm Chiquita's claim. That appearance, however, did little to convince those who say that Chiquita's "ownership" of Honduran politics may be more secure than its title to the land.

Following the February eviction, president Reina explained his decision to remove the squatters in the following terms: "It has not been understood, though I've said it a thousand times, that in Honduras we live under a state of law. That means that when coercion must be used, it must be used within the law. Ungovernability would be chaos, and disrespect for the law is a challenge to democracy."[12] Carl Lindner himself, the president of Chiquita Brands International, cites national concerns for the protection of property as an important factor in deciding for eviction. In a letter to the president of Xavier University in Cincinnati, Lindner wrote, "The Honduran government, the business community, and many other sectors have expressed serious concern about the potential threat of further land invasions if the Tacamiche situation were to continue."[13] Chiquita and property rights also won ready support from some of the conservative Honduran media. Two weeks before the eviction, an editorialist for the influential *El Periódicro* argued that real estate law should take precedence over human rights concerns in the Tacamiche situation.

The legal and economic repercussions of allowing the Tacamiches to remain, however, went far beyond the fears of Honduran property owners: the government of Honduras supported the eviction of the Tacamiches because if it had not, the international community would have perceived Honduras as anti-business. Among other concerns that may have led Honduras to evict the Tacamiches was a pending $700 million loan from the Paris Club of international donor nations.[14] U.S. Ambassador William Pryce alluded to international investors when he expressed his satisfaction that, by evicting the Tacamiches, "the government has complied with the law, since the land is property of the Tela Railroad Company. I have always said that respect for the law helps investment, and national and international investment helps economic development, and that helps the people, including the workers."[15]

But international law may subordinate Honduran property law in the case of Tacamiche. Whether or not Chiquita actually owns the land, Michael Windfuhr of FIAN-International says the eviction violated a United Nations agreement. According to Windfuhr, "Honduras is a party to the International Covenant on Economic, Social, and Cultural Rights, and is therefore duty-bound to respect and protect the right to feed oneself as recognized in Article 11 of the Covenant." The eviction has also been challenged under local law by several Honduran organizations. The Roman Catholic Bishops of Honduras, the Committee for the Defense of Human Rights, the Coordinating Council of Campesino Organizations, and the National Workers Center all argue that the court order that began the February eviction called only for arrests, not for the demolition and confiscation of property and homes.

The Chilly History of Chiquita:
"Machine-Gun" Maloney and Worse

Above all else, Chiquita seems to feel justified in evicting the Tacamiches and other squatters because, according to Lindner, "Our constitutional right to private property is in serious jeopardy."[16] But in the case of Honduras, the private property over which Chiquita asserts its supposed rights seems to have been gained through fraud and violence. While Chiquita may have justified its claim in local courtrooms and among its paid-off politicians, it has failed to do so among historians.

When asked how Chiquita originally came to own the land upon which the town of Tacamiche used to stand, the normally smooth Rodriguez laughed nervously. "I don't know. We're going back now to the beginning of the century. We have 22 farms, and I just don't know how, decades ago, we came to own them." History burns beneath the simmering Honduran opposition to Chiquita's claim, and Rodriguez may have broken a sweat because he knew better than he said. Even a cursory review of Chiquita's acquisition of land in Honduras since the beginning of the century makes local opposition to the company's land claims easy to understand.

For most of its corporate life, the American-controlled company now called Chiquita was known as the United Fruit Company. It changed its name in 1970 to United Brands. The Lindner family, which now holds 46% of Chiquita's stock, took control of United Brands in 1987 and changed the name to Chiquita in

1990.[17] Whether intentional or not, the latest name change was a savvy marketing decision: it distanced the Lindner family interests from the monolithic overtones inherent in the United Brand/United Fruit name and, even more importantly, from the bloody and oppressive history of those companies.

United Fruit, the company that founded the legacy of questionable dealings in Honduras by American business, got a large portion of its land in a railroad giveaway engineered by Samuel Zemurray. With the help of a hired gun named Guy "Machine-Gun" Maloney and other mercenaries, Zemurray personally overthrew Honduran President Miguel Davila in 1911 and installed his own man, Manuel Bonilla, as president.[18]

Bonilla immediately repaid his debt to Zemurray's company with tax breaks, port development rights, railroad concessions, and land. Today the Tela Railroad Company — Chiquita's subsidiary — owns the 1,200 hectares of which the disputed Tacamiche land is a part. They bought it for $1 as part of a railroad contract in 1936. But Tela reneged on that contract on multiple occasions, refusing to lay railroad track to small inland towns or the capital. Also in violation of the contract, the Tela Railroad Company dismantled 125 kilometers of track when it temporarily abandoned its Trujillo division, shipping rails and bridges out of the country.[19]

In addition to this fraud, United Fruit slowly extended its holdings by periodically calling for "re-measurement." Local officials friendly to the company would survey adjoining lands — and characteristically discover and register boundaries more favorable to United Fruit than previously recorded. Another land-grabbing method took full advantage of United Fruit's ownership of the railroads and position as the only local buyer of bananas. United Fruit would simply refuse to buy from, and thus ruin, small independent banana producers. The company could then buy the abandoned or confiscated plantations for a song. In 1912, United Fruit owned 2,400 hectares in Honduras. By 1924, the company had received as cost-free subsidy for railroad construction some 71,000 hectares more and had acquired another 37,000 hectares by other means.[20]

As the Honduran population grew and the amount of non-banana land shrank, land scarcity caused unemployment and fragmentation of holdings, which forced landless peasants into overpopulated urban areas and onto unproductive soil. Such an extension of the cultivated area into wilderness areas led to the erosion of topsoil on hillsides and to the beginnings of deforestation.

United Fruit maintained its control over Honduras and its awesome profits by merging with other banana companies, slashing wages, firing hundreds of workers, and brutally suppressing strikes in 1931 and again in 1935.

Eventually, United Fruit accumulated more fertile land than it knew what to do with. In fact, the company did nothing at all with much of that land. While poor Hondurans scraped at unproductive soil, United Fruit's land ownership in

Honduras had climbed to 166,000 hectares in 1946. It planted only 20% of that land with crops.

The biggest Honduran labor dispute occurred in 1954, when a 69-day general strike led by 25,000 United Fruit workers and 3,700 workers of various trades crippled the country. In addition to the usual strike-breaking methods, United Fruit evicted strikers from company towns.

In the face of 1954's massive union mobilization, the democratically elected administration of President Ramon Villeda Morales promised to staunch the extreme and increasing poverty of the times. Between 1958 and 1960, the government distributed 30,000 hectares to landless Hondurans, most of which came from the enormous holdings of United Fruit. Accompanied by howls of protest from that company and its smaller competitor, Standard Fruit, Morales shepherded through legislature the first Honduran agrarian reform in 1962. In this reformist and permissive atmosphere, a new agrarian workers' organization emerged, the National Federation of Honduran Peasants (FENACH). It began organizing renters and other marginal tenants on United Fruit land.

Faced with increasing rural unrest, United Fruit contacted Col. Oswaldo López Arellano of the Honduran Air Force and convinced him to oust Morales. With United Fruit support, Arellano orchestrated a coup on October 3, 1963, that deposed the Villeda government. Immediately thereafter, Arellano halted the agrarian reform and repressed FENACH.[21]

Given the strong presence of Chiquita/United Brands/United Fruit in the country's politics and history, especially in regard to land, one understands why the Honduran government would think twice before supporting the Tacamiches in their struggle against Chiquita. Bananas account for more than a third of Honduras' export dollars, and Chiquita produces the lion's share. In fact, the company is bigger than the country. Chiquita's total annual sales internationally exceed the Honduran gross national product. The 1990 Chiquita strike cost Chiquita a few cents per share; the Honduran economy, however, was devastated by an estimated $60 million. By 1990, Honduran president Rafael L. Callejas was referring to his country as a "banana republic." After government troops helped defeat a strike, Callejas told the *Los Angeles Times*, "We want to be a banana republic, but not in the pejorative term of the past. We want to produce more bananas. We should become the largest producer of bananas in the world."[22] To continue taxing and profiting from the foreign exchange brought to Honduras by Chiquita, the government and local business interests try to keep the company from fleeing the country. To do this, they tend to support the company in disputes with small groups such as the Tacamiches.[23]

No end to this conflict appears on the horizon. Chiquita owns 51,000 hectares of land worldwide and leases more than 16,000 hectares, mostly in Costa Rica, Panama, and Honduras. The company has 35,000 employees in Central and

South America. As Chiquita warns in a recent shareholder prospectus, further strikes are likely whenever labor contracts expire.[24] Chiquita's apparent acceptance of the labor strike as integral to its business dealings seems to portend plenty of conflict in the future.[25]

IMF Increases Rural Poverty in Honduras

Chiquita's recent evictions highlight a decades-long trend in which large landowners and multinational corporations have steadily eroded the land base of poor Hondurans. A 1974 study found that 4% of the agricultural landholdings in Honduras encompassed 56% of the land, while the other 64% of landholders accounted for only 9% of the land. One hundred and fifty thousand households were landless. To survive, almost 80% of all Hondurans must sell their labor to large landowners. Honduran land reform legislation during the '70s and '80s failed to make a significant dent in this maldistribution because it left most of the largest landowners untouched.[26]

Yet even extremely modest land reforms are being attacked. In 1992, at the height of Chiquita's influence in national politics under the corrupt Callejas administration, the International Monetary Fund (IMF) pushed Honduras to pass a law for the Modernization of the Agricultural Sector. This law withdrew technical aid, loans, and marketing assistance formerly given to small farmers and has severely weakened the country's agrarian reform. The measure confiscates much of the land distributed through the agrarian reform process by designating it as national forest land. According to Windfuhr, government experts in Germany concerned with international development estimate that 100,000 Honduran families will lose their land because of the law.

Implementation of the 1992 law also allowed big landowners like Chiquita to buy reform sector land never meant for ownership by large foreign corporations. "In all of 1992," said Owens, "there was frenetic movement on the part of the big investors and fruit companies to get the best of this land." A similar withdrawal of constitutional protections from communal *ejido* lands in Mexico helped spark the Zapatista rebellion in 1994. Rather than passing *ejido* lands down through the family by inheritance, thus ensuring that each generation would get land, the constitutional reform gutted Article 27 of the constitution and allowed the sale of *ejido* lands to private investors and companies for the first time.

The 1992 "modernization" law in Honduras benefited the buyer of reform sector land, yielded more profit to local elites and foreign agribusiness like Chiquita, and garnered more foreign exchange for Honduras to pay its debt to the IMF and the World Bank. But it is leading to an even more concentrated land ownership pattern and, in the long run, may erode what remains of the relatively dependable and roughly egalitarian food supply provided by small farmers.

Because Honduras devotes a large proportion of its land to export agriculture, the country depends on food imports and is vulnerable to the volatile market swings of agricultural produce. The 1996 drought in the United States, for example, decreased the caloric intake of the average poor Honduran. In the second half of that year, the basic foods in Honduras, beans and corn, tripled or quadrupled in price and made it difficult for many small farmers to buy even seed for the next season's crop.

The Honduran government's turn toward neoliberal policy in the '90s effected a shift in its attitude toward squatters. In the '70s and '80s, landless peasants like Elvia Alvarado squatted vacant land to encourage the government to enforce the agrarian reform law. Government officials at the National Agrarian Reform Institute helped the peasants with creative financing or outright expropriation from large landowners who left the land vacant. Since the modernization law of 1992, which repealed land reform, however, the government almost always uses the might of the Honduran military to help landowners like Chiquita in evictions.

Government repression of land occupations made many in the *campesino* movement more cautious. According to Owens, "I think a general sense of demoralization has affected the popular movements over the past two years. Not just *campesino* organizations, but the trade unions and everybody have fallen into a state of low morale. There is no sense of combativeness, of resistance, of feeling that somehow organizing from the grass-roots will get anyplace. It is really quite discouraging. I believe very much in movement building, but it is very hard to get anybody to do anything in terms of grassroots organization."

When asked what people can do to escape low morale, Owens said that the growing poverty may increase the likelihood of more militant tactics. "I am afraid it will be some extreme crisis. There has been terrific inflation. If the inflation continues and if the shortage of food continues, then there could be some sort of real civil unrest." For over a week in November 1996, local community groups seized and refused passage to anyone on the major highway between the capital and one of the richest agricultural areas of the nation. "That type of thing could happen on a general level if things don't get better somehow," Owens said. "It would tend to be chaotic, and I am not sure that anything great would come from that. There is no easy way." In 1997, a crime wave gripped Honduras, the government electricity company and fast-food outlets were bombed, and unions organized widespread strikes.

Tacamiche Resistance Pays Off

The resistance to eviction and the protest by the Tacamiches garnered widespread attention and support. The media within Honduras covered the story as told

by the Tacamiches, and Honduran human rights and *campesino* organizations
gave moral, tactical, and material support. FIAN-International organized a letter-
writing campaign responsible for 10,000 letters sent to Lindner and President Reina of Honduras. In November, FIAN presented the Tacamiche case to the United
Nations Committee on Economic, Social, and Cultural Human Rights in Geneva.
An article in the *New York Times* and one in a Cincinnati weekly, where Chiquita
has its headquarters, seems to have increased the pressure, as well.

Locals in Cincinnati organized two demonstrations in front of the Chiquita
building, one with about 40 participants, the other with about 70. A frigid winter
day caused low turnout for the first demonstration, at which a waiter emerged
from the Chiquita building with hot chocolate and mugs on a cart. Asked about the
hospitality, the waiter replied that the chocolate was "courtesy of Carl Lindner."
The demonstrators refused such sweet nothings.

The Tacamiches demanded not chocolate, but housing, and after almost a
year their resistance paid handsome dividends when Chiquita and the Honduran
government finally relented. On November 4, 1997, the families moved into the
47 newly constructed shacks; shortly thereafter, Chiquita rebuilt another 76 homes
and two of the three demolished churches. The government invested over $80,000
(a lot of money in Honduras) in self-help industries for the Tacamiches, including
a fish farm and concrete block manufacturing. According to Windfuhr, the Tacamiches made the best of a bad negotiating position. "After no activity for several
months, some of the victims see it as a first victory. They are not totally satisfied,
but at least their protest and the international support led to Chiquita taking the initiative to build more houses and rebuild the destroyed churches."

The Tacamiche case demonstrates both the danger of land occupations and
the power of protest. Chiquita found it expedient to evict 123 families and eradicate an entire town in retaliation for land occupations. But by refusing to move
into the rebuilt housing and by securing assistance from a wide array of community and international groups, the Tacamiches obtained government funding and a
fully rebuilt town. Perhaps most importantly, the Tacamiches profoundly affected
the politics of Honduras by shocking the public with years of headlines. Only time
will reveal the outcome for Chiquita of this intensive public relations debacle.

To cleanse the term "banana republic" of its distasteful meaning, the Honduran government and Chiquita may have to be guided less by the wishes of
shareholders, Honduran tax collectors, and the international investment community, and more by the basic needs of Hondurans impoverished by a century of
American corporate hegemony. Chiquita is the world's largest supplier of bananas, which account for 60% of its sales. The company is trying to diversify into
prepared foods, as well.[27] No company that depends on the good will of consum-
ers can afford to ignore public opinion indefinitely.

C H A P T E R   3

Philosophy to Squat By

The New Challenge to Property

"Thou shalt not steal," we are often told. It is clearer to me that the majority are poor because a few are appropriating more than they need or work
for. We cannot let a few rob us of our birth rights and systematically kill
us by this act of robbery — with our children undernourished and our
bodies weighed down by tuberculosis. God, rather, is the God of life who
wills that we all live, and struggle to live. The land and the water that we
need for life belongs to us all.

Kuya Terio, Filipino peasant, 1976[1]

In the short passage above, Kuya Terio voices the main arguments in favor of
squatting. People have a natural right to land, which belongs to all. The rich are rob-
bing the impoverished of the most basic necessities of life. The struggle to live is an
absolute good. All these arguments lend ethical weight to the mass of people who
every day overflow the boundaries of property to fill vacant land and housing.

One could also argue other points in favor of squatting. To be truly free,
people need a place to call their own, privacy not only from governments but landlords. By inhabiting space, squatting allows the poorest sectors of society to create
culture, community, and employment. Equality demands change in the badly
skewed distribution of property. Not hard work by the rich, but wars, conquest,
theft, and fraud have determined most of this maldistribution of property. All these
arguments figure in this chapter, devoted to the philosophical defense of squatting
and the interrogation of misperceptions of and prejudices against squatters.

Need over Property, Compassion before Accumulation

Fourteen percent of the world's population, 840 million people, are chronically hungry. Every day 11,000 children die of malnutrition — one every eight seconds.[2] Construction of new housing lags far behind world population growth. Homeless people die of exposure even on the gold-paved streets of every major U.S. city. Faced with death and disease from malnutrition and lack of shelter, large sectors of the Third World poor have no choice but to occupy land; build shelter from bits of salvaged cardboard, discarded lumber, or sheets of plastic; and grow food to sustain their malnourished children. "The land all sold, / to the rich sharks, / the poor cannot work any more / to earn their daily bread," sings Saturnino, a balladeer in Mato Grosso, Brazil.[3]

Necessity is the first and culturally most powerful argument in support of squatters. The United Nations Charter on Social and Economic Human Rights defines a right to shelter; all major religions have ministries of charity; common law prioritizes necessity over property. In the '60s, Charles Avila, a seminary student in the Philippines, toured the countryside and recorded the Bible-inspired musings of small farmers in his book *Peasant Theology*. Avila captures the justification of necessity as voiced to him by a very old Filipino peasant:

> The land is like the air. It is just *there* for us to use in accordance with our need and labor. I did not ask to be born, he says, almost mad. But I was born to live — needing land, and air, and other things. The birds of the air and the animals of the field get what they need in order to live. Can anyone of us say they don't have that right? Why then are we denied the right to own the land we need to have a decent living?[4]

Few people accept death without a struggle. By denying need in the name of property, society denies its own humanity and compassion in favor of cold legalism and just deserts. Hard love becomes an excuse for a hard heart. If not revitalized, hardened hearts refuse society and civilization for a dead society of consumerism, materialism, law, and greed — not love, not generosity, not charity. In the following passage, Filipino peasants imagine St. Peter denying a rich but pious landlord entry into heaven.

> In your lifetime, there were so many poor people right in front of your mansion and you hardly lifted a finger to help them because you were so selfish, too busy in self-sanctification. You had many tenants who produced the rice for you and whose children died of undernourishment because you were always opposed to land reform. There was no concern, no love in your heart. Depart from me, because I was hungry and you did not feed me.[5]

Like the teaching of Christ as interpreted by Liberation Theologians, the defense of necessity is ultimately a law of love. It appeals to our common humanity, our sense of the beautiful, and our feelings of family. If one can transcend an understandable cynicism and achieve this ethic of selflessness, of caring for the downtrodden, then one has turned the defense of necessity into the necessity of mutual compassion. Only with compassion can society hope to bridge the terrible gap between economic ideology and the reality of poverty.

Demanding a Fair Share: Squatter Ethics of Equality

On May 13, 1974, a contingent of Mohawk Indians and allies occupied New York's Adirondack Mountains. They called the land Ganienkeh, an assertion of Mohawk national sovereignty. After several months, locals claimed that the occupation impeded the state park's recreational purpose. The native activists conceded the point, but noted that the occupation took very little relative to other big landholders in the area. The Native American periodical *Akwesasne Notes* contrasted Ganienkeh with corporate ownership of land in the neighborhood: "Diamond International has 60,000 acres. Draper Division of Rockwell International has 75,000 acres. Georgia Pacific has 63,609 acres. Finch Pruyer and Co. has 155,000 acres. Ganienkeh: 612 acres."[6]

Just as recreationalists criticized Mohawks and not corporations for taking more than their fair share, critics who call squatters selfish ignore the millions of acres held by the relative few to the exclusion of many. In striving for a more egalitarian distribution, landless squatters exhibit not selfishness, but its opposite. Even those who squat as a matter of principle, much maligned as activists and not truly in need, exhibit generosity. Jeremy Graham of Homes Not Jails, San Francisco, worked to feed and shelter the homeless with such fervor that he no longer had time for the office job that paid his rent. Graham quit and started squatting.

Leo Tolstoy noted a curious phenomenon of society. The impoverished, who have so little, give a greater proportion of their earnings in charitable donations than the very rich. Hunger and homelessness could be eradicated to the extent that the wealthy can overcome what clearly appears to be selfishness. Such generosity is no naive hope for the impossible. In the '50s and early '60s, Vinoba Bhave walked 40,000 miles from Indian village to Indian village to encourage such magnanimity. Convinced landlords donated over 4.5 million hectares of land. This 4.5 million hectares came from the combined generosity of hundreds of landlords across India who took the difficult step of relinquishing privilege. Similar landlords exist around the world, landlords like Butterfly McQueen of Augusta, Georgia, who played Prissy in *Gone With the Wind*. McQueen left her rental homes to the tenants who lived in them when she died in 1996.[7] Also in 1996, a

Christian group called the Mount Hermon Association near Santa Cruz, California, donated the leased land upon which 142 families had built homes. "We are inspired by the Association's willingness to do what is in the best interest of the homeowners without any financial gain for themselves," responded eight of the homeowners. "Thank you for this generous and unselfish gift."[8] In Wyoming, Native Americans have opposed recreational rock climbers who pound bolts into and ascend the 1,200-foot Devil's Tower during Native American spiritual rituals held at the base of the rock every June. "To see the climbers up there is in conflict with what we tell our children about respecting sacred sites," said 78-year-old Johnson Holy Rock of the Pine Ridge Reservation to a reporter. After years of discussion held by the National Park Service, nearly all the climbers agreed to stop ascending the rock during the sacred month of June. Only 193 people climbed the tower in June 1995, compared with 1,293 in June 1994.[9] These few voluntary and admittedly small concessions suggest that generosity does exist, and could theoretically fuel substantial redistribution.

It will require hundreds of millions of Vinoba Bhaves, Butterfly McQueens, Mount Hermon Associations, and sensitive rock climbers to eradicate as much inequity as this world now endures, however. According to the United Nations Food and Agriculture Organization (FAO), the top 2.4% of agricultural landholdings in the world encompassed 76.3% of the acreage in 1980. The 82% of holdings on the bottom covered only 8% of the land. This skewed distribution roughly mirrors the concentrated distribution of wealth in general. According to the United Nations Development Program, the richest 20% of the world's population garnered 79% of the world's income in 1988, while the poorest 20% divided only half a percent of the income. This disparity doubled between 1960 and 1988 and will continue to increase in the early 21st century. In 1996, more than 3 billion people made less than $2 a day, while 358 billionaires controlled assets greater than the combined annual incomes of countries with 45% of the world's people.[10] If the distribution of wealth largely determines access to land, and the rich have more wealth than they did in 1981, then the poor have even less land access today then they did at the time of the FAO study. In other words, the distribution of land is steadily concentrating into the hands of fewer and fewer people.

This bad news is even worse than it seems. Since many people have more than one piece of land, and the FAO did not count the landless, actual land distribution in 1980 was skewed more than figures indicate. The Cornell University Rural Development Committee considers most of the families who own small holdings "near-landless" because their land is of inadequate size or quality to provide a reasonable livelihood. A small land base allows family members few choices other than wage labor, underemployment, or squatting. Those considered "near-landless" include 58.4% of agricultural households in Africa, Asia (excluding China), the Middle East, and Latin America.

Worse yet, the near-landless can count themselves lucky compared to their neighbors who have no land at all. The landless in Africa, Asia (excluding China), the Middle East, and Latin America include 13.3% of agricultural households (173,600,000 people).[11] Combined, 71.7% of rural households in the Third World are landless or near-landless.

Further spheres of concentration and dispossession become evident when considering the scant ownership of land by women. According to the United Nations 1988 *World Economic Survey*, women hold title to only 8.1% of agricultural properties in Africa, 12.1% in Asia, 13.6% in Latin America, and 13.8% in the developed countries. Substantially worse than the current wage gap of women earning only 70 cents to the average man's dollar, U.S. women own only 15.7% of all land, both rural and urban.[12]

Particularly galling is the differing access to land across borders. While Australians and New Zealanders enjoy 2 hectares of arable land per person, their neighbors in Asia have the least arable at 0.18 hectares per person. Likewise, people in the United States luxuriate in approximately 1.7 hectares of arable land per person while South Americans have only 0.44 hectares per person and Central Americans have even less. Lightened border restrictions could ease this garish inequality between continents, but virulent anti-immigrant sentiment in countries such France, Australia, and the United States go largely unchallenged by comfortable liberals.[13]

Any immigrant lucky enough to navigate the treacherous crags placed by the Immigration and Naturalization Service faces tremendous odds against achieving the American Dream of home ownership. Concentration of land and housing within the United States rivals that of most Third World nations. According to a report by the U.S. Congress, the wealthiest half-percent of the population owned 35.6% of all private real estate in 1986, and the wealthiest tenth owned 77.8%.[14]

In 1978, 80% of the U.S. population owned no land at all, according to a U.S. Department of Agriculture study.[15] True, a much larger percentage of *families* own land than do individuals. But this alarming landless figure nevertheless provides an important perspective since it points to the lack of control over land by women and young adults. The oft-cited family statistics of owner-occupied homes masks this gendering of unequal distribution and the inequalities between generations.

Distribution of private land between ethnic groups further exacerbates the concentration of U.S. land. Comparing the 1978 landownership study with 1980 population figures shows that non-Hispanic whites were 77% of the population, but owned 91% of the private land. This gave whites the largest per capita ownership of any ethnic group. Hispanics, who comprised 6.4% of the population in

1980, owned only 0.7% of the private land in 1978.[16] Native Americans comprised 0.6% of the population and owned 0.4% of the private land (precious little of it in Manhattan). Non-Hispanic Blacks, the second-largest U.S. ethnic group, comprised 11.7% of the population but owned only 0.9% of the private land. Lastly, Asians and Pacific Islanders were 1.5% of the population and owned the least absolute private acreage at 0.1%, and also the least per person, just behind Black per capita ownership.[17]

These figures give the distribution of acres, not the distribution of value. They do not show who owns the most valuable land and who the least valuable. If the general distribution of wealth in the United States is any indication, then the above figures adjusted for value would reveal an even more skewed distribution. Consistent with growing inequality of income, land owned by non-whites is decreasing over time. According to the Emergency Land Fund, an Atlanta organization that provides low-interest loans to Black farmers in danger of losing their land, Black landownership has fallen steadily from 16 million acres in 1910 to 3.5 million acres in 1981. Blacks lost this land despite a rate of population growth greater than most other Americans. While an urbanizing Black population sold its land, the Blacks who remained in the South had little capital with which to compete against white mechanized farming.[18]

The U.S. poor also suffer from a maldistribution of housing. A large percentage of the population finds itself renting that most personal of necessities, the family home. The 1990 *Census of Housing* found that 30.9% of white households, 64% of Hispanics, 56.2% of African Americans, 47.5% of Asians or Pacific Islanders, and 45.1% of Native Americans rented.[19]

When looking at the entire U.S. population, 64.2% of occupied housing units were owner-occupied in 1990. At first glance, this figure implies a nation of owner-occupiers. Satisfied economists quote the number as proof of an egalitarian housing structure. The American Dream realized! But even those who do own their homes have lost the independence of the original Jeffersonian homesteaders. To achieve homeownership in 1994, families had to pay a national average of $154,500 for a new, one-family house. The average monthly mortgage payment for these families was $1,028, about 31% of their incomes, payable each month for an average of 29 years. Such a mortgage adds enough interest to the cost of a house to double its price to $354,000, a lifelong burden for most homeowners, even those in the middle class.

Fifty-eight percent of "owner-occupied" homes carried mortgages in 1993. Add those 34.2 million mortgaged homes to the 32.9 million homes rented that year, and this figure reveals that *about 73% of households were paying banks or landlords for their homes.* Only 27% of U.S. households owned their homes fully. Yet 86% of all U.S. adults would prefer to own their home.[20] Whether or not a mortgager likes to think of himself or herself as an owner, he or she pays a monthly check just like the renter. As over-limit credit cards and political slogans remind us, many people are just one paycheck away from debt-default and homelessness.

All the figures cited thus far refer to the distribution of land and housing among *private* owners. Another level of inequality in the United States comes with the distribution of rights to the 42% of U.S. land owned by the public sector, whether federal, state, or local. Not all people benefit equally from supposedly public resources. In his review of land ownership inequality in the United States, Cornell rural sociologist Chuck Geisler documents numerous studies that show how public land policy routinely subsidizes the wealthy, including one-sided access to timber, grazing, water, and mineral rights for well-endowed interest groups, corporations, and private recreational complexes. Meanwhile, the urban poor have difficulties even accessing national parks that affluent tourists routinely use as free retirement get-aways and private luxury resorts.[21] By attacking environmental regulations and public management, the 1996 Republican-led Congress attempted to increase even further the power of cattle interests and loggers over these public lands.[22]

Accusing squatters of selfishness, especially squatters who own no real property, ignores the larger picture of skewed property ownership. If selfishness is understood as devotion to one's own welfare to the exclusion of regard for others, then the ownership of large amounts of vacant land and housing by wealthy landlords more closely resembles the definition than any example of squatting.

Squatting Expresses Personality:
Suppress Squatting, and You Suppress Personhood

Distribution of land and housing may be skewed, but the Bible commands that thou shalt not covet thy neighbor's goods. Most say the smooth working of society requires property, and, if one accepts property, one must accept inequality. Since squatting violates property, grappling with the major arguments against squatting means reconceptualizing the arguments in support of property.

Three major arguments defend property. The personality theory portrays property as a necessity for individual freedom. The labor-desert theory sees the origin of property in hard work. Utilitarian theories see property as the most practical of arrangements for the welfare of all. Critics have used all these arguments against squatters, but squatters have countered by using the same personality, labor-desert, and utilitarian arguments against landlords.

G.W.F. Hegel cooked up the personality theory. To condense 85 grueling pages more radically than even *Reader's Digest* would stoop to, Hegel said owning a little piece of property helps express yourself. In all its modern permutations, the personality theory says that property allows freedom, individuality, privacy, and protection against government expansion at the expense of individuals. Stanford law professor Margaret Jane Radin explains the personality theory this way: "Property is necessary to give people 'roots,' stable surroundings, a context of control over the environment, a context of stable expectations that fosters autonomy and personality. Property is a property of persons; and this understanding of property is held to be necessary for human freedom."[23]

Certainly for the landowner, the current understanding of property allows him (90% likely to be male, as we have seen) to be himself. For an imaginary nation of owner-occupiers, the home is perhaps the ultimate in personal property, where people can most easily express themselves and "feel free." An Englishman's house is his castle.

But as applied to the squatter, tenant, or landless laborer, the property right can seem more of a coercive tool used by landlords and banks rather than an essential freedom. Property does not protect, but rather infringes on individuality, personhood, and liberty. Property means power by the landlord to charge rent and evict the occupier. The landlord's freedom is a double-plus unfreedom (that is, the opposite of freedom) for squatters, tenants, and laborers.

To promote the freedom of not only landlords, but also the landless, society must jettison the freedom of the few to charge rent, evict, and profit at the expense of somebody less fortunate than themselves. As promoted by conservative property theorists, equal freedom means every person's right to express individuality, privacy, stability, and independence. Squatting and small-scale farming express these attributes far more than the landlord/tenant relationship.[24] Squatters or owners of small plots, not tenants or the landless, have the ability to fully allow their personalities to flourish without infringing upon the rights of another. While squatting on unused land owned by large landowners may to a small degree circumscribe the landlord's ability to manifest individuality, it will to a much larger degree allow tenants and squatters the basic necessity for life, and hence personhood. If individuality and personhood are the goals, then the personality theory of property strongly endorses squatting and any other action that expands the number of people who can exhibit their personality through possessing a modest home or plot of land.

I Worked For It, I Get It

If my grandpa heard the personality theory as a justification for squatting, he'd bump his head on the ceiling of his coffin. "Hogwash! Bums who don't pay rent are plain crooks. They take homes that people worked hard to buy. It's too bad some folks are having a hard time, and we all want to help. But whoever doesn't own their place hasn't worked hard enough and should start working harder."

Grandpa had an ethic of just deserts, according to which landlords (including, incidentally, himself) deserve their rents because they worked hard to purchase the land or build the housing in question. Landless persons and tenants should have to work hard like the rest of the landowners if they want to achieve ownership.

Grandpa's belief that the current concentration of land springs from past labor has a long lineage. In the 17th century, John Locke, that founding theorist of modern capitalism, developed the most common justification for property, now known as the "labor theory of property." Locke believed that people held all land in common in a pre-civilization state of nature. When individuals mixed their labor with the land, the common became property.

A similar story of the emergence of property is the common law principle of first possession (also known as "title by grab"). He who achieves first possession has ownership. But over how much land and for how long should society allow ownership to the first possessor? Charles Avila overheard a peasant use the metaphor of a theater to question the idea of first occupancy as a right to ownership:

> And how absurd is the argument ... of those who claim absolute ownership over the land just because they were ahead of the rest in occupying it? They are like a person who went ahead to a theater and claimed exclusive ownership over all the space — all the seats available — in complete disproportion to his or her seating needs. And when the rest of the people arrived trying to get some seats, he forbade them — saying that because he had arrived earlier, he was now absolute owner of all the space.[25]

Locke answered the question about the amount of land that labor could privatize with his famous proviso: "Whatsoever, then, he removes out of the state that Nature hath provided and left it in, he hath mixed his labor with it, and joined to it something that is his own, and thereby makes it his property ... *at least where there is enough, and as good left in common for others*" (italics mine).[26] In other words, individual persons have a clear right to appropriate land as property, as long as more land remains for appropriation. At the end of his chapter on property, Locke unfortunately drew on concepts of consent and differential work to justify concentration. But leaving his ultimate conclusion aside for a moment, this proviso is the perfect justification for squatters. Its common sense justifies a completely egalitarian distribution of land and even squatting. "After all," says Radin, "if property is acquired from the common by a nonowner simply by taking it and using it, can we not sympathize with someone who does likewise with owned but unused property?"[27] At least in Brazil, peasant squatters have the labor-desert argument firmly in mind. Sue Branford and Oriel Glock, who spent years studying the agricultural politics of the region, say this about regional squatters:

> Most of the families still show a perhaps surprising respect for the law of
> the land, coupled with an even stronger faith in their concept of natural
> justice, to which they turn for legitimization of their claim to a holding if
> Brazil's legal system lets them down. For them, land in a wild and unoc-
> cupied region like the Amazon should belong to the people who have
> cleared it and made it bear fruit.[28]

Although the application of this principle to the Amazon forest is perhaps untenable
since the forest is already inhabited by indigenous peoples, the sentiment of these
squatters certainly applies to unused agricultural land.

Joining a Lockean story of original accumulation to a personality theory of
property, should not all unused land be considered common, or jointly owned by
humankind as a whole, since no person has mixed their labor with nor bound their
personality to the land? As long as a person labors and binds their personality to
land, whether a *de jure* owner, renter, or a squatter, should it not be their property?
Says one older peasant in Avila's *Peasant Theology,* "Why should only a few
landlords who do not till the land own the most of it and reap the benefits of our
labor?"[29] The egalitarian interpretation of Locke's proviso justifies squatting on
vacant land by any of the 71.7% of rural households in the Third World who count
themselves among the landless or near-landless.

But returning to Locke's meaning, he reasoned that where lack of land limited use, that is, where two individuals both wanted the same land, they simply
agreed upon a division. Over time, differential labor and ability, consent, and a fair
land market made an inequitable distribution of land, including Locke's own vast
acreage, eminently justifiable.[30] Locke's theory is the foundation of landlords' belief today that an inequitable distribution is justified and that squatting is ethically
wrong. Luckily for squatters, the argument holds no water.

First of all, Locke failed to address the consent of those born into the world
after the division of land into private property. Why should newcomers relinquish
their rights to as much and as good? Are they less than human for being part of a
later generation? Harvard professor Robert Nozick, in his *Anarchy, State, and
Utopia*, dons the Lockean fighting gloves at this point and argues that because the
civilizing benefits of property have improved the plight of the landless from what
it would be in the state of nature, the wealthy can justifiably ignore the poor's right
to enough and as good land.[31]

Perhaps it comes as a surprise to Nozick, but most rational people, if faced
with death by starvation, as are 14% of the world's population, would probably
choose Locke's state of nature over today's highly concentrated ownership of
land. Even many not faced with starvation would choose Locke's state of nature to
the current environmental crises. From Earth First! activists and some in the Native American movement to many of those in the Third World who occupy land

for basic shelter or subsistence agriculture, a substantial percentage of the world's population might feel more at home and have better opportunities to survive in the Lockean state of nature than under today's Hobbesian, dog-eat-dog capitalism. Robert J. Wenke, professor of anthropology at the University of Washington, comments on the poverty of modern arrangements:

> Today, two-thirds of the world's population are "involuntary vegetarians" whose diet, morbidity and mortality rates, and general standard of living compare poorly with those of most Pleistocene hunting and gathering bands: and even in the most industrialized countries, the vast majority labors longer for sustenance than did many of the people of prehistory.[32]

But even for those landless who would choose today's starvation (as long as they can watch "Beverly Hills 90210" on TV), their preference fails to justify inequality. Nozick presents us with double jeopardy: a choice between the current capitalist property system, ensconced in the modern world with all its technology, on one hand, and an imagined state of nature on the other. Other forms of land tenure preferable to both today's capitalism and the state of nature can cancel Nozick's argument and justify squatting. G.A. Cohen at the University of Oxford has noted that because Nozick relies on utilitarianism to support his natural rights argument, he leaves his natural rights theory vulnerable to empirical arguments.[33]

For those who can think of better systems of land tenure than the pure capitalism promoted by Nozick, his justification for violation of the Lockean proviso collapses. Indigenous peasants in Ecuador have organized as the Confederation of Indigenous Nationalities of Ecuador and have delineated a five-point agrarian reform proposal in which they reject the market as a way to distribute land. "While the market acts as a dynamic force and improves the efficiency of many enterprises, it cannot rationally distribute access to land. Rather, if the market is given free rein, land tends to become concentrated in the hands of a few."[34] Abundant examples of better land tenure systems and needed reforms put the lie to Nozick, whose justification for inequitable distribution of land simply repeats Aristotle's crude justification for slavery or Hobbes' justification for monarchy: if better off enslaved than free, total subjection is justified.

Considering the above, and despite Locke's ultimate conclusion, it seems the Lockean proviso justifies squatting in the face of land concentration. The only justification that gives the original privatizers ownership and deprives all latecomers is first acquisition, or title by grab, and this argument implodes when presented with systems preferable to unequal capitalism. Nozick fails to completely convince with his labor-desert argument. If anyone is to own land on the basis of labor, it should be those who actually *work* the land, in other words, squatters, renters, shareholders, and construction workers. The National Campesino Confederation in Mexico declared as much in its 1935 statement of principles, which included "defense of the thesis that the land belongs to those who work it, including ... *peones* [day laborers], *acasillados* [resident laborers], sharecroppers, small farmers, and the rest of the organized workers of the *campo* [rural areas]."[35]

In 1935, as well as today, agricultural laborers in the Third World probably win the prize for the world's hardest workers. While I admit my grandfather earned recognition as a veritable workaholic and thus, according to Locke or Nozick, was justified in owning more property than those who worked less, he got much of his income from buying and selling real estate. Though he improved each property before selling it, the income he received on his rentals certainly outweighed the work he did, if one considers the average income of people worldwide.[36] He owned much more than would someone less fortunately placed, even if the less fortunate person worked at least as hard, for just as long, and just as diligently. The concept of original common and the labor theory of property, therefore, justifies squatters, not absentee landlords. Nature or God created the earth, and therefore landlords do not ultimately own the land. The land should remain common because it began as common, human attempts to privatize it notwithstanding. What is common and unused, even if someone wrongly claims it as property, the squatter may use without infringing on the original state of nature.

Mang Guimo, a landless Filipino peasant, questioned the right of the landlord Don Jose to own 700 hectares. "Before Don Jose and I were born, the land was already there. When Don Jose and I shall die, the land will still be there. Whose is the land really?"[37] Guimo's reflection on death and its consequences for ownership is strikingly similar to Ralph Waldo Emerson's poem "Hamatreya." In the poem, Emerson assumes the voice of the land:

> They called me theirs,
> Who so controlled me;
> Yet every one
> Wished to stay, and is gone,
> How am I theirs,
> If they cannot hold me,
> But I hold them?[38]

How ridiculous for a single landlord, with the inconsequential effect of his momentary life and a title deed akin to the emperor's clothes, to presume ownership of something so fundamental as a portion of the timeless earth. "Earth laughs in flowers," Emerson continues, "to see her boastful boys / Earth-proud, proud of the earth which is not theirs." Ownership is just a relationship between humans, a bundle of rights, as the property theorists say, but the intuition that nobody can really *own* the earth remains. If nobody owns the land, how is the squatter who borrows a vacancy wrong? Is anybody else any different? Because death spirits us from this earth, ultimately nobody owns the land. If nobody owns the land, squatters infringe on no one.

Property Makes Peace?
Ahistorical Fences and Good Neighbors

Locke implied that property makes peace. Rather than fighting over land, Locke's story depicts persons in the state of nature voluntarily consenting to divide land as property. If property derives from voluntary consent, squatting seems to erode this peaceful coexistence. The violence, repression, and even revolutionary movements that sometimes spring from squatting certainly lend credence to such a view. Without property, the argument goes, people would have no reason to forego the use of their neighbor's house, a field, or even national territory. Thus constant war would develop from an international to a local level. Good fences make good neighbors.

The drawing of boundaries and some types of property certainly do make peace. After a successful occupation, most squatter movements subdivide the land to build homes or farm individually, a subdivision that they consider a form of private property. Property in these instances is essentially a mutual recognition of boundaries, and boundaries supposedly help avoid conflict between everything from individuals to nations.

But if voluntary divisions of land and the marking of boundaries can create peace, violent or oppressive division does the opposite. From ethnic cleansing in the Balkans to the battle over land between Israelis and Palestinians, the number of property conflicts that cause bloodshed seem innumerable. But the absence of war does not constitute peace. "Genuine peace is the fruit of justice, as the Bible says," a Filipino peasant woman told Avila. "And true peace is not a dead kind of peace, like the tenant's surrender to the landlord. It is a living, dynamic one which can often be accompanied by struggle and conflict."[39] For this peasant, peace is a state of mind, rather than the absence of conflict. Peace is justice, or the struggle for justice, a feeling or condition of mind, regardless of outward struggle. The context of property determines whether it makes peace. In his 1914 poem "Mending Wall," Robert Frost makes fun of the adage, "good fences make good neighbors."

> Before I built a wall I'd ask to know
> What I was walling in or walling out,
> And to whom I was like to give offense.
> Something there is that doesn't love a wall,
> That wants it down.[40]

Frost questions the nature of the fence before he agrees that it could improve the relation between neighbors. The nature of a wall — equal or unequal, imposed or agreed upon — determines whether or not the wall is "good" and promotes peace.

The legal construct of property allows for an inequitable distribution of resources and the ill will it engenders. Landless and near-landless would understandably resent walls that kept them from vast acreage, thus leaving them little or no space. While good fences can make good neighbors, bad fences often make bad neighbors. Fences based on inequality and violence beget more violence. Fences based on equality and agreement provide for peaceful coexistence. By definition, squatting is conflict, and the conflict should be resolved. But resolution rarely finds release in elision and suppression; it more often finds freedom in asking what was the origin of this conflict: the conflict itself (squatting) or an inequitable distribution of land and housing, a theft from the impoverished?

Landless squatters usually locate the beginning of the conflict at the original theft of land. Jesse John Roe Whitecloud, a homeless Chippewa Indian, called on history to justify the 1992 Santa Cruz Union of the Homeless occupation at River and Josephine streets.

> I own this fucking country. How can they say I am homeless when I've been here all the time? First they take away my land, now they take away my home, and then they say I can't even sleep on my own land. It has been mine the whole fucking time.[41]

History invariably reveals the source of conflict that gives rise to squatting: violent theft of land and unjust economic systems that have impoverished large sectors of the population. When one looks through history and finds that a particular piece of property sprang from violence or theft and not labor, and that inequitable property resulted in violence, not peace, squatting by the dispossessed becomes not only understandable but imperative for justice and ultimately for amicable coexistence. The history of Chiquita's land acquisition in Honduras, explained in chapter two, justifies the land occupation by the Tacamiches.

History is key, and popular squatting movements make this clear by using language to describe themselves as rightful owners retaking property that landlords stole. In Cuba, the slang term for squatters around Havana is *palestinos,* or "Palestinians." Popular opinion in Cuba sees the squatters, like the Palestinians, as having been unfairly dispossessed of their rural homesteads and as enduring adverse conditions in refugee camps while they fight for a just cause.[42] In Puerto Rico, squatters from the 1960s to the 1980s described themselves as *rescatadores,* or "rescuers." Many other squatters in Latin America, like landless Mexican peasants during the Zapatista rebellion, call their occupations *recuperaciónes de tierra,* translated as "land recoveries" or "land recuperations."[43] Movement language historicizes the struggle, pointing to governments, colonists, large landowners, and foreign corporations as the real thieves of property that rightfully belongs to the "recuperators."

> You read in the paper, "*Campesinos* invade such and such a piece of land." That's not true. We don't invade land, we recover land that belongs to us by law but was invaded by the big landowners or the foreign companies. They're the invaders. By what right did they take the land from our families to begin with?[44]

Just as the newspaper twisted history in the case of Elvia Alvarado's occupation in Honduras, reporters, landlords, and government officials try to label squatting negatively with words like "occupation," "takeover," "seizure," or "invasion," all of which are ahistorical, stress the transgression of propertied boundaries, and conjure up violent images. The writing of Charles Abrams in *Man's Struggle for Shelter in an Urbanizing World,* first published in 1964, is a particularly stark example of this use of this value-laden invasion language:

> Human history has been an endless struggle for control of the earth's surface; and conquest, or the acquisition of property by force, has been one of its more ruthless expedients. With the surge of population from the rural lands to the cities, a new type of conquest has been manifesting itself in the cities of the developing world. Its form is squatting, and it is evidencing itself in the forcible preemption of land by landless and homeless people in search of a haven. Unlike other forms of conquest that were propelled by the pursuit of glory, trade routes, or revenues, squatting is part of a desperate contest for shelter and land.... As in a military campaign, some would bivouac during the night with their stock of materials behind a newly placed billboard. Next day, the horizon would be dotted with new rows of hovels, to which others would be added shack by shack, until the expansion was checked by a road, by a canal, or by an owner prepared to spill blood.[45]

Abrams depicts squatters as the aggressors, using battle and conquest imagery to define squatting generally. To Abrams, squatters are the invaders, fearsome foreign troops attacking and encroaching until civilization, whether road or canal, can stop them; the "owner prepared to spill blood" seems almost justified. By using the language of invasion and takeover, the media puts a negative slant on squatters and subtly prepares the public to accept violent repression as justified.

Because many activists, along with Nozick, believe that the history of property should determine to some extent its current distribution, it matters if "invasion" more accurately depicts squatting than does "recovery." If all the big landowners really did gain their property through hard work and mutual agreement, as my grandfather, Locke, and Nozick imply, anyone who needs a house or land should simply work harder. Nozick theorizes, "What each person gets, he gets from others who give to him in exchange for something, or as a gift. In a free society, diverse persons control different resources, and new holdings arise out of the voluntary exchanges and actions of persons."[46] Nozick continually allows his readers to entertain the idea that "existing society was led to by an actual history that was just."[47]

To test this key ideological defense of property against squatting, we can use Nozick's very fair criteria for a just distribution: its origin and the intervening steps of transfer. Each step along the line must be just for the final distribution to be just. Nozick states,

> A distribution is just if it arises from another just distribution by legiti-
> mate means.... The legitimate first "moves" are specified by the principle
> of justice in acquisition. Whatever arises from a just situation by just steps
> is itself just.[48]

Nozick leaves vague the specifics of how his principles of justice would apply to real life situations. The Pit River Tribe in California lost 3.2 million acres by 1853, part of the 64 million acres taken from California Indians when settlers massacred 90% of the California Indian population in the 19th century. In 1959, the tribe refused a cash settlement offered by the U.S. Indian Claims Commission in lieu of the land, much of which large corporations, including Pacific Gas and Electric, now own. Because the Commission refused to return even a small portion of the land itself, the Pit River Nation decided to occupy the P.G. & E. campsite on June 4, 1970.

Who should own the disputed P.G. & E. campsite? Nozick does say that a thief is not entitled to his "ill-gotten gains." "Justice in holdings is historical; it depends on what actually has happened."[49] If the theft of 64 million acres from the Pit River Tribe violates justice in transfer, it counts as an injustice. If one could trace any ownership claim back and find an illegitimate transfer, then the land would have to be returned to the rightful owners or their heirs. Mang Fabio, a Filipino peasant, saw himself as one of these dispossessed heirs in 1976:

> Where is it written that God gave the land only to Don Jose and the land-
> lords? Nowhere! Where then did the landlords get the land they now
> own? From their parent landlords, you'll say, and these, where did they
> get the land? From their landlord forbears, you'll also say, who got them
> from their landlord ancestors. But I tell you, my friends, if we continue
> tracing the origin of landlord ownership, we must arrive at a time when
> the lands were grabbed by force from our own great-great grandparents.[50]

Nozick recognizes that unjust distributions must be rectified, even after several generations had become used to their new benefits. Time does not absolve an injustice, especially when current owners continue to profit off the impoverishment of the original owner's progeny.

The catch with Nozick and many landlords is that they do not acknowledge the massive injustices that have shaped the worldwide distribution of land and income. In light of the violent history of ownership, Nozick would find it difficult to show how his principles of acquisition and transfer actually adhere to written history. And without this adherence, the current distribution of property has no legitimate claim. Without legitimacy, landowners cannot credibly claim the sanctity of property as a defense against squatters. Indeed, squatters can claim that the current large landowners are the beneficiaries of unjust violence and theft in the past, and should therefore return a substantial proportion of land to the dispossessed.

Nearly every social movement for land or housing has some sense of historical injustice, and most have members who research the details extensively.[51] The reader now knows the historical details in the case of Tacamiche against Chiquita, but a broader history of dispossession and inequitable land distribution justifies squatting more generally.

Rousseau believed inequitable distribution originated in the use of violence.[52] One of the Tacamiche plantation workers evicted for squatting on Chiquita land theorized the same origin of private property. As the first nomadic farmers came to know the areas with the most fertile soil, the Tacamiche said, they settled down.

> After a while, some of the people got tired of working, and so they set about trying to gain control over others so that others would do their work for them. They also set out to take control of the best lands, so that others who had no land would have to work for them even harder, just to survive. This was called private property.[53]

Thus, contrary to Locke's and Nozick's stories, we have a competing theory of property that undercuts the legitimacy of its present concentration: the violent origin of property for the purpose of inequality. If the origin of land ownership can be traced to violence and not consent, then the property rights of current large landowners are revealed as unjust impositions.

Rousseau and the Tacamiche plantation worker were guessing when they theorized violent origins, as did Locke when he theorized consent. Nobody really knows how property and its inequitable distribution began. Most archaeologists guess that property in land originated with agriculture in the Neolithic era between 10,000 and 6,000 B.C.E. Primitive agriculture led to a more sedentary culture than the transitory pastoralism of hunter-gatherer societies could provide. The early "complex societies," that is, Mesopotamia, Egypt, China, the Indus Valley civilization, Inca, and Maya, all blossomed only after evidence of agriculture. The greater stability of agriculture allowed wealth accumulation and permanent shelters.

Whether inequality during the formation of complex societies originated from hard work or violence is anyone's guess, since the ancients left thin archaeological records and few hints of social organization other than a few skulls bashed in by blunt instruments. Once we pass the prehistoric period, more reliable snapshots of social organization have been found in fragments of written language, which give well-known evidence of violence as the basis of inequality.

"Historically, as ethically, private property in land is robbery," argues the American economist Henry George in *Progress and Poverty*. "It nowhere springs from contract; it can nowhere be traced to perceptions of justice or expediency; it has everywhere had its birth in war and conquest, and in the selfish use which the cunning have made of superstition and law."[54] George saw the "original equal right to land" extinguished by violence in ancient Greece and Rome when warfare concentrated power in the hands of chieftains and the military class. This enabled them to monopolize common lands, divide small plots among themselves, and reduce the conquered to a state of serfdom.[55]

Early Greek and Roman societies based their division of land on the strongest male in the family. The Roman Empire conquered land of neighboring communities and divided it among the Roman elite. Germans between the fourth and sixth centuries A.D. won their lands by invading the Romans. Feudal lords in the middle ages maintained their ascendant position over serfs by laws with penalties of torture and death. The depopulation of the countryside during the enclosures in Europe depended on forceful expulsion of entire families and the military suppression of spontaneous revolts among family farmers. The imposition of Western concepts of absolute land ownership during colonial and imperial periods in Asia, Africa, North America, Latin America, and the Middle East succeeded only through forced expulsion or suppression of the inhabitants by foreign armies. History texts make the case most clearly that without violence, no substantially inequitable distribution of land could exist.

Water Under the Bridge:
Adverse Possession and the Drowning of the Past?

Violence, corruption, and theft marred the distribution of land and property from ancient Greece to postcolonial societies. Steering their pretty yachts from this mucky history, philosophers and legal scholars who recognize these historical facts say past injustices are water under the bridge.

They argue for adverse possession, a double-edged principle for squatters. Adverse possession absolves the current occupier when an injustice occurred long ago. The original occupier's title should last only so long, after which the statute of limitations wipes the historical slate clean and current occupiers become rightful owners. Current occupiers may have invested heavily in their property, lack knowledge of its stolen nature, or, under the influence of copious John Wayne films, even consider the violence justified. To dispossess hard workers or the uninformed of their life savings for abstract historical justice would, the philosophers argue, add injury to injury.

Adverse possession laws can theoretically protect squatters from landowners after a certain number of years. More often, though, adverse possession is used to absolve current landowners in cases where their titles can be traced to a past injustice. Beyond a sense of compassion for current landowners, the theorists say, adverse possession makes economic sense now, since it frees occupiers to make long-term investments without fear of losing title. "Barring old valid claims is the price worth paying to protect valid titles against ceaseless attack," asserts Richard Epstein, law professor at the University of Chicago. "The social gains from forcing quick resolution of disputes are so enormous that everyone is better off with the limitation than without it."[56]

Here you may recall from chapter two the argument made against the Tacamiches by Chiquita's Carl Lindner: "The Honduran government, the business community, and many other sectors, have expressed serious concern about the potential threat of further land invasions if the Tacamiche situation were to continue."[57] In other words, if you let the Tacamiches get away with occupying land, everyone else in Honduras will want to occupy land, as well. Even in the most glaring cases of recent injustice, relenting on one case creates a precedent. In Brazil they call it the Copacabana syndrome. "Indigenous land could be anywhere … give the indigenous people this area, and next they'll want Copacabana beach."[58] Since the return of Copacabana to rectify past wrongs seems preposterous, property theorists preclude any return of land at all. Righting past wrongs would only lead to chaos and conflict. "My own judgment," comments Epstein, "is that any effort to use massive social transfers to right past wrongs will create far more tensions than it is worth, so treating all errors as a giant wash is the best of a bad lot."[59]

But Epstein's giant wash capsizes his utilitarian argument, because squatting has immediate utilitarian benefits for national economies. Epstein says that the current distribution is "the best of a bad lot." But is a world where 840 million go hungry and where 1 billion adults were either unemployed or underemployed in 1995 really the best we can do?[60] Most land and housing direct action occupies previously unoccupied land and housing, improves its value, and brings it into the economy as a productive asset. "If the 'wrongdoers' are productive and the titleholders are passive," Radin questions, "are the 'wrongdoers' so wrong in the utilitarian sense?"[61] Far from decreasing the real gross national product of their nation, squatters use appropriate technology to alleviate unemployment, increase the housing stock, and produce food crops. Without squatters and their unconventional forms of production, a much larger proportion of the world's poor would depend on charity or starve to death. Would Epstein and other property theorists prefer that these landless persons quietly die?

Epstein says current owners should remain owners because they were ignorant of the stolen nature of their goods, but no courtroom would allow such an argument for anything but land. If a person unknowingly buys stolen artwork, his or her ignorance fails to protect his or her ill-gotten gain from the claims of those from whom it was stolen. In the case of landlords, most have long since received the land's purchase price plus interest in rents and other fees collected over the years or, in the case of railroad lands, for example, in actual use. "Even granting that landlords invested in the land a hundred years ago," a Filipino peasant told Avila, "who will deny that investment has already been recovered by now — not twice but at least a hundred times over?"[62]

If a particular landlord purchased stolen land and then received enough income from that land to pay back the purchase price, then it follows that any claim for compensation after a squatting incident approaches the ludicrous. Indeed, if the landowner had received more than the original purchase price, those from whom the land was stolen have a civil claim against the landlord.

Epstein says hearings and litigation to trace injustice in individual titles would be impossibly onerous. But in many cases the injustice happened within the last hundred or so years and victims have documentary evidence. In cases where descendants of the original victims are attempting litigation against the very corporation that took wrongful action, Epstein's argument utterly fails. Even in the case of injustice lost in the mists of history, we know that group activity (racism, sexism, wars of conquest, etc.) led to group advantage and group disadvantage. Courts could use class-action suits to rectify these injustices without an unreasonable outlay of resources. Social movements have successfully used rectification arguments on this historical basis. Even conservative Nozick grudgingly concedes that past injustices should be rectified on a macro basis.[63] Native Americans as a group have suffered because of their land loss, while wealthy Euro-Americans have benefited. The perpetrating and victimized entities still exist on a group level and are still affected by the past on a group level. A transfer to the poor of one group from the wealthy of the other group would begin rectification, moving society toward the goal of equity without creating disincentives to production.

To ignore a past wrong encourages future wrongs, a principle war crimes tribunals in the late 1940s forged into a law that would be used against the ethnic cleansing of land in the late 1990s. The validation of past violence actually harms society more than any irregularity caused by nonviolent squatting. Only by rectifying past land theft can we dissuade today's land theft and its consequent violence.

Culture, Neighborhood, and Squatting

Squatter settlements provide essential shelter to the poor and historical justice to us all, but whether in the "third" or "first" world, wealthy neighbors commonly complain of street crime and drugs. An acquaintance of mine once associated squatting with a broken-down crack house next to her home. The entire neighborhood felt threatened by these squatters, who left trash strewn about their yard, played loud music with disregard for quieter neighbors, and made residents more fearful of street crime.

These neighbors had an acceptable grievance against squatters. Yet evicting squatters has less of an effect on general anti-social behavior than does targeting the anti-social behavior itself. If squatters litter their yards and play loud music more than their rent-paying or homeowning neighbors, if they steal from neighbors, this behavior should itself be targeted. To evict an entire household of squatters when one or two of their number are responsible for anti-social behavior violates the basic legal principle that rejects group punishment for the crimes of an individual.

Even though most urban squatters take a position against crack houses, neighbors associate squatters of any stripe with the deterioration of a neighborhood, as wealthier and more stable neighbors sell their homes to speculators who leave them vacant. Yet neighborhood deterioration invites squatters more than squatters deteriorate a neighborhood. One of the biggest squatting operations in the United States was started by a group of neighborhood organizations that decided to recruit squatters as a way to *improve* their neighborhood. The Association of Community Organizations for Reform Now (ACORN) began in 1982 as a neighborhood organization in New York City committed to lowering the crime rate and increasing property values. Abandonment in the neighborhood caused tax delinquency, government takeover of buildings, and the auction of tax-delinquent buildings to speculators who left them vacant. The vacant buildings attracted drug dealers and crime, and many became crack houses.

ACORN first pressured the city to stop selling buildings to speculators. They lobbied the city to begin a homesteading program, in which low-income families would receive ownership of the buildings in exchange for sweat-equity improvements. A land trust would retain ownership of the land. When the city refused, ACORN started advertising for squatters to move into the neighborhood. Dozens of squatter families, mostly Latinos, moved into and repaired the broken-down houses while ACORN pressured the city and finally succeeded in legalizing the squatters' tenancy in 1987. Eric Hirsch, assistant professor of sociology at Columbia University, and Peter Wood, the executive director of the Mutual Housing Association of New York, describe the ACORN movement and squatting not as deterioration, but as an important method of improving New York's low-income housing stock:

> The rehabilitation of old housing stock is generally cheaper than new construction. If the buildings are allowed to stand vacant, however, they will suffer vandalism and physical deterioration from the elements, making them too costly to rehabilitate.[64]

ACORN fostered a highly organized squatters' movement to improve their neighborhood, but just by removing plywood from the windows of an abandoned home and making it look lived-in, even unorganized squatters improve an area's image and the real estate value of surrounding homes. The longer squatters live in a neighborhood and the more stable they become, the more squatters meet their neighbors, form friendships, and bring a greater sense of security to pedestrians who must walk past a block of abandoned homes and vacant lots.

Improvements that squatters make to a neighborhood can even bridge racial differences. Aisha Stone, an African American squatter from Philadelphia, said that her white "squatmates" initially had problems with the Black neighbors at one of her squats. But through community projects, they eventually grew to respect each other and live harmoniously.

> Doing stuff in the neighborhood and interacting changed the attitude of the neighborhood a lot. The neighbors started accepting us and not looking at the other people in the squat as all these white people who had moved into the neighborhood. People in the squat decided to go and clean up the street and the cops came and started bothering them because they knew they were squatting. The neighbors came and said leave them alone, they are cleaning up the block.[65]

While true in the case of many crack houses, the argument that squatting destroys neighborhood community seems totally untenable in the case of responsible and interactive squatters.

In the Third World, urban squatter settlements and large-scale, coordinated rural land occupations do more than improve neighborhoods. They start from scratch on vacant land and *create* brand-new neighborhoods. Likewise, in the case of former renters or owner-occupiers resisting eviction or eminent domain, the community resists the landlord or government, entities that have the legal power of eviction. The Sanrizuka struggle against airport construction in Japan and the Larzac farmers struggling against the expansion of a military base in France are examples of communities that resisted their demise by resisting eviction.

Many individual landlords acting independently can wreak the same destruction of a neighborhood. "Gentrification" is the gradual eviction of lower-income people from entire urban areas by the higher bidding of upper-income people. Ruth Glass first used the term "gentrify" in 1964 to describe the English gentry buying and renovating old buildings in the '60s.[66] Because of landlord willingness to raise rent beyond levels affordable to longtime residents, my former neighborhood in San Francisco, the Mission District, is undergoing a process of gentrification in which young Euro-Americans are displacing the former Chicano and Mexicano community. Though not as obvious as mass evictions, gentrification is more common and dangerous to community since it targets individual households one at a time, a big obstacle to effective organizing.

Where money can force the deterioration of neighborhood character through gentrification, society should protect renters. Where government threatens a neighborhood through eminent domain, as in Sanrizuka, society should protect resident homeowners. Where landlords abandon buildings and cause distress for residents, society should protect squatters. From urban punks in rich countries to indigenous Indians in Brazil, squatting and land struggle defends existing neighborhoods and provides fertile ground for the emergence or reemergence of incipient or threatened cultures.

Lazy Squatters: The Case of Dissolute Youth

Squatters steal housing or land, goes my grandfather's argument, because they don't work hard enough to buy. Their own laziness and individual shortcomings lead to squatting. But this tired argument hits short of the mark in many, if not most, instances. Obviously, in the Third World, squatters work harder than most, not on the most fertile flatlands, but on the rocky soil of mountainsides and the sandy soil near deserts, all several days' travel from transportation and markets. Squatters must contend not only with the vagaries of weather, but also with the vagaries of eviction. Rigoberta Menchú and her family squatted in the Altiplano of Guatemala. Calling her and her community lazy would be like calling the prodigal son industrious. To survive in the face of hunger, they had to marshal even their youngest children for long hours of clearing, digging, planting, hoeing, and weeding. When the landowners tried to evict their community, they had to expend additional energy in political organizing.

Calling Third World squatters lazy ignores their work and substantial contribution to society, but the laziness argument can at first appear sensible as applied in urban areas of the more affluent nations. Editors at the *New York Times* supported a May 1995 eviction of New York City squatters on East 13th Street because the city offered to sell the housing to a nonprofit housing provider and return it to the tax rolls.[67] True, the housing crisis would improve greatly if community groups that renovate housing for low-income families had access to more buildings. But too often city governments use this excuse to justify the eviction of squatted buildings when they could have donated hundreds of other vacant buildings with no resident squatters. The evicted homes referred to by the *New York Times* already housed low-income individuals and families who, with no help from the New York Police Department or funding from the city treasury, had done renovations over the previous ten years.

The city made no guarantee that the evicted squat would become inhabited anytime soon. In San Francisco, hundreds of Filipino tenants at the International Hotel, a single-room-occupancy building, fought eviction in the 1970s. The landlord said he wanted to renovate the building. When he finally evicted the tenants in 1977, he tore the building down. It remains a rat-infested, foul-smelling hole. How did that eviction help society, generate taxable revenue, or increase employment?

Between the lines of the *New York Times* editorial, one imagines a group of squatters too lazy to fix their decrepit buildings, who leach from society by refusing to provide profits to landlords, property taxes to their local governments, or mortgage interest to banks. Here we come to the crux of the conservative argument against squatting: squatters lead dissolute lives and should get real jobs. In a 1987 article in the *National Review*, Peter Weber dismisses New York's Lower East Side squatters variously as being political dilettantes, drug users, and thieves, childish and "not truly needy."

> For the most part, they were kids, college-age, white, articulate, pausing to speak on the housing problem, but then rushing off to lectures at [New York University] or to eat the food churches give out for the truly poor. One of them, a young woman, was dressed in leather and sported an attractive plastic spider in her ear. Four years' college, year in Italy, corporate job, which she quit, hadn't had a shower in nine days.... She does what other kids around do. Work, maybe. Maybe hand out passes for [nightclubs]. Get drunk, do drugs.[68]

Weber's depiction holds an important truth. Squatting allows young adults a lifestyle without home ownership, taxes, or full-time employment. But Weber portrays this lifestyle as purely nonproductive. For those who prefer devoting their time to the unremunerated production of alternative culture through music, fine arts, or political activism, the argument that they fail to contribute rings false. Squatters may not have ordinary responsibilities, but they have responsibilities nonetheless to a political movement, musical band, or artists' collective. This kind of squatter sees alternative forms of production as far preferable to the industrial and often environmentally destructive type of "production" that the gross domestic product (GDP) registers. Some join the war-tax resistance movement, consciously limiting their income to deprive the government of funding for militarism, jails, prisons, and law enforcement, all of which go to ensure the unjust distribution of wealth and an overly intrusive legal system.

As if activist rich "kids" can do nothing to make social change, Weber has contempt for youthful squatters from middle- or upper-class families. But, by becoming squatters, these youth take one of the biggest possible steps toward radical social change: they abdicate privilege, even if temporarily. I met Miguel Wooding, a committed Homes Not Jails activist, as he handed out leaflets in favor of rent control at the prostitute-filled and addict-ridden corner of 16th Street and Mission, perhaps the seediest patch of pavement in all of San Francisco. He quit a physics program and guaranteed six-digit salary to start working with Homes Not Jails when he could no longer endure the sad daily stares of homeless people. The phenomenon of voluntarily abdicating resources is just as important to social change as the struggle of the dispossessed to acquire resources. For those who hope for nonviolent social change, fighting for justice and voluntary abdication of privilege must become opposite sides of the same precious coin.

Addressing his arguments to a conservative, presumably adult audience, Weber's critique of squatting was derailed by a description of alternative youth culture. Alternative forms of culture, the new and the *avant-garde*, pay notoriously little. Yet penniless movements like the 19th-century French Impressionists and the Beat generation in the 1950s contributed priceless gifts to culture as a whole. If society exercised a greater magnanimity toward these unconventional workers, cultural and political innovation might more rapidly develop, with parallel cultural and political benefits. Even if payment of taxes and expansion of the GDP were seen as a positive good, a distinction must be made between the general character of squatters and the nature of squatting itself. Anyone can point to particular lazy squatters, but others are highly industrious. Anyone can condemn squatting in general by focusing on the stereotypical squatter, whether youthful, crack-addicted, or otherwise. But most squatters substantially improve broken-down houses or work harder raising crops in Third World nations than any corporate executive works at his or her desk. Squatting gives the unemployed an opportunity to work, improve a neighborhood's housing stock, or increase the nation's food production. Rather than through taxation, squatting contributes to the national well-being by housing individuals who might otherwise need public housing.

Landlords who leave their land or housing vacant, however, deprive society of its most productive assets. Shock at these wasted resources recurs as a prime impetus for squatter action. In his book, *Alcatraz! Alcatraz!,* Adam Fortunate Eagle outlined the resentment he felt while planning the Alcatraz occupation in 1969: "Those twenty acres and all those buildings, all empty, falling apart from neglect. And we have nothing."[69] Feelings aroused by the juxtaposition of scarcity and abundance, hunger and opulence, and landlessness and vast expanses of arable land are powerful galvanizing agents for potential squatters.

In contrast to squatters' attempts to improve derelict housing, local governments in some urban areas go so far as to restrict the supply of housing by purchasing and destroying buildings. In the late 1970s, New York City bought hundreds of buildings when landlords found them unprofitable. They poured cement down the toilets, punched holes in the roofs, and left the structures to rot in the elements. All this was done to ensure that homeless people would not sleep in them. Although some crack houses have drawn people who have strewn trash about or even stolen fixtures and copper wiring for resale, none approached the extensive, malicious, and permanent damage wreaked by city housing agencies. In the '80s New York's housing policy became even more destructive. Officials completely demolished 300 buildings, leaving entire blocks vacant. Rick Van Savage, who currently squats in New York, calls it "warehousing":

> The idea behind warehousing is that the city aids the real estate/landlord
> industry by creating an artificial shortage in housing and simultaneously
> building an asset portfolio that the city can sell at large profits during peri
> ods of economic growth and gentrification.[70]

Landlords and governments, not squatters, have destroyed the most housing and deprived society of some of its most valuable assets. Homeless people, farmers, workers, and householders — everybody, in short — must have land and housing to live and produce. Where maldistribution encourages destruction and creates an impediment to production, squatting affords an important bridge not only to survival but to the expansion of both physical and cultural productivity.

If life is justified, squatting is justified. In a world where property bars people from basic necessities, people who lack shelter or food have, by defense of necessity, a right to survive, even if that means stealing the requisite resources. By natural law, argued 18th-century philosopher William Ogilvie, no society has the right to deprive any animal, including humans, of the right to shelter.[71] By taking vacant land and housing, squatters exhibit not selfishness but their right to survival. The selfish, rather, are those who take more land and housing than they can use, leaving it vacant in the face of homelessness, unemployment, and starvation. Squatting squares better with the classical justifications of property than does inequitable distribution. Squatting increases the number of people who can enjoy freedom and the ability to express culture and Hegelian personality. Squatting takes less than a fair share of vacant land, which should be considered common under Locke's proviso. Squatting rectifies historical wrongs. Squatting even makes sense on a purely economic and utilitarian level, since it transforms unproductive vacant land into housing, crops, and a basis for community. Despite the obfuscation offered by generations of property theorists beholden to inequitable property, people have every right, and every justification, to continue squatting.

CHAPTER 4

Tell It to the Judge

Direct Action and the Law

The costs of running for office are enormous for average people in terms of time and money, and the impediments to change built into the legislative process make it very hard to sustain a pressure-group coalition or legislative social movement that does not have a great amount of money and patience. But if average people have very little power through voting or lobbying, at least when things are quiet, they do have power when they disrupt the system.... Liberals, labor, and minorities, despite their great numbers, never win much against the conservative coalition unless there is a fear of disruption and violence loose in the land due to the actions of strikers, civil rights demonstrators, angry rioters in northern ghettos, or students demonstrating against wars.... I am asserting that social disruption, whether violent or nonviolent, is an essential factor in any successful challenge to the power structure in the United States.

William Domhoff, *The Power Elite and the State*[1]

Disruption makes change where normal channels fail. Professor William Domhoff's observation applies not only to the United States, but to land and housing movements in most parts of the world. Renters, landless, and homeless persons face overwhelming odds in making change solely through legal channels, so they embrace unconventional tactics such as squatting, rent strikes, land occupations, demonstrations, and riots. This chapter addresses the difficulties tenants and the landless face trying to make change through legal channels, whether because of strong real estate lobbying during the legislative process or because of undue influence of landowners on police and judges. Finally, this chapter looks at successful and unsuccessful legal strategies as they relate to direct action.

Litigation and electoral movements have successfully created and enforced rent controls and land reforms. These legal rewards of struggle and organizing endure far longer than most social movements. They have the long-lasting and far-reaching effects that inspire activist movements in the first place. But landowner and property interests can pressure government either into reversing land reform or rent control or into allowing only showpiece reforms with little substance. In partnership with corporations, industrialists, and other property holders, landowners use their wealth to contribute to candidates who maximize the power of property. This financial skewing of democracy protects absentee land ownership from laws that might favor tenants, small agriculturists, redistribution of land rights, or protection of the environment.

"In Britain," wrote the editor of the *New Internationalist*'s land issue in 1986, "where about 1,700 individuals own one-third of the country, you only have to look down the list of landholdings of Oxford-educated Members of Parliament to see the persistent connection between land and power."[2] On a local level, too, landowners skew politics in their favor. "City councils have typically been dominated by owners and investors," according to Stella Capek and John Gilderbloom, "while tenants have been viewed as transients and noncitizens in their own communities." Capek and Gilderbloom found that homeowners voted twice as often as renters.[3]

Tenants may hesitate to vote because they feel the political system ignores them in deference to the large campaign donations regularly contributed by landowners and real estate interests. Three percent of South Bronx landowners own 90% of the housing. "Not surprisingly," notes Rick Van Savage, a New York City squatter, "they also finance over 80% of the political campaign budgets."[4] More explicitly, real estate associations in most states donate money to defeat rent control referenda in any city that dares put one on the ballot.

In the Third World, too, landowners control much of local government, especially where agriculture puts a premium on control of land. According to Inderjit Singh, "In rural South Asia, as in other developing areas, disparities in land holdings produce disparities in incomes, and control of land usually coincides with control of local institutions."[5] Where local governments lack adequate police power, or where landowners lack control of this power, landowners sometimes create parallel institutions of government outside the regular rule of law. Landowners in much of Latin America hire their own paramilitary forces, such as the *Guardias Blancas* (White Guards) and *Mano Blanco* (White Hand); landowners use these gangs to evict rent defaulters and squatters and to terrorize dissident movements. A landowner forced Rigoberta Menchú and others in her indigenous community in Guatemala to vote for his favored candidate. "He warned us that anyone who didn't mark the paper would be thrown out of work at the end of the month. Anyone who was thrown out would not be paid."[6]

From the viewpoint of squatters and tenants, the bond between landowner and government can be so seamless as to blur the distinction between the two. In a discussion on her indigenous community's resistance to eviction and its attempts to appeal to the Guatemalan agrarian reform authorities, Menchú explained, "We didn't realize then that going to the government authorities was the same as going to the landowners. They are the same."[7]

The undue influence that landowners exert over the legislative process makes it difficult to make major economic changes, such as rent control or land reform, through legal channels. Though the occasional virtuous landowner voluntarily grants her or his holdings to land trusts or organizations, such as Vinoba Bhave's Bodhgaya movement in India during the 1950s, most landowners simply try to amass more earning potential with more acreage and more rental units.

Even when tenant or landless movements do achieve rent control or land reform, landowner political power decreases the gains. In Bangladesh, alluvial deposition constantly creates new land with rich soil called *khas*. By law, the government must lease *khas* land to the landless. More commonly, however, large landowners illegally obtain leases through government connections by using names of non-existent people or of dependents presented as being landless. Once the government agency grants the land, landowners protect themselves from landless movements by hiring private thugs and bribing local officials.[8]

When land does get redistributed to the landless by land reform, it almost never gets distributed evenly among the population. Women benefit much less frequently than men from land reform, yet women have less land on average. In the 1980s, women amounted to only 3% of land reform beneficiaries in Honduras, 4.8% in the Dominican Republic, 5% in Peru, and 11.2% in Colombia.[9] Although reforms have made the distribution of land and housing more equal, they remain woefully inadequate, and land reform enacted in one decade is frequently repealed in the next.

Direct Action Grows from Frustrated Legal Change

When legal channels of change appear closed, the dissatisfied seek other means. In the 1980s, an out-of-state development company claimed ownership of a ranch in Tierra Amarilla, New Mexico, which had been owned for 23 years by the Flores family. Rather than go to court, the Flores family constructed booby-traps, bunkers, and roadblocks. "We took an armed position," said supporter Pedro Arechuleta of the occupation, "because we knew the court system in the U.S.

would never give justice to our people."[10] At the end of the conflict in 1990, the company ceded 200 acres to the Flores family.

Not surprisingly, participants in land and housing movements widely acknowledge that direct action works when legal means fail. In 1974, public housing tenants went on a rent strike in Barking, England. Most strikers possessed little confidence in electoral channels: 77% felt their opinions were not taken into account in the way the country was run, and over 70% thought their opinions were not taken into account in the running of their own housing project. In response to the question, "In your opinion, what are the most effective ways by which people like yourself can influence the government?" 49% chose collective action, such as strikes and demonstrations, and solidarity as the most effective means; 1% even subscribed to revolutionary means and violence.[11]

These figures came from a modern liberal democracy. The perceived inaccessibility of legal means, both electoral and through litigation, affects land and housing struggles in the Third World to an even greater degree. "The government is not listening, and for that reason various forms of resistance have been and continue to be practiced," stated Elda Broilo, a Brazilian Catholic nun and organizer of land occupations. "This inconveniences the government, but from our point of view, it is through these forms of resistance that the movement is going forward."[12]

The more often legal attempts fail and the longer they take to grind through a hostile legal system, the greater is the pressure to try other means. Increasing frustration and desperation combine to drive the tenant or landless peasant to more vigorous tactics. A land occupation can provide fields to plant this season; squatting means a house to live in tonight. A 1993 Long Beach, California, flier on squatting by Homes Not Jails said, "After years of protesting, trying to get houses through the Stewart McKinney Act and other legal means, we have very little 'affordable' housing available.... Taking housing is necessary today because we cannot wait any longer to address this issue head on." To many, waiting for long legal processes could even mean death by starvation or exposure. Squatting may offer the only realistic alternative.

The Union de Campesinos de Queretaro seized land in San Martin, Mexico, on February 22, 1977. Even after police and armed men beat and arrested 100 *campesinos* on the second day of their occupation, the peasants still spoke of direct action as their only viable option.

> During the past few years, there have been many groups applying for land in the State of Queretaro under the laws of the Mexican Government. We wandered about much in the agrarian office, and received deceit and reprimands from functionaries. Hunger in the stomach followed. Because of this situation, we sat down with members of five other groups that had ap-

plied for land and organized the UCEQ [Union of Queretaro Campesi-nos]. We have continued in struggle, and on March 21st of last year [1976] captured the agrarian delegation [representatives of the agrarian reform department]. However, though we now have still more people, they still do not pay attention to us, and they continue deceiving us. Be-cause of this we have decided, in general assembly, to take the land. We can no longer endure our hunger and our anger.[13]

Racism often exacerbates the inaccessibility of legal channels to tenants and the landless. The predominantly African American tenants of East Park Manor in the City of Muskegon Heights, Michigan, "pulled" a rent strike in 1967 and 1968. They had attempted unsuccessfully to redress housing grievances through the manager beforehand. According to activist George Neagu, who took an active part in the strike,

Efforts to remedy the problems through the project director, who was white, not only were fruitless but led to a feeling on the part of the tenants that he was unconcerned about them. Efforts to involve the councilmen were unsuccessful. Letters to the mayor were unanswered. The tenants clearly perceived that they were faced with institutional indifference.[14]

It is often a combination of factors that leads groups to choose direct ac-tion. Llanquitray, a leader of Mapuche Indian land occupations during the popu-lar presidency of Salvador Allende Gossens in Chile from 1970 to 1973, told researcher Ximena Bunster why she supports land occupations. Included in her reasoning is the lack of time and money for litigation, a legislative and judicial bias towards the rich, and a refusal by the courts to recognize traditional forms of land tenure unique to the Mapuche.

So, what does the Mapuche do? If he makes a juridical claim for a piece of land usurped by a rich man twenty or thirty years ago, it can take fif-teen, twenty, or thirty years to reclaim it through the Court. He can sell everything he owns and be out on the streets, and he will never win his claim. Why? Because a poor person cannot put himself before a rich one. Impossible! ... He realizes that the laws which exist are useless to him: they protect the powerful, because they were made by them to protect themselves.... The old ones can explain how the land was taken from the Mapuche and subdivided. But the declarations of the elders are not ac-cepted by the authorities. So, what does the Mapuche do? He resorts to violence. It is necessary to resort to violence![15]

To discourage direct action, some governments foster false hope or pretend to yield legal or political victory. When people think they may get land in the fu-ture through legal means, government reasoning goes, they are less likely to break the law today. In the 1970s, the Puerto Rican government owned huge

quantities of land. For those who requested a plot, the government started a waiting list. "The governor's people said we would have to enroll on a waiting list.
But some of our people had been waiting eighteen years already," said spokesperson Miguel González. "We told them we needed our land now."[16]

In the fall of 1980, González and 350 families occupied a 65-acre parcel
that they named Villa Sin Miedo (Village Without Fear). The movement grew,
and by 1981, hundreds of occupations housed 18,000 Puerto Rican families.
González felt no surprise at a court ruling that ordered the eviction of the squatters. "We knew all the time the court would rule against us. Because we understand the laws are made to protect the rich people and not the poor people."

The similar thoughts mentioned earlier by Llanquitray, the Mapuche
leader, suggest that the more access one has to government power, the less reason
one has to risk direct action. Conversely, the less access one has to government
decision-making, the more compelling direct action becomes. Different ethnici-
ties and genders, with varying levels of access to government power, therefore
often have different attitudes toward direct action.

Ronald Lawson and Stephen E. Barton's essay "Sex Roles in Social Movements: A Case Study of the Tenant Movement in New York City" drew on sur-
veys conducted in the mid-1970s and historical research.[17] The authors found that
women disproportionately chose direct action for making changes rather than legal
action. Men more often chose legal action. This preference explained why women
led direct action at the grassroots level but men captured leadership in the larger
tenant organizations. In the 1904 New York City strike, as well as the larger strike
of 1907-08, women (who lacked the vote nationally) started rent strikes as building leaders, spreading the strike from building to building. After the number and
breadth of rent strikes grew, however, Socialist men began broader neighborhood
organizations in which they dominated. The neighborhood organizations spent
much less time on direct action, preferring legal activities, such as lobbying.

Between 1963 and 1964, women also led the primary activist organizations
during strikes. A survey of 238 tenant organizations by Lawson and Barton indicated that women were the majority of core activists at every level of organization (building, neighborhood, and city-wide federation) between 1976 and 1977.
But women held the majority of leadership positions only in buildings, not in
neighborhood or city-wide federations, most of which had strong ties to male-
dominated organizations such as labor unions, churches, and political parties.

Women only attained leadership positions on the neighborhood level when
they fought institutional gender barriers. In 1904, the president of a New York
neighborhood organization vetoed a proposal that Bertha Liebson, the most
prominent of the rent strike organizers, take a position as treasurer of a neighborhood organization. He said women lack the necessary qualifications to hold such

a post. More recently, according to Lawson and Barton, New York City court bureaucracies and city housing agencies have refused to deal with organizers and movement personnel, who tend to be poor women and are generally not professionals. Instead, these city institutions have demanded the professional packaging of lawyers or architects, who are more frequently male and middle-class. Poor women may have taken a more confrontational attitude toward their adversaries in negotiations, while the professional men generally exhibited a more polished and subservient manner.

Lawson and Barton found that, in addition to playing a greater role in organizations that developed interactive ties with formal organizations such as legislatures, banks, courts, and government bureaucracies, men exhibited a much greater tendency to vault from their tenant organizing into political or administrative careers, jeopardizing their loyalty to movement interests.

In their leadership of building organizations, whose primary role and source of power is direct action, women exhibited a greater willingness to aid the struggles of other buildings than men exhibited. "Relatively few tenants active in their own building organizations are drawn into efforts to help other buildings, but those doing so are much more apt to be women than men."[18]

When women did organize more broadly on a neighborhood level, according to Lawson and Barton, they eschewed bureaucratic lobbying in favor of mass tenant mobilization more often than their male counterparts. Lawson and Barton described the Metropolitan Council on Housing, led for over 18 years by Jane Benedict:

> Met Council uses lobbying trips to the state capital as a tool to educate its members concerning the futility of expecting changes to be given when they must be forced by direct action. It also emphasizes that tenants must rely on the strength provided by organization and unity rather than the expertise of lawyers and other professionals. Indeed, though a federation, over the last eight years it has rejected the usual political role of federations and has instead poured most of its resources into organizing rent strikes in buildings. Thus by rejecting professionals and refusing to enter the established political arena, Met Council has avoided the main avenues of male domination within the tenant movement.[19]

Women's emphasis on direct action in New York City tenant struggles parallels testimony from activists in other parts of the world. Though exceptions exist, male leaders tend to surrender during land and housing campaigns and make concessions with authorities earlier than women. In the Sanrizuka struggle against airport expansion by Japanese farmers, women took more militant positions than men took, and engaged in direct action more readily. "Members of the Women's Corps would jeer at their husbands and goad them to action," wrote researchers David Apter and Nagaya Sawa.[20] The movement held Oki Yone, a very old woman who had lived at Sanrizuka for decades, in highest esteem for her courageous acts. The police carried her away on a stretcher after her resistance to the demolition of her cottage. Apter and Sawa asserted:

> In the original Hantai Domei, women were among the most militant....
> The women who visited from the Kita-Fuji movement taught the San-
> rizuka women their techniques of violent protest, such as chaining them-
> selves to bulldozers or trees, and standing well in front of the men in
> confrontations with the police so that they took the first blows.[21]

In addition to gender, race affects the level of participant militancy. During the New York City rent strike of 1963-64, African American organizers con-flicted with organizations led by whites. "The two major rent strike powers — [African American] Jesse Gray's Community Council on Housing and the [pre-dominantly white and pre-Benedict] Metropolitan Council on Housing (MCH) — were at cultural and tactical odds."[22] Gray refused a request by MCH to as-sume leadership of a proposed city-wide rent strike coordinating committee be-cause he viewed them as a white, middle-class organization and did not want his ten years of hard work in the Black ghettos (with their rising spirit of race con-sciousness and nationalism) diluted by MCH's polite and reformist tactics. In general, campaigns composed of more impoverished or disadvantaged individu-als will wage more militant campaigns, in a continuum from land occupations by destitute and malnourished peasants in the Third World to rent strikes by lower-middle-class tenants in wealthy, Northern nations.

Morality and Power

Faced with intimidating legal hurdles, activists of all stripes have success-fully utilized not only direct action, but a discourse on rights and morality. Chap-ter three details some of these arguments in favor of squatting. The appeal to ethics strengthens the resolve of activists, wins new recruits from the community, and has even changed the hearts of landowners or government officials who pro-ceed to yield voluntary concessions. In June 1996, at Habitat II, the Second United Nations Conference on Human Settlements in Istanbul, many Third World and European nations prioritized inclusion of the right to shelter into UN documents. The United States, as has become customary at such conferences, in-cluded itself among the few nations that voted against the measure.

The right to land and housing and other forms of moral argument help gain public approval for squatters. Law-abiding citizens see that higher forms of ethi-cal reasoning can countermand local or national laws that violate basic human rights. Chants extolling the right to housing or references to UN documents that mandate the provision of decent housing for all citizens help embolden otherwise law-abiding persons to risk arrest for rights to land and housing.

Relying on the philosophical justification of one's cause alone, however, fails to provide all the resources needed for success. To increase the chances of gaining concessions, movements also emphasize the importance of power. "Power is the key ingredient," activists in the East Orange Tenants Association and the New Jersey Tenants Organization wrote in 1976. "How much a tenant union will achieve through negotiation does not depend on 'justice,' 'fairness,' 'equities,' or 'truth,' but on power, economic intimidation, and exposure."[23] Ben Cirlin, a school bus driver and organizer of the 60,000-person Co-op City rent strike in the Bronx (1975-76), similarly locates tenant power in raw economic strength. "Money is the name of the game — it's the only thing the financiers and the politicians understand."[24] Withhold the money and, though you risk getting thrown out on your ear, you at least have their ear. One tenant group likened landlords to a wild animal that rent strikers must dominate.

> Your landlord does not want to do what you want. In fact, the idea that you have the gall to try to tell him what to do will drive the landlord mad. The landlord is like a bucking bronco, mean and fierce and raring to take you apart. Tenants have to ride landlords out until you've got them tamed.25

A street theater company in a Mexico City squatter settlement pits "Superbarrio" in free wrestling against greedy landlord Catalino Creel.[26] The metaphor of Superbarrio communicates the importance of tenant power and encourages those who feel powerless in the presence of landowners and police. Showing that tenants can win through tactics of power helps participants understand this nonmoral dynamic that underlies success. "We depend on ourselves, and on those who share our broad interests, for the power to express and advance those interests," wrote the Cambridge Tenants Organizing Committee (CTOC) in 1972. "We believe that tenants can have power as tenants through our numbers and through the economic weight of our rents. Our job is to make that power real by organizing it."[27]

The CTOC offers an understanding of power conducive to direct action. Landlords are weak, but tenant power is unorganized. To win a struggle requires the reorganization of this power to benefit the tenants themselves, not the landlord. Nonviolence strategist Gene Sharp explains:

> Nonviolent sanctions are based upon the following perception of power: the ruler's power has sources; these can be located; they depend upon the cooperation of people and institutions; this cooperation can be restricted or cut off, with the result that the ruler's power is weakened. If the resisters' noncooperation can be maintained in face of repression, the ruler's power may be disintegrated. Hence any given institution, policy, or re-

gime can be controlled, limited, or destroyed by the application of nonviolent sanctions. This is, in highly simplified terms, the theory of power
upon which nonviolent struggle is based.[28]

Sharp's theory of nonviolent power differs substantially from the standard
understanding of power, which sees some people (the landlords) as having power
and some people (the tenants) as powerless. When we point out that tenants already have power (via their rents) and that the question is how best to use this
power for tenant advantage, then the possibilities of collective organization
spring immediately to mind.

Stephen Barton co-chaired the 945-946 Tenants Union, an organization of
squatters and tenants that saved two buildings in New York City from abandonment in 1975. He wrote that tenant organizing "involves delegitimizing the established authorities, creating new cooperative social relationships among the
tenants, and hopefully creating a basis for a new legitimate authority, the tenants'
association."[29]

Power also comes from the actual location where tenants or squatters wage
a struggle. By ending a lobbying campaign (probably in a business district or
government building intimidating to some activists) and instead organizing direct
action, activists move a struggle to their own neighborhood. Deemphasizing lobbying tactics shifts geographical space from benefiting the adversary to benefiting the activists. Officials must leave their sphere of power, where they are
surrounded by grand architecture, judges in robes, landlords behind big desks,
and other symbols meant to infuse "regular people" with fear. Direct action takes
full advantage of the home court: nearby supporters, easy supply lines, and a
strong defensive instinct. The media comes to the community, where neighbors
and homes give context and a sympathetic backdrop to the struggle. In a movement against resort development to save a Canadian island neighborhood from
destruction, Linda Rosenbaum rejected as ineffectual delegations to the park su-
perintendent "on *his* turf, around *his* desk, at *his* convenience." The superinten-
dent met demands when forced to meet with a room-full of islanders on "*our* turf,
in *our* time, in *our* office."[30] When tenants and the landless can force government
officials to come to the contested neighborhood, activists win a small tactical victory, if nothing else.

To achieve success, direct action campaigns have had to use all the tools at
their disposal, including tactics that rely on morality and those that rely on power.
To use morality without power, that is, to hold only legal demonstrations or make
speeches, is likely to reach a few people and might even gain some concessions
from those adversaries willing to listen. But to use power without morality, by,
say, occupying land without developing a justification, will yield gains threatened by popular indignation. Successful movements combine moral arguments

with the power of numbers, militancy, and even courtroom and legislative strategies.

Dual Use of Law and Direct Action

Authorities exclude land and housing activists from effective use of the law in official legal channels to some extent, but activists can extend the use of law beyond the courtroom and appeal to public opinion. To buttress their legitimacy, indigenous nations use treaty rights, rent strikers cite building codes, and squatters appeal to land reform laws. Broadcasting government failure to follow its own laws strengthens the legitimacy of direct action in the eyes of the public.

Brazilian organizer Elda Broilo says, "The Constitution says land reform must take place, and the movement has taken advantage of this law on paper to demand that land reform be enforced in actuality."[31] Broilo's use of the Brazilian Constitution as a platform from which to argue is powerful rhetorically and has garnered much Brazilian support for her movement. Constitutional arguments also pave the way for litigation.

In a study of the Pit River Nation land occupations in the 1970s, M. Annette Jaimes describes this dual technique of direct action and litigation "not in terms of civil disobedience in the sense that it is conventionally understood, but as a means of employing the American juridical tradition in its own terms (e.g., illegality ultimately rationalized by law)."[32] Ward Churchill maintains that American Indian Movement occupations on the Pine Ridge Reservation had a

> positive bearing on the evolution of litigation in the [Black Hills land claim], and helped bring vital public attention to and understanding of the issues. In this sense, the legal and extralegal battles fought by Lakotas for Paha Sapa have been — perhaps inadvertently — mutually reinforcing. These two efforts may have finally created the context in which a genuine solution can finally be achieved.[33]

The Colombian peasant leagues in 1929 devised an ingenious use of the law. Initially, the leagues occupied and used violence to defend a mountainous area of over 500 square kilometers as an independent communist republic. But once on the land, they used legal strategies to maintain their position for over 20 years. According to nonviolence strategist Gene Sharp, "In 1933, the peasants took advantage of a Colombian law which made the landlord financially obligated to his tenants for improvements they made on his land. With and without permission, tenants planted coffee trees, making repossession by the landlord impossible without payment to the tenants." Eventually the Colombian Congress passed an agrarian reform law that compensated the landowners and sold the land to the peasants on long-term credit for favorable prices.[34]

When the military and police fail to follow law, in cases where they refuse to obey positive court rulings, or when the court falsely defends the landowner, direct action becomes a mechanism for popular enforcement. In 1985, Samata Samaj Kalyan Samity, a social welfare society in Bangladesh, filed charges against 18 landlords who had illegally occupied *khas* land. While landlords attempted to bribe members of Samata and exclude them from relief wheat distribution, "Food for Work" programs, and bank loans, a court finally awarded the society 21 hectares of land. But the landlord hired more than 100 armed men to flaunt the court order. The Samata ultimately had to transcend regular police procedure to create their own extra-legal enforcement apparatus. Taking the land required a march of 3,000 persons carrying clubs, spades, and scythes to scare the landlord's small army into flight.

This success spread the movement to more than 100 villages involving 20,000 members, but landlords and government officials began a new legal offensive. The courts trumped up charges of theft, rape, looting, and arson against over 200 Samata workers and supporters, many of whom the police held in jail for long periods of time. In January 1986, another landlord's private army (aided by police) burnt and ransacked several houses in the area, beat and arrested children and adults, and forced 3,000 landless persons to hide in the nearby jungle.[35] While the peasants' legal defense freed them from most of the baseless charges, won them legally recognized land rights, and mobilized thousands of people, the Samata members faced a landlord with extensive influence among local police and a willingness to hire armed thugs. The initial legal campaign failed to actually gain the land. Samata only gained possession with the additional strategy of direct action, and even then the landlord inflicted retaliation and scattered the Samata forces.

Like the government-mandated distribution of *khas* land, countries with land reform distribute very little land very inefficiently. In Latin America, most governments have failed to achieve an enduring redistribution that affects anything over 20% of agricultural land (Mexico, Cuba, Peru, and Nicaragua are exceptions).[36] With lax enforcement of land reform, land occupations play an important role in keeping society in accordance with its own laws. Where land reform does not yet exist, land occupations motivate the public to pass necessary legislation. Land occupation campaigns in colonial Zimbabwe, colonial East Africa, Chile in the late 1960s, Mexico and Honduras in the '70s, and Nicaragua in the early '80s all precipitated the adoption or enforcement of land reform.

As a result of Honduran peasant demonstrations in the early '70s, leftist General Oswaldo López Arellano issued an emergency land reform measure in 1972. When a paramilitary organization of top landowners quashed the temporary reform, Arellano issued a much stronger reform in 1975. Peasants ensured that Arellano could honor his promise by organizing about 100 occupations in May, involving 10,000 Honduran peasants. These occupations provided the leftist regime with enough power to overcome its more conservative leaders and earmark 32,000 hectares for distribution.

A common theme in Latin American history is the ouster of pro-land reform governments by landowners allied with international interests. By early 1977, all the progressive military leaders in Honduras had retreated from politics in response to threats by opponents of land reform.[37] Undeterred, Honduran voters elected a civilian government in 1982 that allowed land reform to resurface. But the revitalized reform provided for less than 1% of the estimated 150,000 families seeking land.[38] After waiting years in vain, peasants undertook a nationally coordinated effort to increase land distribution in 1984. Members of three national *campesino* unions occupied more than 50 properties, 350 families in the north occupied a municipal hall, and over 300 peasants occupied a regional office of the National Agrarian Reform Institute (INA).[39]

The idea caught on, as most successful occupations do, and the next year 30,000 peasants took 30,000 hectares of land in yet another nationally coordinated string of occupations. Regarding these, National Peasant Union Secretary General Marcial Caballero told *In These Times,* "we are convinced that the little that has been done about agrarian reform in Honduras has come about because of sacrifices by the peasants and pressure from their organizations."[40] Indeed, the *Progressive* reported in April 1989 that land occupations initially claimed 93% of the land redistributed to *campesinos* by INA since 1962. The director of INA even admitted this privately in 1984. "The lands that are given are almost always given to peasants who carry out invasions."[41] Land occupations with an ultimate sanction by land reform continued throughout the '80s in Honduras.[42] In 1992, an International Monetary Fund plan overturned the land reform law, but 50,000 landless families remained successfully "seated" on their occupied land.[43]

Honduras in the 1980s exemplifies how direct action nudges recalcitrant bureaucracy to follow an already existing law. The same principle applied in New York City during the 50,000-person rent strike from 1963 to 1964. Instead of land reform, direct action encouraged lower rents and the enforcement of building codes. At the time, New York City rent control law required landlords to apply to the City Rent and Rehabilitation Administration (CRRA) for rent increases on rent-controlled buildings. Buildings that participated in the strike enjoyed a lower incidence of rental increase by the CRRA on average, when the CRRA did not reduce rents drastically to promote repairs by landowners. Half the buildings in a study by Michael Lipsky won rent reductions of over 50% during the strike.[44]

Non-striking tenants also benefited from the strike. According to the rent control law, tenants of particularly decrepit buildings could receive rent reductions to as low as $1 until their landlord made repairs. For 18 months previous to the strike, the District Office for Upper Manhattan reduced rents to $1 in only 21 units, but at the beginning of the strike in October 1963, 532 units were so reduced, and the trend continued into the following months. For those who did not receive rent reductions to $1 during this period, many received reductions of over 50%. Comparisons with the non-strike neighborhood of Brooklyn during the rent strike period indicate that strike activity caused these reductions.

Members of rent strike buildings and organizations enjoyed greater access to city housing maintenance agencies than similar non-strike buildings, individuals, and civic groups. Otherwise inaccessible bureaucrats encouraged strike leaders to phone them, rent strike tenants appeared without appointments and were ushered into offices of the highest agency officials, and agency personnel took quick action and ordered immediate inspections to beat the predictable inquiries from reporters. In December, for example, tenant pressure forced the city to reinspect 35 Harlem tenements, many of which were on rent strike, for code violation. Even in Brooklyn, where the strike failed to reach critical mass, a CRRA interoffice memo dated January 6, 1965, mandated that rent strike buildings were "to be expedited and classified as emergencies."[45]

While strikers found their cases expedited, non-strike tenants with equally serious complaints only received inspections after passage of a few weeks, and then by a regular inspector whose report received only routine attention. This bias in scrutiny caused some agency officials to criticize rent strikers for cutting in line. But, as Lipsky points out, "it is interesting to speculate on the results if all buildings worthy of departmental attention were suddenly referred to the departments with urgency and the prospect of publicity."[46]

Problems with Litigation

Direct action leads to greater success in winning concessions from government agencies and the courts, but excessive reliance on litigation can also slow a direct action campaign. The National Tenants Organization wrote in 1972 that laws providing some legal protection against the retaliatory eviction of strikers do not necessarily help given that in many cases "such laws are more trouble than they're worth because of complicated court escrow arrangements, other legal procedures, and extensive delays."[47]

Tenant use of rent strike laws during the New York City strike of 1963-64 illustrates the problem with courtroom strategies. Tenants primarily invoked "Section 755" of the buildings code as a defense against litigation by landlords. Section

755 provided for the payment of rent to the court until the landlord made repairs. Legal prospects initially looked good. The first two court decisions in December 1963 favored tenants and triggered a wave of landlords willing to make concessions and seeking to settle out of court.[48] In neighborhoods where the rent strike attained massive proportions and attracted media attention, even unorganized buildings experienced temporary improvement in services. The positive court ruling caused the movement to expand, as many more tenants began withholding rent because of the greater prospects for success.

But when cases began appearing in large numbers and publicity lagged, politically sensitive judges who had responded to the media turned against the tenants.[49] Mark Naison captured the new mood:

> In some cases, judges made no attempt to hide their contempt for the tenants and their opposition to the rent strike, and didn't try to separate their legal arguments from their personal biases. But more common was a strict adherence to legal technicalities on the part of "objective" judges, which, given the nature of the housing laws and the peculiar problems of the low-income person in a court situation, proved to be a frustrating and confusing barrier to effective action.[50]

Lipsky concurred. He attributed legal failure during the 1963-64 strike to tenants' unfamiliarity with highly ritualized and intricate courtroom procedure and their financial inability to hire adequate representation.[51] Landlords purposely magnified the tenants' confusion by leaving their own cases unprepared or demanding new witnesses — legal maneuvers that caused temporary adjournments and forced tenants to return to court again and again. For workers and homemakers with economic and familial responsibilities, repeated court appearances meant unaffordable childcare or the loss of a day's salary.

Once tenants presented the evidence, judges found oral testimony and photographs of housing conditions inadmissible. To present legal evidence, tenants had to seek early inspections from an intransigent bureaucracy. Even when tenants managed this, inspectors often missed the relevant violations or forgot to record them at the Hall of Records. For tenants to check the Hall of Records cost $2 and a trip downtown. Then they had to subpoena the records on trial day.

When tenants faithfully jumped through each legal hoop in the correct order, plain corruption could still ruin their case. According to Naison, "inspectors were notoriously corrupt and amenable to bribes, and would often slant their inspection reports to favor the landlord."[52] In the final ruling, judges usually found evidence contained in inspection reports insufficient to issue a Section 755 and ordered tenants to pay all back rents and resume regular payment or face eviction.

The Lower East Side Rent Strike lost three-fifths of its cases during March and April 1964, with only slight improvement in the following months. With the exception of Brooklyn's Congress of Racial Equality, none of the other rent strike organizations did much better.[53] From December 30, 1963, until March 22, 1965, only 182 tenants in 68 buildings successfully paid rent to the court instead of the landlord.[54] On seven court days in March, tenants received favorable rulings in only three cases, while the judge ordered eviction in 31. This pattern recurred in 100 cases handled by the Mobilization for Youth, in which tenants won only three cases for every 14 orders of eviction.[55] Lipsky's examination of 20 strike buildings found that tenants in seven paid rent to the court and received repairs (though two buildings first deteriorated to such an extent that the city took ownership) and in two buildings paid rent to the court but never received repairs, while landlords won eviction notices in most of the other 11 buildings.[56]

Even when judges actually granted a Section 755, they only required landlords to correct violations recorded on Buildings Department forms. If landlords fixed a certain percentage (and in only the most perfunctory manner), they received the withheld rents. Once the landlord received rents held by the court, he had no reason to make further repairs. If tenants vacated the premises during the strike or paid late, even if the landlord made no repairs, the landlord received the entire amount held by the courts.[57]

Given anti-tenant laws, Naison attributes the 1963-64 rent strike failure to organizers' concentration on lengthy and unrewarding legal procedures. Court action imposed a "nonmilitant psychology" on leaders, according to Naison, and subtly steered them from strike expansion and mass direct action. Naison notes that such an expansion similarly occurred during the depression, when 4,000 New Yorkers resisted the eviction of an Olinville Avenue building on strike in 1933. The 1963-64 strike organizations "were pushed into the safe and legitimate style of organizing, which would not put themselves, or the tenants, in danger," argued Naison. "They did not know enough about housing work, or perhaps about American society in general, to realize that major economic changes could not be effected by the courts."[58]

Though they lost power in the courts, rent strikes on the massive scale of New York City during the winter of 1963-64 carried enough public support that they impacted state-wide legislation. Initially, this legislation seemed to be one of the major rewards to the movement in the wake of courtroom failure. The state legislature made three laws regarding rent strikes in the 1965 session. It amended the law under which tenants paid rents to the court instead of the landlord so that this money could immediately be used to hire contractors for repairs, it made rent strikes easier by allowing tenants to take the legal initiative before the landlord, and it produced a list of building violations sufficiently serious to make rent strikes legal.[59]

However, these laws proved fatally cumbersome when rent strikers actually tried to use them. Well-intentioned legislators might have initiated the laws in response to pressing social needs, but legislators funded by real estate interests riddled them with loopholes and revisions. Once laws went into effect, tenant organizations discovered them to be time-consuming and expensive. Strikers had to serve more documents than under Section 755, and a "new law" strike cost a minimum of $500 at standard legal rates. "For the unorganized, unsubsidized poor who compose the vast majority of the slums' inhabitants," wrote Naison, "the new law did nothing, illustrating once again the depths of the chasm separating the poor from the democratic process."[60]

Governments have recognized the ways in which protracted legal cases can devastate a social movement, and they sometimes consciously encourage movements to sink funds and energy into litigation. In the early 1970s the Puerto Rican government provided free legal services to squatters in their fight for land title and against evictions that the government itself ordered. "The increasing intervention of Legal Services transformed the social struggle into a battle fought by lawyers," wrote researcher Liliana Cotto, and "had a demobilizing effect."[61] Communities formerly united against eviction became individualized by the legal process, which subsumed other organizational tasks and non-institutional popular struggle.

The challenge facing rent strikes today, according to Lawson, is to avoid becoming institutionalized by legalization and uninventiveness. Whereas large rent strikes previously threatened social stability in that they challenged established structures of law, now the legal process has normalized them into landlord-tenant relations, resolved in court like any other small-claims dispute. Jurisprudence codifies a rebellion by offering minor concessions, such as a smaller risk of eviction, while at the same time bringing rebellion under control. Lawson expressed what seems to approach a consensus of social movement researchers: "As strategies become less unruly, they are also less successful."[62]

Refusal to Litigate

When litigation bankrupts a campaign, activists often change their strategy. Having learned from the 1963-64 strike, the next wave of New York City tenant action, which started in 1971, adopted a strategy of decentralization and avoidance of the courts. Activists organized rent strikes in thousands of buildings and formed a tenant association in virtually every neighborhood.[63] In reaction to the failure of litigation by Section 755, according to Lawson, New York City tenant groups began in 1973 to promote the "rolling rent strike," which denied rent money not only to the landlords, but also to the courts.

Strikers strove to postpone court appearances, to negotiate directly with their landlords, and, if ordered to place rents in escrow, to pay them instead to the landlord and withhold the next month's rent. The rolling rent strike proved successful, especially in housing affected by landlord abandonment and neighborhood decay. While conventional rent strikes failed to gain needed services and repairs, tenants began direct and illegal spending of accumulated rolling strike funds on building improvement. Lawson observes that this led to the "incorporation of tenant control and even plans for tenant ownership in several programs."[64]

The rolling rent strike followed New York law and avoided fruitless legal battles. Another tactic was to allow the landlord to win court battles, but to resist enforcement. Predominantly African American tenants of East Park Manor in the city of Muskegon Heights, Michigan, went on rent strike in late January 1967. The strike had a strong base of support: an enthusiastic meeting that included two-thirds of the tenants decided unanimously to strike. One hundred and fifty-five tenants — over 70% of all tenants in the housing project — placed their rent money in escrow. When a judge ordered them evicted, tenants held a mass meeting and unanimously decided to risk arrest rather than appeal the decision and lose time and energy to litigation. On the eve of a threatened 89-family eviction following a total of six months on strike and extensive negotiations, the mayor (who before the strike neglected even to answer letters) granted the tenant organization's primary demands.[65] In an essay written by the National Tenants Organization for other tenant groups, the East Park Manor strike is featured as worthy of emulation. "The decision not to fight the eviction cases but to use political confrontation instead was probably the main factor in the tenant union victory."[66]

Squatters have also refused to litigate for tactical reasons. In an atmosphere of mass land occupations in Mexico during the mid-'70s, 600 Mexican peasants in the Farm Workers Association of Self-Defense (AIAC), armed with machetes and shotguns, occupied more than 1,800 hectares on October 7, 1978. An *Excelsior* correspondent reported, "for more than 40 years the farmworkers have been applying with the proper agrarian authorities in reference to the return of land that belongs to them, but nothing has been resolved," so, instead of continuing their fruitless legal overtures, the farmworkers decided "to take the land over by force." Leaders of the AIAC refused to litigate or dialogue with representatives of the state government or agrarian reform authorities. Rather, they occupied two additional small properties, causing sentiment in favor of occupations to grow. Fearful that the landless peasants would increase the rate of occupation, a group of landowners from the region promised to donate 25% of the occupied land.[67] The offer came within three days of the initial occupation, a very quick victory.

Direct action produces better results than ordinary legal means because it tends to seek redistribution not only of the immediate land or housing at issue but of wealth, industry, and investments more generally. Because governments, corporations, and others who depend on political and economic stability fear widespread unrest, they make concessions to stop the unrestrained growth of campaigns for radical redistribution of any type. As already noted, squatter organizations in Puerto Rico from the late '60s to the mid-'70s eschewed conventional methods of political participation, at least when divorced from taking and defending land by occupation and community organization. Rather than legalistic petitions, applications, meetings, and committees, they preferred to augment their occupations with pickets, vigils, caravans, and mass mobilizations. "These popular sectors acknowledged that mass actions were the most effective form of political pressure outside electoral periods," Cotto wrote. "The threatening potential of these mass demonstrations lay in their strength for carrying out direct action, thus alarming the regime and frightening possible investors."[68]

Even when revolutionary or Social-Democratic governments take power, tenants and the landless have organized direct action as the best way to get results. Reform-minded government officials may have progressive ideas about land and housing law, but they often need direct action outside of legislative channels to gain an audience within a government administration for progressive policy proposals.

Rather than a silver platter, revolutionary or leftist governments provide windows of opportunity for successful struggle. When the Popular Unity government of Salvador Allende took power in Chile, the government failed to provide housing for all the poor and even evicted some of the squatter settlements. The poorest only got housing when the frequency and extent of land occupations multiplied rapidly: occupations increased tenfold in less than three years. In 1971 alone, squatters occupied 560 parcels of land in Chile. By May 1972, according to the Ministry of Housing, 15% of Santiago's population, or about 83,000 households, lived in settlements that had originated by occupation.[69]

From Chile to England, tenants and the landless choose direct action because of its history of success. Propertied interests since the ancient Romans have crafted much of the law, which government officials administer to favor landowners. These landowners continue to have an undue influence over governmental processes, making change difficult by electoral or legislative means. Popular campaigns have used existing laws to buttress their direct action, and direct action has helped enforce neglected land reform or rent control. However, activists have found it prudent to avoid legal battles except in the rare instances when it does not overly deplete their energy and resources. In most cases, a focus on direct action tactics have provided better results.

So that government power does not appear compromised, most governments will create or enforce land reform to legalize land occupations and distribute housing plots to legalize urban squatter settlements; likewise landlords re-write rental contracts to legalize rental deficits caused by rent strikes. Authorities legalize existing conditions to preserve the law, which direct action has the power to change. To take part in this creation of law, activists lobby the government. Direct action, though by definition a violation of law, usually attempts to reconfigure that law in accordance with the needs of activists. Legalizing the *de facto* success of a movement ensures that success for the future.

CHAPTER 5

Violence
and Cycles of Reform

Direct action augments the chances of success for electoral or courtroom strategies, but activists often use legal strategies alone in the early stages of a particular struggle. They prefer this less confrontational approach primarily because the legal system sometimes works and because they fear the brutal forms of repression used against direct action. Such repression can include seizure of assets, eviction, beatings, imprisonment, rape, execution, and murder.

While describing direct action, organizers can minimize the possibility of these negative consequences, knowing that participants avoid direct action for fear of bodily or economic harm. But as nonviolence trainings teach, those who know and come prepared for the worst of all possible outcomes develop a stronger commitment to their campaigns. In the long run, bonds of trust tie activists and organizers together in a way that enhances the strength of the activist organization. Frances Goldin, a longtime New York City housing activist, found honesty and a measure of pessimism important in her work.

> We wanted to be honest, completely honest with tenants. No longer could we tell them that if they got together with other tenants in their building, they would overcome. That's just bullshit when the banks and real-estate oriented city and state agencies are all lined up against them. It's bullshit as long as corporate and absentee landlords walk off with the profits and leave them stranded in practically abandoned buildings.[1]

Because the eviction of squatters poses a formidable task, especially when a squatter settlement houses hundreds or thousands of people who have literally no other place to go, officials use ruthless tactics. On February 19, 1969, the Rhodesian government ordered 36 families in the Tangwena community to be relocated from their homes and fields to the relatively infertile Holdenby Tribal Trust Lands. Chief Rekayi responded by pointing to government as the aggressor and refusing to capitulate. "I have not provoked the struggle," he said. "I do not want to fight, but I shall under no circumstances cooperate." In 1931, the Rhodesian Land Apportionment Act had relegated Africans to the most barren areas of the country and established the most fertile lands exclusively for Europeans. Between 1936 and 1959, the government evicted about 113,000 Africans. The Tangwena community resisted and endured this predecessor to what is now called "ethnic cleansing."

Seven months after the eviction notice, officials arrested Rekayi and then those who demanded his release, bulldozed 11 huts, and confiscated property. Most of the village fled into the mountains. About three weeks later, officials destroyed much more property and chased residents into the hills again, this time with helicopters and dogs. Residents eventually returned, but officials again burned their huts down. The next year, many were fined, beaten, and jailed for 30 days. The government impounded and then sold the community's cows.

With this sort of repression, thousands chose to hide in the hills yet again, but living in the wilderness took its toll. Rugged conditions caused one boy to die of pneumonia, so parents returned 157 of the smaller children to the village.[2]

In less than four years, the Tangwena experienced six violent evictions. Communities throughout the world have, like the Tangwena, endured repeated evictions. And, like the Tangwena, they have demonstrated that despite violence, imprisonment, and multiple evictions, a resilient and united community can endure multiple trials. But the varieties of repression they have faced are as numerous and sickeningly creative as the number of landlords and enforcement agencies.

Because of social movement resilience, landlords sometimes combat land occupations through a more covert and surgical use of violence than experienced by the Tangwena community. According to the Pastoral Land Commission of the Brazilian Catholic Church, over 1,684 Brazilian rural workers were assassinated between 1964 and 1992.[3] Assassination is especially common in Latin America, where cash crop landowners and landless peasants suffering from malnutrition compete with greater ferocity and frequency than anywhere in the world. Nonetheless, landlords and government in Latin America usually reserve assassination as the culmination to many attempts at repression. A Salvadoran named Susana explains the occupation in which she took part:

> In the first place, we asked for a salary rise, a reduction in land rents and
> more fertile land. We went on strike in support of our demands but nothing came of it. So we decided to occupy some unused land owned by the
> big landowner of our region. We worked very hard in the fields for about
> four months. We cultivated maize and water melons, and the crops were

just about ripe when the army came one night without warning and destroyed everything. They captured all the leaders. They didn't find my husband at home but I was there and they beat me terribly. They even put a rifle in my mouth and threatened to kill me. They tied me up, ransacked the house and burnt our grain store. They killed an enormous number of people that night because nearly the whole canton had joined [the occupation]. The repression there became well known. Four days later, Monsignor Romero came to visit us. He held a special mass and gave me and another woman some money so we could go to see a doctor because we had both been so badly beaten. We had to move into the capital afterwards, because we feared they would come back to look for my husband and I began to suffer from my nerves, thinking about all I had seen. They killed my husband in the end, in 1982. He was found near Aguilares, naked, nothing but his body. We never found his head. Soon afterwards I had to leave the country.[4]

While this repression occurred in the context of a civil war, the trajectory of Susana's experience shares characteristics with many land struggles. As in Tacamiche, Susana's community occupied land midway through a difficult labor strike to provide themselves with food. In response, and to exact maximum punishment, the army destroyed the crops right before harvest.

The army also murdered many people, and most of those they did not murder, they beat and threatened with death. Land and housing movements that face the death of participants have prepared themselves for this possibility. Elvia Alvarado of Honduras, who witnessed the deaths of several rural activists and received death threats, probably originating from the Honduran secret police, writes of the extreme emotional pain she felt: "We all feel a great loss when someone we love dies. When the four *campesinos* died in the land recuperation, I cried and cried. And when an older person dies, someone you've been close to all your life, of course it hurts. It hurts a lot."[5]

Because of this heavy repression, peasants sometimes attempt to remove conflict from the location of community members. They reason that if they travel to a capital or large urban area away from their community, the action poses less risk for those back home. Even in these cases, however, governments have inflicted collective punishment. In March 1980, Paraguayan peasants from a community of 200 families chose a desperate course of action. The landowner had used connections with a government agency to "misplace" land documents that would have barred him from evicting the community. With two revolvers and a rifle, 22 of the *campesinos* hijacked a bus and demanded passage to the capital. "We are farmers who have been driven from our land," they told passengers. The police blocked the path of the bus and killed 13 of the peasants as they fled into the hills. Back in their community, the landowner arrived with truckloads of military police.

These police beat villagers, destroyed huts and crops, and jailed all males in the community over 15 years old. The civil militia then arrived, raped many of the women, and looted the village. The police jailed 250 peasants in neighboring regions.

As in Paraguay, a widespread method of repression used against some movements is mass imprisonment. The government of India broke the record in 1970 when it arrested 20,000 landless peasants and agricultural laborers who participated in a massive occupation of 6,100 hectares of unused government and private land.[6] As Mahatma Gandhi suggested, such mass imprisonment is particularly unsustainable for governments because it requires a substantial budget to hire prison guards and provide food. Also, government officials must make the choice between freeing other regular prisoners (thus losing some power in deterring common crimes) and constructing temporary holding facilities with additional public expenditure. For these reasons, mass imprisonment often turns public opinion against the government.

Because of public opinion, governments and landlords have tried to use forms of repression that mask their own involvement, whether through vigilantes, death squads, or low-intensity coercion, such as denying food aid or agricultural outreach services. On May 27, 1989, 200 families occupied U.S. Navy land on the Puerto Rican island of Vieques and built makeshift shelters of plywood and plastic. Through the summer and early fall of 1989, the government decided not to evict the squatters because of the delicate political situation created by the presence of the base. In the confusion following Hurricane Hugo, however, the Navy erected a wall to bar the squatters from their destroyed shacks. Hugo not only destroyed the settlement, but also diverted media attention. To much of the public, Hurricane Hugo, not the U.S. Navy, seemed the main culprit.[7] While the Navy ejected squatters who attempted to rebuild their community, the national media was focusing on the wreckage of nearby towns.

Again and again, throughout the world, land and housing struggles have faced terrible repercussions. Because even severe violence rarely stops large national squatter campaigns completely, governments have also tried the divide-and-conquer technique. The government announces that it will legalize present squatter settlements and outlaw any future squatter settlements. In 1973, the Puerto Rican government legalized all settlements squatted prior to January 18 of that year. It threatened, however, to evict new squatters immediately. This legalization aimed to divide present from future squatters, but squatting continued. Between 1973 and 1975, at least 17,000 more families took land. In 1976, government officials used stronger anti-squatter laws and court decisions to evict five spontaneous occupations. The well-publicized evictions seemed to chill the creation of new settlements by mass invasions, but during the rest of the '70s, new squatters individually joined existing settlements. People must have a place to live. A real estate system that allows for landlessness and homelessness guarantees unrest by the most economically marginal. Given landlessness, the best a government can hope to do is direct the flow of squatters onto less valuable land.

At times, the level of repression exceeds the resources of a community. In these cases, the community at least provisionally surrenders to the will of the government and landowners, whether that means community dispersion, low wages, high rents, or heavy share-cropping burdens. In one instance, however, an entire village of indigenous Kaiowá families in Brazil threatened mass suicide. The conflict started when a rancher from the city of São Paulo displaced the 250-person indigenous community of Jaguapiré three times in five years over a title dispute that left the village with only a third of its federally guaranteed land. In November 1993, local farmers at the behest of a large São Paulo landowner invaded the community, forced people into trucks, and dumped them at the side of a highway. Many Kaiowá eventually lived at that spot in plastic tents and suffered from starvation. Their companions at the village told a visiting delegation that the Kaiowá planned to defend the land with shotguns and spears if the court ordered them to move again. If these efforts were to fail, however, the companions revealed religious structures in which almost the entire community, including 22 tribal leaders from neighboring villages and encampments, had pledged to commit suicide. Between 1991 and 1994, 120 Kaiowá killed themselves, following traditional custom. "We're tired of being threatened," said the chief of Jaguapiré, Rosalindo Ximenes Guarani. "We can't take care of our crops because at any moment we may be expelled by the police. Therefore, we prefer to die, rather than give up our land."[8]

Repression in the United States: Native Americans

Indigenous participants in Northern land struggles have also faced imprisonment and death. At the Pine Ridge Reservation in South Dakota alone, activists endured 500 trials between 1973 and 1976. Most of the original leadership of the American Indian Movement (AIM) was imprisoned or exiled. At least 342 members of AIM sustained serious physical assault, and 69 were killed.[9] Pine Ridge assaults included rapes and at least two children wounded by gunshot.[10]

Vigilantes supplement the repression that governments use against land and housing activists. One can especially expect vigilantism during long struggles or when a government has communicated that it does not intend to enforce property laws. From 1974 until 1977, snipers repeatedly fired on a group of Mohawk occupiers at Ganienkeh in New York State.

> In several shooting incidents, according to Iroquois spokesmen, women doing laundry by Moss Lake and children swimming were pinned down,

not by an occasional shot from a passing car, but by intense firing from fixed positions.[11]

A major attack by conventional police or military forces can legitimize repression in the minds of vigilantes. If occupiers are left unprotected following such an attack and the media is absent, these vigilantes can emerge from the woodwork and take advantage of an isolated campaign. In 1970, several dozen Puyallup Indians and their supporters erected a campsite near the Puyallup River from which they proceeded to assert their fishing rights against state regulations. On September 9, over 200 police stormed the camp with tear gas and clubs, beat and dragged people, some by their hair, and arrested 60, including five children. The police then bulldozed cars, teepees, and other personal property; smashed windows; and slashed the tires of nearly all vehicles at the camp. After the police action, hundreds of white vigilantes raided other Puyallup fishing camps, sunk Indian boats, stole and destroyed nets, and took pot-shots at Indians. A half-year later, on January 19, 1971, two white vigilantes approached Hank Adams, a leader of the fishing struggle, while he tended his fishing nets. They shot him point-blank in the stomach.[12]

Repression of Native American land struggle continues unabated even in the last decade of the 20th century. A September 1990 offensive by Canadian troops against a road blockade on a Kahnawake reservation hospitalized 75 Mohawks.[13] Native Americans have experienced the brunt of repression in the United States, a fact that may be explained by their strong vulnerability to racism, their militant demonstration tactics, the degree to which they effectively threaten elite economic and cultural power, and the unwillingness of institutional and established political groups to extend them sufficient support.

Other U.S. Repression:
People's Park, Tompkins Square, and Rent Strikes

Although to a much lesser extent than against Native Americans, the U.S. government has used violence against white activists, as well. A major conflict over development has simmered in Berkeley since 1969, when the University of California used eminent domain to purchase at lower than market-value and then demolish an entire block of houses behind the 2400 block of Telegraph Avenue. Officially, the university claimed it needed the space for a new sports field. Neighborhood activists questioned the truth of this statement, however, and suggested that the university really wanted to eliminate inexpensive housing used by a politicized and countercultural community of leftists.

On April 20, 1969, about 200 people occupied the gutted lot, from which they created "People's Park." After three weeks of community-directed gardening and cultural activity, Berkeley police evicted a 50-person camp and built a cyclone fence on May 15. Enraged demonstrators responded by opening a fire hydrant and pelting police with rocks and bottles. The police escalated the conflict with gunfire and tear gas. They killed one young man with gunshot, inflicted a 20-stitch bayonet wound into the forearm of a 12-year old child, wounded at least 100, and arrested more than 700.[14]

Activists sustained their presence at People's Park during the '70s and '80s, but the university doggedly made attempts to recover gradually and develop the valuable downtown property. On July 27, 1991, riots flared once again when the university constructed a volleyball court in an attempt to capture a beachhead at the park. A crowd of 1,000 faced police who used helicopters, tear gas, motorcycles, and clubs. Demonstrators retaliated by breaking windows on Telegraph Avenue and smashing police car windows. On August 1, after six days of sporadic rioting, the police suppressed demonstrators with rubber and wooden bullets.[15]

Urban parks, one of the last forms of commons remaining on the rapidly privatizing landscape of the 20th century, are flashpoints of struggle for the increasing number of poor people who defend these green havens from encroaching gentrification and the value real estate agents place on sterile cleanliness. On the Lower East Side of New York City, several struggles over land use and gentrification have erupted at Tompkins Square Park, one of the last non-institutional places in New York City for homeless persons to sleep at night. On August 8, 1988, 450 mounted police and a helicopter attacked 500 squatters, punks, homeless people, and supporters engaged in a demonstration against the curfew law for Tompkins Square Park. Many demonstrators retaliated with bottles and stones. Fifty-two people, including 14 police, were treated at hospitals, and nearly twice that many received minor injuries. One participant, who received a sprained arm and stitches in his lip, told the *Guardian*, "They had already cleared out the park with sticks, and they just all of a sudden stampeded. I stepped into a phone booth and they came up. There were five of them. They hit me in the groin and they just kept hitting me. I still can't walk straight."[16] Shortly thereafter, the department of parks erected a chainlink fence around the square, only allowing renters or property owners, not homeless people or squatters who had lived there for years, to use the park.

Squatting and land occupations more often face repression than do rent strikes. Repression for rent strikers would mean eviction, which is more assiduously avoided by people who have the resources to rent a home. Nevertheless, exceptions occur when landlords impose unreasonable conditions and tenants are particularly organized. New York City tenants of Anderson Equities Company at 1197 Anderson Avenue faced landlord abandonment in 1970. The landlord refused to provide heat and hot water, workable elevators, or a watertight roof, and the city recorded 151 housing violations at the address. After three months of withholding rent, the tenants decided to use their escrow account to repair the elevator, roof, boiler, plumbing, and doors. When tenants completed the repairs (and thus made their strike money accessible in the form of improvements), the East New York Savings Bank took the property from the landlord with a lien and ordered evictions. The tenants refused to vacate. On April 7, 1972, police armed with machine guns, shotguns, shields, and helmets used tear gas and gunfire to force tenants, including women with infants, out of the building. The police arrested all of the tenants, five of whom the district attorney later singled out to face multiple charges.[17]

Repression falls heaviest on the poor, people of color, women, the landless, and those who live in Third World squatter settlements. In addition to outright discrimination, this is because such groups are in greater need of land and housing and are closer to debilitating poverty than other more affluent sectors of society. Desperation leads poor people to more sustained resistance and greater risks than are acceptable to other groups who might have better alternatives.

Repression in International Context

Not only landowners and governments have a stake in repressing land and housing campaigns. International investors have similar interests, as became clear for the Tacamiches in Honduras when the U.S. ambassador and the Honduran media began linking the eviction of Tacamiche to creating a business atmosphere conducive to foreign investment. Competition among Third World states for foreign investment tends to guarantee the repression of squatter movements in these regions, even by the most sympathetic or revolutionary of governments. When leftist governments ignore the concerns of their wealthy constituents, for example, by turning a blind eye to rent strikers and squatters, they often get deposed. International interests combine with local elites to plan coups or revolutions from within. It takes more than leniency toward squatters to create the conditions necessary for right-wing forces to depose a government, but it usually plays a role.[18]

In one of the most famous examples of the international guarantee of repression, the leftist government of Jacobo Arbenz in Guatemala legalized some peasant land occupations during the early 1950s. He set legal limits on the amount of land that a single person could own and empowered *campesino* unions to enforce the laws by takeover. In 1954, when this law freed 152,000 hectares of United Fruit's total land area of 90,000,000 hectares, President Eisenhower authorized a CIA-backed invasion force of mercenaries who overthrew the Arbenz government and ended its land reform program.

A similar end befell the leftist government of President João Goulart in Brazil. In the northeast the Peasant League, led by Francisco Julião, staged extensive land occupations between 1963 and 1964. A threatened railway strike lent credence to Goulart's attempt to help some of these occupiers gain land under a new agrarian reform law. But the United States saw Julião as the most dangerous leader in the region and the Peasant League as a potential guerrilla threat, and local landowners feared a general upheaval. These factors, among many others, led to a CIA-backed coup in April 1964 that installed a right-wing dictator who exiled Julião and brutally suppressed the Peasant League.[19]

The overthrow of Salvador Allende's Popular Unity government of Chile in 1973 also sprang from several of his socialist policies, including his refusal to repress land occupations vigorously. Even though President Allende ostensibly discouraged land occupations in speeches and evicted a few settlements, he ignored far more. News of his lenience multiplied occupations from seven in 1965, before his election, to 456 in 1970, when he was elected,[20] and to 1,278 occupations in just four provinces of south-central Chile in 1971. Prior to the Allende government, peasants and Indians had occupied land for small concessions, such as better salaries and benefits. After he gained power, the landless organized occupations aimed at direct expropriation and often were successful.[21] In addition, Allende used land reform laws to expropriate many large landed estates, including a 1.4 million-hectare sheep farm, the world's largest. Because of these and other well-known infractions against local and international property owners by the Popular Unity government, the United States outfitted Pinochet's military to overthrow Allende in a 1973 coup.[22]

Thus, even when governments might condone occupations and the redistribution of land, such support is risky, given the prospect of overthrow by a coalition of local elites and foreign interests. This makes even the threat of a coup or military action sufficient to influence a leftist government to repress land movements.

Mexican Squatters of the 1970s

In Mexico, the government repressed land occupations in the '70s after rumors of a right-wing coup circulated. The repressed occupations had roots in the late '60s, when conservative President Diaz Ordaz declared the termination of land reform at a time of severe agricultural crisis.

Having no legal recourse, and after a period of dormancy, peasants occupied lands and involved themselves in guerrilla warfare during the presidency of Luis Echeverría in the '70s. Spontaneous groups, independent unions, and collectives, often against the wishes of more established *campesino* unions, formed to occupy landed estates belonging to large growers.[23] In July 1972, hundreds of peasants invaded land belonging to several *haciendas* in Tlaxcalla, and 400 peasants, in coalition with students, took 2,100 hectares to establish the Campamento Emiliano Zapata, named after the famous Mexican revolutionary who demanded land with the battle cry *Tierra y Libertad* (Land and Freedom). In December, 1,000 marching peasants demanded official action on their land claims, then occupied ten *latifundia* in Tepeaca, Atlixco, and Tecamachalco. Under mounting rural pressure, the government took title to some big farms in northwest Mexico, assigned them to *campesinos*, and legalized some urban squatter settlements. Echeverría strengthened agrarian reform laws, increased rural expenditure from 10% of the national budget in 1970 to 20% in 1975, and began nominal support of the embattled *ejido* system,[24] which previous administrations had actively attacked.

Though a definite improvement, Echeverría's reforms failed to address adequately landlessness and poverty in the countryside. Over half of all Mexicans employed in agriculture remained landless, less than 1% of arable farms used 30% of all arable land, and in Sinaloa and Sonora, *ejidatarios* rented from 40-80% of their land to large agribusiness. Though officials at the Institute of Agrarian Reform received petitions from the landless to redistribute 66,000 parcels of land, officials took very little action.

Encouraged by Echeverría's initial reforms, in 1975 peasants throughout Mexico occupied tens of thousands more hectares in Zacatecas, Veracruz, Hidalgo, Chiapas, Tamaulipas, Sonora, Nuevo Leon, and Oaxaca. Seventy-six occupations took place in Sinaloa alone, where just 85 rich families owned nearly one-quarter of the irrigated land and 126,000 farmworkers were landless.[25] In another region, nearly 300 armed peasants seized 310 hectares to begin communal farming near Ensenada, only 40 miles from the U.S. border, a prime beachfront resort favored by American tourists.[26]

In 1976, land occupations and political turbulence increased further. Nine thousand peasants organized in 130 groups took over 100,000 hectares spanning eight municipalities, including Sonora, Sinaloa, Chihuahua, and Baja California.

To prevent repression, some of the occupiers took hostages as well as land. In the Yaqui Valley, they kidnapped the regional representative of the land reform commission when he appeared for negotiations. A peasant spokesperson said his group decided on the kidnapping as an act of "self-defense because of the repressive brutality of the army and police, as manifested at San Antonio Rio Muerte," where troops murdered six peasants while attempting to retake occupied land on October 24, 1975.[27]

To appease this growing unrest, President Echeverría again attempted reform. He ordered the expropriation (with compensation) of 100,000 hectares on November 18, 1976. Echeverría intended to distribute most of this land to those already in occupation. With a new-found mantle of government acceptance, though, occupations accelerated, especially on lands the president had mentioned.

That month, however, voters elected a new conservative president. The days of transition between presidents seemed the last chance for the peasant organizations to take land. *Campesinos* in Durango occupied 260,000 hectares on November 28. Tens of thousands more occupied over 400,000 hectares of land as José López Portillo prepared to take the presidency on December 1. Agrarian reform official Morales Mora estimated that 10,000 families, consisting of 50,000 to 60,000 persons, squatted the land during this period.[28]

The political atmosphere, needless to say, became highly volatile. Pressure among the middle and upper classes mounted against government tolerance toward the occupations. Landowners and financiers responded to Echeverría's sympathy for the landless by staging an employee lock-out in 50 cities, blockading roads with farm equipment, and transferring hundreds of millions of dollars to banks in the United States. Some threatened violence, and, for the first time in years, Mexicans talked seriously about the possibility of a military coup. "Many people are ready to put their finger to the trigger," one grower warned.[29] James K. Wilson, an Arizona businessman with heavy landed interests in Mexico, said the big landowners "aren't going to have their lands taken away without making a stand."[30]

With this increasing threat from property owners, a federal court overturned the expropriation law on December 7, forcing the removal of 8,000 peasants from 1 million hectares of occupied land. Even with this repression, however, land occupations on the scale of Mexico in the '70s usually succeed in at least some permanent redistribution. Though the private landowner paramilitaries, Mexican police, and Mexican army used brutal measures to repress occupations (killing over 120 peasants between 1975 and 1976), the occupations permanently redistributed 12,000 hectares in Sinaloa and 37,000 hectares in Sonora. This relatively small amount of land did little to alleviate the massive need; but, if nothing else, *campesinos* during the mid-'70s tested their tremendous political strength against that of landowners, business, and government, and walked away with at least a few concrete successes.[31]

Rather than bring a country to the brink of revolution or civil war, as in Mexico, most governments immediately repress nascent land and housing occupations as part of their courtship of foreign capital. This is especially evident whenever international attention might be focused on a region. At these times, governments have repressed squatter movements prior to large events to present an unblemished landscape to international audiences. The government of the Philippines demolished the houses of 100,000 squatters along the Miss Universe parade route in 1974 and demolished the houses of 65,000 more in 1976 to prepare for an IMF/World Bank conference.[32] Governments desperately court international investors, and any international attention to squalid conditions or social movements that threaten property can give investors cold feet. In the race to repay foreign debts and gain hard currency for the purchase of luxury imports, Third World governments go to almost any length to present the image of being a secure place for investments.

Revolutions that Evict Squatters: Portugal and Nicaragua

When a revolution completely alters the government, this does not necessarily nullify the power of foreign interests and local property holders. Foreign interests that have existing investments in a country will want to ensure the security of those investments even after a revolution. As in the cases of Guatemala and Chile, if a revolutionary government fails to provide that security, foreign governments and businesses can encourage military aid to counter-revolutionaries. Small- and medium-sized property holders may provide popular support to this counter-revolution.

Appeasing these sectors is uppermost in the minds of revolutionary governments when they evict squatters. In 1974, a group of left-wing officers startled the world by orchestrating a coup in Portugal. According to Nancy Gina Bermeo, author of *The Revolution Within the Revolution,* the new left-wing government (called the "fourth provisional government") "feared — quite rightly — that the spontaneous seizure of property would panic small- and medium-sized farmers and drive them into the ranks of reactionaries." In its land reform proclamation, the fourth provisional government announced, "From this moment on, land occupations will no longer be tolerated, as they are damaging to the agrarian reform and therefore reactionary."

The government, however, did not have the power actually to stop or evict the occupations. According to Bermeo, the government "could not pay the high political price of putting them to an end," given the extraordinary strength of the cooperative associations involved in previous land occupations. In addition, many in the army lent the occupations active support, including the leader of the powerful internal police, leftist Otelo Saraiva de Carvalho.[33]

In response to the military support of occupations, large landowners organized the Confederation of Portuguese Farmers (CAP). "Citizens' militias" openly affiliated with CAP blockaded roads with huge and militant demonstrations of up to 25,000 people and inundated the local and international press with bold press releases that included complaints against land occupations and veiled threats of a counter-coup.[34]

The day after the 25,000-person CAP demonstration, rightists within the military arrested about 100 far-left officers, including the much beloved "Otelo." Without military support, the land occupations came to a halt in less than two weeks.[35] The Portuguese governments that followed were increasingly hostile to the land occupations and their cooperative structure, partly because they were actively courting loans from West Germany, the European Economic Community, and the United States. Western economic powers made these loans contingent upon, among other things, the return of land to former owners.

In November 1976, António Barreto took power as the first CAP-approved president. Within a year, he added several loopholes to the land reform law, putting at least some portion of the land of most cooperatives in jeopardy of re-expropriation. By January 1981, riot police (with orders to shoot to kill any resistors) had returned farm equipment, livestock, and 569,000 hectares of the most valuable land to private hands.[36]

The Portuguese land occupations did maintain some gains, however. Bermeo wrote in 1986 that "The loss of land, livestock, and machinery is a crippling blow. But both government officials and union leaders estimate that at least one-third to one-half of the original cooperatives will survive."[37]

In Nicaragua, as in post-coup Portugal, the revolutionary government generally opposed land occupations. Even before they overthrew right-wing President Anastasio Somoza Debayle in 1979, the Sandinistas promised not to confiscate the land of supportive landowners. When peasants occupied land, writes Joseph Collins of Food First,

> Sandinistas worked to ensure that farms around León belonging to landowners aiding in the fight against Somoza were *not* taken over....To a truly remarkable extent, the Sandinista Front succeeded in using its moral authority with the *campesinos* and landless agricultural workers to restrain their wrath against landowners, including the Somocistas, and to await due process.[38]

Full support of land occupations, the Sandinistas reasoned, might have pushed the quiescent sector of landowners into aiding Somoza or, after the Sandinista victory, helping the Contras (U.S.-supported counter-revolutionaries). "To resist any U.S. destabilization pressures," writes Collins, "the Sandinistas knew they had to do everything within reason to build support among all social classes for the future of the revolution."[39] When President Ronald Reagan's pugnacity replaced Jimmy Carter's policy of coexistence with Nicaragua, many of Nicaragua's big growers began to employ direct sabotage. The need to maintain internal stability became paramount for the Sandinista government,[40] which also feared that Reagan might impose an embargo (which later took place) or even invade Nicaragua.

Not paying the foreign debt contracted by Somoza would increase the chances of such punitive international actions. To repay the debt and also buy food, medicine, oil, machinery, and imported luxuries (to pacify the remaining Nicaraguan upper class), the Sandinistas needed to grow export crops exchangeable for foreign currency. "While 'Land to whoever works it!' might have been an effective rallying cry during the war of liberation," writes Collins, "it got quietly buried once the victorious leadership had to confront the urgent need to get the capitalist farmers and ranchers controlling most of the country's exports back into production."

During the first land reform, in July 1979, the Sandinistas resisted popular land occupations meant to divide the large export-oriented farms formerly owned by Somocistas into small, subsistence farms. Instead, the Sandinistas assumed control of these lucrative assets. About 20% of the nation's agricultural land became state farms; 65% stayed in the hands of large landowners. *Campesinos* controlled only 15% of the nation's farmland after the first land reform — about the same as during Somoza's regime.[41]

To grow export crops, the Sandinistas had to attract wage labor, which meant keeping a certain number of peasants landless. For this reason also, Sandinistas opposed land occupations. If all the peasants occupied land and became small private farmers, the big farms would have no cheap labor. Because small farming of food crops produced a higher standard of living for the small farmer compared to wage labor in the export sector under both Somoza *and* the Sandinistas, both governments had to bar a significant portion of landless laborers from becoming *campesinos*, even though capitalist and state farms had excess land.

Because of increasing agitation and rural disillusionment with the revolution (30,000 protesters marched in 1980, and land occupations increased in the following years),[42] however, the Sandinistas instituted a second land reform program in August 1981. As officials realized the inefficiencies of state farms, they granted land in this and future land reforms to worker-owned cooperatives. By the start of 1986, 60% of the nation's *campesinos* had received land titles to more than 1.8 million hectares, or one-third of the nation's farmland. Before the revolution, all of the nation's poor had owned a total of less than 120,000 hectares.[43]

The Sandinistas won the revolution, instituted a land reform that made land holdings more egalitarian, and protected, to some extent, land occupations. Even though the Sandinistas took power, however, the former large landowners, remnants of the Somoza regime, and foreign governments continued indirectly to repress land occupiers and land reform beneficiaries by financing and training the Contras. In 1983 alone, the Contras killed 811 farmworkers and *campesinos* and spread fear by rape and torture.[44] To devastate squatters and land reform beneficiaries economically, the Contras destroyed crops, buildings, and machinery.[45]

Because of this repression, according to Collins, "some families [were] afraid to join cooperatives or even to receive land through the agrarian reform."[46] By 1984, more than 120,000 peasants in the war zones had fled Contra raids, abandoning their homes and fields.[47] Eventually, under such pressure, a bare majority of the Nicaraguan electorate voted for U.S.-supported candidate Violeta Chamorro, who opposed land reform.

Revolutionary governments faced with peasant land occupations must balance their desire to implement land reforms against the possibility of inflaming a counter-revolution among local elites and international investors. Communists during the Spanish Civil War, Allende in Chile, Echeverría in Mexico, the Sandinistas in Nicaragua, and the fourth provisional government in Portugal after the 1974 revolution all chose to evict some peasant land occupations and deploy deterrents against others.

While these evictions seem justified to some extent, given international and local pressures, all of the governments noted above were eventually defeated, overthrown, or voted out of office. After their fall, the new governments usually reversed the land reforms and evicted many, if not most, of the land occupiers. Immediately following the coups against Arbenz and Allende, former owners of expropriated lands initiated counter-reforms that returned practically all lands, reinstituted feudal share-cropping in Guatemala, and reduced the Chilean reform sector from 39% of total agricultural land area in 1973 to 9% in 1975.[48]

The same has happened with capitalist incursions into other former socialist countries. Threatened with loosing foreign aid from the United States and loans from the World Bank, the Chamorro government in Nicaragua began expropriating land from families who had benefited from Sandinista agrarian reform. In June 1992, the new Nicaraguan security forces (many of them ex-Contras) violently evicted inhabitants of 21 farms slated for return to former owners, 11 of which went to family members of Somoza.[49] By 1995, 3,000 claims by former landowners remained unresolved, one-third of them filed by members of the Somoza family or their supporters. The claims included a quarter of Nicaragua's arable land, upon which 170,000 families had settled, most of them impoverished squatters and war refugees to whom the Sandinista government had promised land titles.[50] Chamorro also violated the truce agreed to by Sumo Indians and the Sandinistas after the Indians waged a guerrilla war in the 1980s to protect their tropical forests from commercial incursions. Chamorro gave foreign companies lucrative concessions to log 62,000 hectares of that forest in March 1996, more than half of which is in the Sumo reserve.[51]

Arnoldo Alemán, who won the Nicaraguan presidency in October 1996, has promised to repossess land from those who benefited from Sandinista reforms at an even quicker rate. Alemán still smarts at the confiscation of his own property

by the Sandinista government in 1989. He led landowner associations that opposed land occupations during Sandinista rule and denounced Chamorro as running a co-government with the Sandinistas because he considered her
counter-reforms insufficiently zealous.[52]

Fear and the Deactivation of Movements

The counter-reforms in Nicaragua and other post-socialist Latin American
nations are implemented under threat of repression. Through the use of repression,
landlords and government officials hope to dissuade land and housing activists
from taking direct action. Often the repression required to deactivate a movement
is very small. With a minimum of force and by this principle, the British government ended one of the largest rent strikes in history, against the Housing Finance
Act (HFA) of 1972. The HFA brought all public housing in England and Wales to
market rates by de-subsidizing rents. It mandated rent increases of up to 100% for
every unit. Initially local Labour Party councilors refused to implement the act, but
politicians buckled shortly after the national government threatened them with
fines.

Led by decentralized and relatively independent tenants' associations,
100,000 public housing tenants continued the struggle by refusing to pay the increases, while some even staged a "total rent strike" (refusal to pay any rent at all).
Ancillary tactics included the publication of broadsheets, the staging of demonstrations, and the blocking of roads. When ordered to appear in court, strikers
scrawled "on rent strike" or "we won't pay" on subpoenas and returned them to
the court *en masse*.[53] At one demonstration, tenants used the tactic of humiliation.
Television cameras filmed 3,000 marchers spitting on the names of 31 politicians
responsible for implementing the increase.

In response to these tactics, government officials targeted organizers and
those on total rent strike. The government threw some in jail, coopted tenant leaders by incorporating them into local Labour Parties, initiated court proceedings,
seized furniture, garnished wages, evicted tenants, and forcefully ejected tenants
from government meetings.[54] Although tenants organized warning systems, anti-
eviction committees, and mobile pickets to blockade evictions, they rarely brought
such tactics to bear when actual evictions took place.

Thus the government managed the situation predominantly by threat rather
than actual force, effectively intimidating tenants into abandoning risky tactics
against eviction. When the government went beyond court orders to make eviction
seem imminent, most tenants paid the increases and arrears. In the end, the mere
threat of repression succeeded in squelching the rent strikes against the HFA. The
law remained unchanged, and rent increases took effect.[55]

When not completely ending a movement, as in the English rent strike above, repression can steer it toward less confrontational tactics. Participant Art Goldberg analyzed the emergence of pacifism during the Berkeley People's Park protests in 1969.

> The willingness of the police to shoot at people has for the most part forced demonstrators to deescalate their tactics. Few rocks have been thrown since "Bloody Thursday," May 15. Almost no windows have been broken, and not many barricades have been erected. Nonviolence has not been a conscious tactic, but one which evolved on the streets.[56]

People's Park activists remained active two weeks after "Bloody Thursday," organizing a nonviolent demonstration of 25,000 to 30,000. According to Todd Gitlin, "A small minority of radicals wanted to tear down the fence with their bare hands; the Guard wouldn't shoot — or would they? The balloons, the nervous festivity, reminded the militants of a funeral procession. They saw May 30 as the day they lost control to liberals and pacifists."[57] This nonviolence seemed to work, coupled with some riots in the '90s: People's Park is still green almost 30 years later.

Though nonviolent demonstration in liberal democracies rarely brings violent repression, pacifists in developing nations have not enjoyed such privilege. In April 1984, Saul Mkize, the leader of Driefontein, a South African community resisting eviction, was shot and killed. Although people attended more meetings afterwards, according to a local lawyer, "if it came down to passive resistance, people would be scared that they would be shot."[58] In the case of Driefontein, the assassination strengthened an underground network, but stifled public expressions of dissent.

Deactivation does not necessarily require an assassination; subduing a campaign can be done by mere suggestion. In Santiago de Chile, the city-wide Committee of the Homeless organized the Manuel Rodriguez squatter settlement in 1969. Because of their success in resisting removal, by 1975 the government began helping residents improve the settlement. The population remained small, however, probably because of the potential threat of dictator Augusto Pinochet's housing officials, who called for evictions and the construction of high-rise buildings on the land. A mere credible threat of eviction deterred the settlement's growth.

But anytime that obvious squatting, land occupations, or radical political activity appears to be repressed, smaller and less detectable measures are probably taking place. In his book *Weapons of the Weak: Everyday Forms of Peasant Resistance*, James Scott details his experiences living for several years in a small Malaysian rice-growing village. Over time, the other members of his village community, many of them landless, confided in Scott their methods of resisting landlords and the combine harvesters that replaced their labor. These included not the overt political acts of land occupation and squatting, but the more subtle and apparently depoliticized tactics of "foot dragging, dissimulation, desertion, false compliance, pilfering, feigned ignorance, slander, arson, and sabotage."[59] Thus, even when peasants do not have the power or organization to combat landlords overtly, when landlords have repressed popular peasant movements, a close study of peasant communities will nonetheless find an active subterranean culture of both material and ideological resistance.[60]

Reinvigoration of Struggle

A widely recognized symbol for squatting in Europe and North America is a lightning-shaped arrow through a circle. One sees this symbol painted in murals on the sides of squats in Berlin, as the central motif of many emblems adopted by squatters'-aid groups, in squatter comics, and generally in any place in the North where squatters congregate. The symbol originated long ago with hobos, who assigned to it the meaning "continue on" or "safe haven ahead." Squatters in the Netherlands borrowed the symbol during the 1970s when faced with persistent evictions. "This fearless preparation for the unknown," writes an Amsterdam squatter, "kept alive that rage which made a motley group of neighborhoods, houses, and individuals 'the collected Amsterdam squat groups.' As a sign that they would 'go on' to the bitter end, the circle with the arrow borrowed from hobo language was elevated to the squatting symbol."[61]

For squatting, a predominantly nonviolent method of struggle, the hidden "continue on" meaning of the hobo symbol has particular importance. When repression becomes intense, the most common strategy for achieving success in land and housing struggles is to "continue on" with all nonviolent resources at hand, including increased media outreach, lobbying, demonstrations, leafleting, boycotts, sympathy strikes by labor allies, hiding in the hills, and, most importantly, continued squatting, land occupation, or rent strike. "Faced with repression," writes nonviolence strategist Gene Sharp in his three-volume *Politics of Nonviolent Action,* "nonviolent actionists have only one acceptable response: to overcome they must persist in their action and refuse to submit or retreat…. Without willingness to face repression as the price of struggle, the nonviolent action movement cannot hope to succeed."[62] Such continuing struggle in the face of repression has proven an extremely effective tactic for gaining public sympathy and ultimately for gaining land and housing concessions.

While repression can dampen and even end a movement, it can also sow the seeds of future struggle or strengthen the movement it meant to destroy. Repression tends to inflame any already existing sense of injustice and spurs a feeling of righteous indignation. As a particularly painful ordeal, repressive incidents can

bring into stark focus a previously obscured adversary, cementing solidarity between activists and those previously uninvolved. During a Bronx rent strike in
1971, an organizer confronted two men illegally serving eviction notices to tenants. They broke her nose and dragged her outside to their automobile, where they
claimed she was under "arrest." After other tenants challenged their authority, the
thugs released the organizer and sped away. Before the attack, only half the tenants had pledged themselves to strike; shortly after, all the tenants joined.[63]

In the most extreme of situations, even the killing of participants can
strengthen a land movement's resolve. In 1973 and 1974, the Regional Indian
Council of Cauca (CRIC) in Colombia organized land occupations and held mass
marches from forests and highland regions to urban areas. In response, local landowners and politicians assassinated the agrarian leader Gustavo Mejíea González
and the Indian leader Venancio Taquinaz, slaughtered peasants, evicted people
from the land (some subsequently died of malnutrition), blacklisted employees,
and threatened jail and death to those CRIC members who remained. Activist
commitment only increased after the repression, and the communities developed a
vigorous campaign to build public pressure against the violence. In a March 1974
demonstration against the deaths, people called for continued struggle. "If they kill
one of us," a placard read, "one hundred more will be born. They will not be able
to kill us all." [64]

Beyond strengthening the resolve of already existing movement participants
or those tenants who stand to benefit, repression sometimes galvanizes wider community support. Repression injects news of an occupation into informal discussion, periodicals, and television, making it real for the uninvolved. This can
activate community members and increase participation in a movement by more
mainstream groups that have influence with governments and landlords. The Tacamiches benefited from this dynamic in Honduras. Germany witnessed this phenomenon too, according to a study of that country's squatting by Margit Mayer.

> The occupation and subsequent violent eviction of a building in Septem-
> ber 1971 encouraged more squats, because widespread indignation over
> brutal police actions and bloody street battles forced the Frankfurt mayor
> to rescind his earlier eviction order. Similar sympathies arose in Hamburg
> over the city government's repressive and criminalizing response to their
> first squats. Citizens' initiatives, tenant groups, and professionals came to
> the support of the squatters and formed a broad housing movement.[65]

This diversity of movement and coalition of forces, as developed in chapter six,
greatly increases a campaign's chance of success.

One of the most renowned instances of repression in recent Guatemalan history also galvanized community support. The infamous Panzós Massacre of May
29, 1978, is named after the town in which it took place. On that day, a group of

700 Kekchi Indians marched to Panzós and attempted to petition the mayor. They demanded the protection of their land rights, which oil prospectors were in the process of eroding. They also wanted to investigate the whereabouts of three peasant leaders kidnapped some weeks earlier.

At the behest of a group of eight landlords, 150 soldiers of the Guatemalan Army attacked the demonstration with sustained gunfire. Many of the peasants, including five women with babies, drowned as they tried to escape across the Polochíc River. The army hunted down others in the surrounding hills, and many died for lack of medical attention when the military denied the Red Cross access. In total, the soldiers killed 140, wounded 300, and then buried the dead in a mass grave.

This brutality caused a week of protests by student, labor, church, peasant, and professional groups, culminating on June 8, 1978, when 80,000 people marched through Guatemala City. Rigoberta Menchú remembers the effect that the massacre had on her indigenous squatter community. "We felt this was a direct attack on us. It was as if they'd murdered us, as if we were being tortured when they killed those people."[66]

The community support that repression elicits can go beyond a particular land or housing issue and threaten the popularity of the government in power. The guerrilla tactics of Sumatran squatters in the 1950s and their relentless persistence in the face of eviction proved quite effective against the forces of large plantation owners and the government. When ordered off the land by patrols, squatters simply returned the next night, and children and women blockaded bulldozers that attempted to demolish huts and irrigation trenches. By 1951, government interdiction and limited repression was clearly ineffective, so tobacco companies agreed to return 130,000 of their 250,000 leased hectares to the government's holdings. Of the land returned, 20,000 hectares belonged to long-standing squatter settlements and 30,000 hectares belonged to newer settlements.

Land retained by tobacco companies in this agreement was to be cleared of squatters, but when police killed four in a 1953 attempted eviction on the Tanjung Morawa estate, public opinion swung against the government. "The Wilopo cabinet's support of the eviction," writes researcher Laura Ann Stoler, "and its unequivocal siding with foreign capital, made this notorious Tanjung Morawa affair an immediate and principal cause of that cabinet's fall."[67] The movement grew, and half a million people were squatting in Sumatra by 1957.

Persistence in the face of repression, as Gene Sharp notes with regard to nonviolent struggles in general, is of principal importance for social movements wishing to gain land and housing concessions. The amount of persistence displayed, however, depends on the solidarity of the participants, the ruthlessness of the adversary, the degree of community support, and the elasticity of the move-

ment. Weighing these factors, participants gauge the relative merit of tactical retreat compared with continued struggle.

Elasticity of Squatting

Where large numbers of people squat, governments have difficulty making
evictions permanent. Police evict squatters, who then return or simply squat another area. In South Africa, a squatter camp called KTC began in 1983 with 20
houses framed with sticks and covered with plastic trash bags. KTC grew due to
demolitions at other squatter camps, but every day the police demolished and
burned people's shelters. The settlement became a focus for women's political action,[68] and, within a few weeks, 10,000 people, mostly women, moved in. The police raided methodically, staging evictions even on rainy days. But after each
eviction, squatters rebuilt their demolished huts at nightfall. Some squatters buried
their houses before the police came or dug underground houses that escaped police
bulldozers. Police failed to dislodge KTC until they demolished the shacks and
ringed the area with barbed wire, search lights, and tanks. But this only squeezed
KTC inhabitants into Crossroads, a squatter settlement famous for militant politics.

Squatters, by definition, have no legal place to live. This makes any form of
removal, except for massacre, ultimately ineffective. Unfortunately, some governments or business interests may have consciously undertaken such a sinister tactic.
In Rio de Janeiro, the 1993 murder of eight homeless children (known as the Candelária killings) started a rash of similar murders. Before Candelária, the average
number of young people killed was 285 a year from 1985 to 1992. Since 1993,
however, the average has risen to 1,172 a year. Some allege that shopowners pay
police to kill homeless youths who congregate in commercial zones. A *New York
Times* article refers to a "consensus that Rio residents are thankful that the police
clear the streets of poor children and the petty crimes they rely on to survive."[69]

Barring outright massacre, however, eviction of a squatter from one place
almost always means she or he squats somewhere else or waits until the police
leave and then reoccupies the original land. Squatters are elastic like a water balloon. When you squeeze one spot, it bulges in another. Eviction only succeeds in
moving poor people from one squatter settlement to the next, never in defeating
the phenomena of squatting and poverty.

The elastic quality of Third World squatting approximates the elasticity of
homelessness in the more affluent nations. As diligently as politicians attempt to
invent new anti-homeless legislation to eradicate the poor from one city or neighborhood, the homeless only migrate to the next and shortly thereafter get repelled
back to their origin. After New York City Mayor David Dinkins ordered the

eviction of Tompkins Square Park in June 1991, most of the residents simply rebuilt encampments elsewhere, one of which they named "Dinkinsville," where
200 lived for about four months. According to Lower East Side activist Bill Weinberg, squatters built "shanties" with found materials, and the encampments
"started to look like the slums of Mexico City or Rio de Janeiro."[70]

In 1998, I witnessed the supposedly liberal San Francisco Mayor Willie
Brown buckle under to neighborhood and business pressures to "clean up the
homeless problem." A few blocks from my home in the Haight district, he evicted
homeless people from their campsites in Golden Gate Park and erected fences
around their places of congregation. Ironically, the homeless had nowhere to go
except the nearby residential and business neighborhoods from which the complaints originated.

Movement Use of Violence

Most land and housing struggles succeed through elastic response to repression and persistent nonviolence. But like a water balloon squeezed so forcefully
that it bursts, tenants and the landless can lose patience and use violence or the
threat of violence as an ancillary tactic.

Some go underground to form clandestine organizations when authorities
repress their nonviolent demonstrations. On January 26, 1972, aboriginal activists
erected a tent city on the lawn of the Australian Parliament House in Canberra and
dubbed their encampment the "Aboriginal Embassy." They demanded, among
other things, better housing and land rights. Six months later, after 100 police
evicted the embassy and arrested eight people, John Newfong, one of the original
Aboriginal Embassy staff, announced that the land rights campaign would continue to operate, but would increasingly go underground. Urban guerrillas, according to Newfong, were training in several Australian cities.[71] The training may or
may not have produced Newfong's promised guerrillas, but the impulse is clear:
repression of nonviolence tends to intensify the violent elements of a movement.

In the case of the Aboriginal Embassy, repression caused a land struggle to
threaten violence. For a campaign waged by residents that attempts to defend a
stationary resource, such as a particular piece of agricultural land or housing development, the transition from legality to violence follows a logical progression. Following repression, the initial impulse toward violence can appear in its most
harmless manifestation: property destruction.

The 1971 rent strike by tenants of East Main Street in Bridgeport, Connecticut, to force the landlord to replace a broken boiler, shows how violence begins
small and develops. After five months of tenants nonviolently withholding rent,
police created a crisis. They arrested Willie Matos, a tenant leader and captain of

the Bridgeport Young Lords Party (a radical Latino political organization), and forcibly evicted the Lords from their office for refusal to pay rent. The police then arrested 18 people and injured 20 in a failed attempt to disperse a large crowd in front of the office. Four people required hospitalization and one couple, according to the *Guardian,* "signed an affidavit testifying that police broke into their apartment, hit them with rifle butts, and threw their 18-month-old boy to the floor."[72] After police arrested Matos, a friend of the landlord entered the Young Lords office, tore down posters, ripped out phones, broke a temporary wall partition, and threw furniture and office supplies onto the street. The illegal destruction of the office, the eviction, and the police violence all spurred some tenants to become more militant. They lit a police car on fire, returned the ousted furniture to the Lords' office, and danced to drums in the street.

Another round of repression lurked around the corner. When a young white man ran down the street yelling insults and a fight broke out, police re-evicted the Young Lords, cordoned off a 15-block area, made sweeps through the neighborhood, and injured a number of people on side streets. "One older man was asked by the police if he was Puerto Rican," reported the *Guardian.* "When he said he was, they hit him with their rifle butts."

Whereas tenants damaged only property in response to the first round of repression, in response to the second, harsher repression, tenants escalated in kind. After the eviction, 1,000 people marched from a nearby housing project to the Young Lords office, and someone lit a nearby building on fire. When fire engines arrived, angry tenants pelted firefighters with rocks and bottles. This rent strike by tenants in Bridgeport illustrates how, as police repression increases against larger numbers of people, small acts of violence by groups of tenants can escalate into large-scale riots like the ones that engulfed urban areas in the '60s.

Housing struggles throughout the world have also escalated into riots. In *Cracking the Movement: Squatting Beyond the Media*, the Foundation for the Advancement of Illegal Knowledge (ADILKNO) describes a squatters movement in Amsterdam during the 1970s and '80s. ADILKNO explains the transformation of nonviolence into violence from the perspective of participants:

> The 1978 eviction of the Nicolaas Beetstraat-Jacob van Lennepstraat corner house on the west side of Amsterdam is praised in current creation narratives as the step up to a squatters' movement which no longer steered clear of violent resistance. You can see it on film. Squatters standing three rows deep with arms linked in passive resistance to eviction had been beaten up with batons while chanting, "No violence, no violence!" It was clear that this was not to happen again: "In response to the senseless provocations of the authorities it's difficult to stay a bit reasonable yourself. A stirred-up crowd has such an energy, if that's unleashed the profes-

sional brawlers [police] will be nowhere," stated the nonviolent activists afterwards. When the Groote Keyser got an eviction notice at the end of '79 and was rebuilt into a fortress, the collective feeling was that the lesson of '78 now had to be taken as far as it could go.[73]

Following the initial use of nonviolence in Amsterdam, Dutch squatters increasingly deployed physical violence against the police. On October 25, 1985, 200 squatters "outfitted with helmets, clubs, and leather jackets" were just beginning to fight the police when they heard news over a radio. In a riot the day before, a friend named Hans Kok had been severely beaten and arrested along with dozens of others. News of Kok's death in his cell shocked and momentarily demobilized the 200 squatters. According to Paul, one of the rioters,

> It was like a bomb had dropped on the square. First everyone was standing close together listening, but then everyone suddenly backed away.... Actually you'd expect that the reaction to the news would be a huge outburst of rage, but instead it seemed like people didn't know what to do anymore. The motivation to go on with the resquat had disappeared in a flash.... People couldn't believe it, it hit harder than a crack with a baton. Maybe part of it was like, shit, if they destroy someone who's already in a cell, then they can shoot us down here on the street like that too.[74]

But news of the death stopped the Amsterdam squatters for only a few hours. At a meeting later that evening, thoughts turned toward rioting. The squatters planned a mass demonstration for the next day and encouraged rioters to take small group actions against municipal targets that evening. Paul told an interviewer,

> It was really strange that night. Suddenly everyone seemed to have the same kind of click. Everyone had the idea, now we'll use the ultimate means, just before guns anyway: mollies [Molotov cocktails]. Even people who were generally moderate said, now it's gone too far, this has to stop.... The fear threshold was gone. It didn't matter if you got picked up either. I think there was really a feeling of justification, like, I'm within my rights. You can bust me but it doesn't matter a fuck anyway. Normally you don't set cop cars on fire in front of a police station, you think it over a couple of weeks, how you'll go about it. That night it happened spontaneously, wham. I ran into people Saturday who said, I thought we were the only ones who would do something so heavy. But everyone did it.[75]

Certain gas stations refused to make sales to "suspicious types" as the number of attacks increased and spread as a far as Utrecht and Nijmegan. "At least 40 lightning strikes took place," according to ADILKNO, "including arson attacks on the traffic police (damage 1.2 million guilders), municipal outposts, an empty prison, the city records office, builders' huts, garbage cans, a tour boat, and city hall."[76]

The use of sabotage and violence by land and housing movements can lead to success or utter failure, depending on the circumstances. Some groups who use violence have enjoyed clear successes. One such group is the Xavante Indians, who live in the rainforests of Mato Grosso, Brazil. Starting in 1975, they drove cattle companies off their lands on multiple occasions and with much international media attention by fielding as many as 100 warriors in full traditional war dress and attacking company camps. In May 1980, 40 Xavante warriors, armed with modern weapons, occupied the headquarters of Brazil's Bureau of Indian Affairs (FUNAI). They vacated the premises only after extracting a promise from the head of FUNAI to add an extra 60,000 hectares of land to their reserve.[77] The Xavante were lucky and politically astute, and took their actions at the right moment. Their success led other indigenous groups in Brazil to use violent tactics, as well, with mixed results.

Increased use of violence by a movement usually means an increase of repression. But repression has costs for the repressor, as well as repressed. Even when repressive tactics eventually extinguish a particular campaign, excessive political and economic costs for landlords and police can dissuade them from using such repressive tactics in future struggles. In the context of criminal justice, legal theory considers this the "deterrent effect" of sanctions. Tenants, the landless, and indigenous communities have also benefited by using the concept of deterrence. Just as repression chills the resistance of not only the repressed, but also anyone who might follow their example, violent resistance that accompanies repression can make government agencies and landlords hesitate. In this way, even a repressed direct action can lead to the success of future campaigns.

In 1973, AIM held hundreds of federal marshals at bay for 71 days at the small Pine Ridge hamlet of Wounded Knee. One of the marshals died, probably from friendly fire. The marshals eventually evicted the armed occupiers, but, in later AIM occupations, government officials thought twice about using violence. Memories of Wounded Knee led to a positive resolution of the armed encampment of the Mohawks at Ganienkeh in 1974 when the tribe received a large parcel of land as a concession. In a rare admission of outside radical influence on government policy, a spokesperson for the Department of Environmental Conservation in Albany said, "We consciously avoided a direct conflict with the Indians.... We didn't want another Wounded Knee."[78]

Land and housing activists have recognized and acted on the principle of deterrence. In the context of massive riots, a squatter in West Berlin spoke to an interviewer in 1981 regarding searches of squats and evictions by the police. "We decided we must always react to these attacks by the police, we can't just let them happen, because if we do, next week they come knocking on this door and we will be out on the street."[79]

Squatters in Amsterdam also used the tactic of deterrence. During the July 3, 1980, Vogelstruys riot, 30 to 40 demonstrators barricaded in a squat threw household items (including chairs, tables, heaters, bricks, and bed springs) at approaching riot police. Dozens of other street demonstrators fought with rocks and steel bars against about 120 riot police who used tear gas, swung clubs, and, in what may have been a spontaneous innovation in police science, threw rocks back at the rioters. Eventually police lobbed tear gas through the windows, then severely beat and arrested the fleeing squatters.

Reflecting on the events, ADILKNO notes, squatters "had no reason to go so far again. But at the same time, the outside world thought that from now on squatters were prepared to defend their houses like this forever. This was an ace up their sleeves in future evictions."[80] Squatters reoccupied the Vogelstruys squat and held meetings to prepare for the next eviction. According to ADILKNO,

> Six intervening weeks of city-wide meetings decided for a change in course. A direct confrontation with the riot police could be prevented by placing evictions in an economic context; from now on they had to start costing the authorities as much money as possible. The strategy was two-pronged: on one hand, the house had to pose enough of a threat that the police would be forced to deploy the maximum amount of personnel and equipment. On the other, there had to be a riot in order to do as much damage as possible to banks, the city, real estate agents and other nasties.[81]

The eviction attempt came in September, but instead of fighting in front of the squat, small groups spread across the city according to the new realpolitik that harkened back to American suffragettes who smashed business windows with hammers. ADILKNO describes how, in a constantly moving evasion of 200 riot police, squatters smashed windows in malls, banks, and upscale shops; looted; and started fires in the middle of streets.

> By the next evictions, the "bank spree" strategy was preferred over a scuffle in and around the squat. But to this end, the squat groups had to disregard the neighborhood- and house-bound local experience that had started it all. The houses, stripped of their excess value of being part of one's "own" space, could be staked in negotiations over purchase, renovation and rent settlements. Threats and use of violence during evictions and other ways of getting into the media were meant to secure a strong position in current or future negotiations.[82]

On October 6, only one month after the second Vogelstruys riot, the "bank spree" strategy seemed to pay off. The city unexpectedly purchased the Groote

Keyser (a house squatted since the late '70s) from the landlord and began negotiating with squatters on the mechanics of legalization, which eventually took place.[83]

To utilize the factor of deterrence for a current struggle, as did the Amsterdam squatters in 1980, activists have broadcasted the threat of violence to adversaries. During the massive public housing strike of 1973 in Newark, New Jersey, Toby Henry, the president of the Newark Tenant Organization, said, "There will be a revolution in this city if they try to evict the tenants." The strike consisted primarily of African American and Puerto Rican tenants. Later, the Newark Tenant Organization became even more specific, saying that "The tenants have threatened resistance and mass solidarity if sheriffs try to padlock any tenant out of their apartment. The thought always lingers that in 1967, race riots started in public housing."[84] Though only talk, such statements are provocative fighting words when coming from a tenant organization president and may cause police chiefs to at least reconsider the efficacy of eviction. Newark tenants won management positions in their public housing, $1.3 million in housing funds, and three years' free rent after their strike.

Even more mainstream groups will use the violence or potential violence of social movements as a way to encourage reforms. Whether knowingly or not, their references to violence are veiled threats that have a chance of drawing the attention of governments that want to maintain political stability. FIAN-International is an international human rights group based in Heidelberg, Germany. Its coordinator for Latin America, Martin Wolpold, has described violence as the inevitable recourse of deprived peoples:

> In many regions, as in Latin America, the peace process has advanced but the social and economic situation has deteriorated. There is a growing amount of violence which will lead to even greater conflict if the necessary structural changes are not made. One of those structural changes is of course land tenure reform.... In the late 1990s there was a lot of criminality in Central America. This is an expression of poverty, as it is in other regions where you see the paradoxical phenomenon of a simultaneously growing economy and growing poverty. The distribution model must change, and those who are excluded are very clear about this process and want their economic share, if necessary by violence.[85]

Wolpold's reference to violence, if conveyed to state actors with whom he has had contact (such as the head of the World Bank's Latin America division), would presumably augment the persuasiveness of his policy suggestions. In other words, the threat of social movements causing instability strengthens the hands of progressive policy advocates.

Though the reference to or use of violence can sometimes encourage governments to make concessions, this usually goes unacknowledged in the mainstream media. In mid-December 1995, Mayor Henning Voscherau announced that the city of Hamburg in Germany would sell the entire Hafenstrasse block to 120 squatters for only one-third of market value. In response, the *New York Times* headlined a January 5 article on the Hamburg struggle, "Squatters Win! (A Checkbook Did It)." Closer examination of the movement, however, and even of the article in question, forces one to reconsider the accuracy of the headline, the only text seen by most of the 1 million *New York Times* readers.

A headline that stated simply "Squatters Win!" without the parenthetical phrase would have at least omitted the mistake. Or, to more fully reflect the text, perhaps editors could have changed the secondary phrase to "(A Mass Movement Plus a Checkbook, Riots, and Arson Did It)." Activists initiated the first squats of Hamburg in 1973 as a protest against the demolition of neighborhoods and homes that had become historical landmarks.[86] Housing movements opposed urban renewal when it threatened existing social networks.

Out of the early '70s movement grew community and tenant organizations that not only prevented many demolitions, but also built an organizational basis for the second massive mobilization. This began in October 1981, when about 100 activists occupied a block of empty houses owned by the city. In the hope of selling at a big profit to developers, the city of Hamburg left the Hafenstrasse houses vacant while waiting for land prices to inflate.

Early attempts to remove the squatters failed in the face of fierce resistance. "Rather than risk an all-out battle, the city agreed to give them a temporary rental contract…. When the rental agreement expired in 1986, more than 10,000 supporters of the squatters marched through downtown Hamburg demanding that it be extended." After the city announced plans to evict, several department stores were firebombed, causing millions of dollars worth of damage. One year later, in 1987, hundreds of masked squatters behind barricades and burning cars defended themselves from eviction with volleys of bottles and bricks lobbed at thousands of advancing police.

The mayor resigned as a result of the massive riot, but even the law-and-order successor had to start negotiating; in mid-December 1995, he granted ownership of the housing to the squatters. In turn, they agreed to pay $1.5 million, less than one-third of market value, and only half of the $260,000 in overdue rent and utility bills, with the city paying the balance.

Though money did play a role, a reappraisal of the story as related in the *New York Times* suggests that it takes much more than a checkbook to win gains for a squatting movement. In the case of the Hafenstrasse, it took persistence over dozens of years by a militant mass movement. Said one squatter, "We won. We struggled for years, and now we've reached our goal."

Deterrence may help some movements in the long run, but the adoption of violent resistance usually means only a more repressive form of eviction. Few isolated squatters or rent strikers will have the capacity to successfully confront the police or military. In Puerto Rico, with the path cleared for eviction by a 1981 court order, the police proceeded to utilize the divide-and-conquer tactic, bulldozing eight squatter settlements one by one.[87] Seven hundred squatter families of the final settlement facing eviction, Villa Sin Miedo, had earlier decided to fight the police instead of willingly vacating the premises. They built barricades made of old cars and tree stumps and dug trenches to prevent the passage of unwanted vehicles. Squatters even surrounded the village with tires, which they planned to set aflame as a protective smoke screen upon attack.[88]

During the confrontation, police opened fire and wounded one man in the leg. Police also dragged two women by the hair to a police station where four officers beat them during interrogation. Despite an initial success, as whole families armed with machetes, sticks, and rocks forced police and bulldozers to retreat,[89] the government evicted Villa Sin Miedo within a year.

Though violent resistance may yield positive results in some instances, social movements that use violence have experienced the harshest forms of repression.

Direct Action and the Birth of Revolutionary Movements

As land or housing movements escalate their tactics, repression often causes the goals of a campaign to change from reform to more radical or even revolutionary solutions. Because isolated land occupations that resist eviction with violence rarely win without allies, and movements have not engaged in violent resistance consistently enough to create a substantial deterrent effect, occupations and campaigns sometimes go beyond sporadic violence to create or ally with revolutionary movements that seek the overthrow of particular governments. Writes Jeffery Paige in his *Agrarian Revolution,* a study of Peru, Angola, and Vietnam,

> The conflict over landed property, which is the fundamental political issue in any system dependent on a landed elite, leads directly to conflicts involving the ultimate control of the political system. There are no other political options open to cultivators who are denied participation in politics, access to the legal system, or the right to engage in the pursuit of profit through small-scale farming.[90]

The process of revolutionizing land movements has followed a similar pattern in many countries. Peasants occupy a piece of land, the army or landowner-hired mercenaries arrive to evict the new community, and peasants hide in nearby hills until the belligerent forces leave. These steps are retraced repeatedly until the occupiers defend themselves with a few ancient firearms. As the government and landlords kill people over many years, or as agricultural activity proves too difficult in an atmosphere of recurrent flight, people leave their communities to live in the jungle permanently, returning only on occasion to their rural communities. In this way, land movements, along with other social movements that experience similarly harsh repression, give birth to rural revolutionary movements.

The Zapatista guerrillas assumed control of large parts of Chiapas, Mexico, on January 1, 1994.[91] They gained mass support in large part from indigenous *campesinos* and their peasant unions, which had experienced violent government and vigilante responses to their nonviolent attempts at land occupation. The roots of this support reach to the Portillo presidency starting in 1976.

A well-known case of repression occurred in Golonchan, Chiapas. Several hundred Tzeltal Indians burned brush, planted fields, and built homes on 80 hectares of land owned by a non-Indian rancher in the summer of 1980. This particular occupation formed part of a nationally coordinated takeover organized by the Partido Socialista de los Trabajadores (Socialist Party of the Workers), in which 3,200 families occupied nine ranches in the Tzeltal region alone. When the Golonchan occupiers heard that the governor of Chiapas promised to communalize their lands, a huge celebration ensued. But what started as a day of jubilation ended in a massacre. Mexican soldiers and ranchers trapped the *fiesta* against a swollen river and opened fire with machine guns, killing 12 and wounding over 40 others. The army then looted and burned the huts and killed the dogs, cats, and chickens of the community.[92]

In response to state and vigilante violence such as the Golonchan massacre, established peasant unions such as the Confederación Nacional de Campesinos (National Confederation of Peasants) became more conservative; other groups went underground and utilized increasingly militant tactics, holding hostages and occupying town halls to gain concessions. Many of these independent peasant unions allied themselves with a coalition called the Comité Nacional Plan de Ayala (CNPA, National Plan of Ayala Network),[93] which became active beginning in the late 1970s. "The CNPA was a loose national network which permitted each group to retain its autonomy while uniting around basic demands and confrontational mobilization for land and against repression."[94] When they decided to militarize their formerly nonviolent tactics in 1983, the Zapatistas got many of their initial supporters from various splinter groups of the CNPA. Many of these supporters came directly from land occupation campaigns and wanted to defend their communities concretely against massacres, assassinations, and many other instances of repression. These rural activists created the first Zapatista guerrilla cells.[95] Major Ana María of the Zapatistas explained the group's evolution from land occupation to guerrilla warfare tactics:

We are told the land belongs to so-and-so, and we don't even know them. But we see, there is the land, and we work on it.... It's been called an invasion; we invaded the land. And then they sent the Public Security forces, to burn the houses that had been built, to evict the people with canes and beat the people. They took our leaders. They put them in jail. They dragged them with horses to torture them. That is how they responded.... And so we took up arms. We cannot do this peacefully.[96]

While the first Zapatista guerrillas trained in the Lacandon jungle, conditions for peasants worsened. From the mid-1980s to the mid-'90s, banks foreclosed about 10,000 peasant landholdings in Mexico. Land occupations and solicitation for agrarian reform by peasants led landlord vigilante groups and the military to massacre peasant communities and burn entire villages on multiple occasions in the '80s.[97] After organizing for ten years, the Zapatistas got a surge of support in 1993. This support grew from outrage over the blatantly corrupt 1988 Chiapas elections, cooptation of established peasant groups, worsening economic conditions for peasants, the threat to local corn production by the liberalized trade policies of the North American Free Trade Agreement (NAFTA), and the cutting of Article 27 from the constitution. Article 27 provided for land reform and the *ejido* system of land tenure, and its loss dispelled the remnants of hope for established government reforms.[98]

In other countries, as well, the classic revolutions gained much of their power from rural discontent. In China, landlords charging exorbitant rents and high interest forced many tenants to flee and squat land in the hills. According to Ralph Thaxton, these squatters coalesced with "friends and relatives to ignite rebellion in their old home localities ... to realize a popular idea of redistributive justice." Mao Zedong first harnessed these already existing forces in the Autumn Harvest Uprising of 1927. After his defeat and the loss of Communist Party posts, the Mao group retreated to the Jinggangshan hills and "was able to survive and grow in part by resonating with itinerant hill-peasant fraternities."[99]

In Africa, many of the anti-colonial armies arose from land movements. When the Germans introduced large cotton plantations in Tanganyika (now Tanzania) and forced Africans into 28 days of corvée labor a year, the 1905 Maji Maji rebellion spread over 10,000 square miles and involved over 20 different ethnic groups.[100] In South Africa, the 1906 Bambatha Rebellion arose in part from exorbitant rents charged by absentee landlords.[101] In Kenya, the Mau Mau rebellion developed from repressed agricultural squatter settlements in the white highlands.[102] One of the songs used by the rebels to mobilize potential guerrilla fighters went, "Tell the young to rise up in arms / So that this land may be returned to us.... / Our whole country is in darkness / And the squatters increase daily..."[103]

In Rhodesia, the Ndebele and Shona precipitated the African Risings of 1896 in an attempt to retrieve some of the 6.4 million hectares of land lost to Europeans (one-sixth of the country's total area). After a severe famine in 1922, during which the Rhodesian government continued to charge exorbitant rents, Africans at Inyanga began a nonviolent rent strike that successfully withheld 70% of the rent demanded. But pressures built until 1972 when, in response to evictions, many turned to guerrilla warfare.[104] This group of guerrillas eventually grew large enough to unseat the Rhodesian government and create the independent nation of Zimbabwe in 1980.

Even in urban areas, squatter settlements form a base of support for revolutionary movements. Squatters often choose names for their settlements that indicate their revolutionary ideology, such as the Tierra y Libertad settlement in Mexico, the Bairro Resistência (Town of Resistance) settlement in Vitória, Brazil, and the Nueva la Habana (New Havana, in reference to the Cuban revolution) settlement in Chile.

Beyond a name, however, urban squatters have helped to form the cutting edge of revolutionary movements in Third World cities. Early 1970s scholarship portrayed squatters as quiescent and politically passive, but recent studies have acknowledged that squatter settlements have launched militant student, labor, food price, and political movements, forming an urban base for demonstrations, riots, and even guerrilla units.[105] Mountain guerrillas regularly visited the shanty of an acquaintance of mine, for example, when he researched a Latin American squatter settlement for two years.

The experience of my acquaintance seems widespread. I have already noted that the Philippine government evicted huge squatter communities in the mid-'70s, once preceding the Miss Universe parade and once before an IMF conference. These evictions curtailed only the visible manifestation of conflict. While squatters organized fewer mass mobilizations and direct confrontations with government agencies, the repression had a deep and radicalizing influence on the squatters' character and ideology. According to analyst J. Rüland, "Whereas formerly the movement pursued reformist goals within the political system, the view now prevailing is that better living conditions can only be achieved when the present authoritarian regime has been overthrown."[106] Parts of the Manila squatter movement started to support the National Democratic Front (NDF), which favored armed struggle in the countryside. Shortly thereafter, in 1978, the NDF deployed an urban army,[107] probably composed at least in part of urban squatters, if the composition of other urban guerrilla movements offers any clues.

In San Salvador, the offensive of the Farabundo Martí National Liberation Front in the early '90s depended on extensive support and cover provided by the surrounding squatter settlements. In the first few years after President Ferdinand

Marcos of the Philippines declared martial law in September 1972, a squatter group from Tondo Foreshore was one of the only organizations that held demonstrations.[108] In Peru, Susan Stokes found a high level of militancy in Lima squatter settlements. Regarding Latin American squatters in general, she noted that "Residents of Santiago's *poblaciones* reportedly became central protagonists in the struggles against military rule; residents of Rio's *favelas* have turned to new institutions like Christian base communities to express a recently acquired sense of social injustice; and the urban poor of Managua under the Somoza regime [in Nicaragua] threw their support behind an openly revolutionary movement."[109]

As noted in the case of Amsterdam, even in the urban areas of Europe and North America, some squatter and rent strike activists have turned to violence, though not to the degree visible in the Third World. Capek and Gilderbloom cite a comprehensive study that positively correlated the severity of Black urban riots in the United States with increased urban renewal and lack of low-rent housing. They also note that during the late '70s and early '80s in West Germany, the Netherlands, Switzerland, and England, people rioted over housing.[110]

In addition to rioting, land and housing activists in the West have sometimes supported terrorist organizations. In 1982 and 1983, the French urban guerrilla organization Action Directe recruited several members from the Paris squatting scene. Likewise, the terrorist Red Army Faction (RAF) in Germany found extensive support among German squatters. When the German government prompted RAF member Astrid Proll to flee the country in 1974, she hid with squatters in London for ten years.[111] Karl-Heinz Dellwo, one of the six RAF members who occupied and later bombed the West German Embassy in Stockholm on April 25, 1975, had earlier been a squatter in Hamburg.[112] In 1981, squatters from the Kreuzberg district of West Berlin smashed 80% of the windows on the Kurfürstendamm, a two-mile outdoor mall, when RAF member Sigmund Depus died while on hunger strike in prison.[113]

The large number of references to squatters in the communiqués of later RAF generations suggest that the RAF probably continued to include squatters in its organization. In an April 4, 1991, communiqué claiming responsibility for the assassination of Detlev Rohwedder, "Bonn's governor in East Berlin," the RAF referred to the "evictions of squatters in East Berlin's Mainzerstrasse" as one reason it would continue its attacks. In a communiqué dated six days later, in which the RAF offered its historic cease-fire, the RAF threatened to renew terrorist actions if the government continued to harass the Haffenstrasse squatters in Hamburg. Four years later, the government granted legal ownership of the Haffenstrasse homes to the squatters.[114]

Squatters not only get and give support to terrorists, at times housing issues actually spark terrorist campaigns. Such was the case with the resurgence in the late '60s, after a ten-year lull, of the Irish Republican Army (IRA). A unionist councillor who had opposed the construction of housing for Catholic tenants evicted Catholic squatters in 1968 from public housing in Caledon. He replaced them with Protestant families that had no priority of need. In response, Catholics held large, nonviolent demonstrations. The police banned some of these demonstrations, which by then had broadened their demands from housing to include civil rights in general. Demonstrators ignored the ban, and police attacked the processions with water-cannon and baton charges. Groups of Protestant counter-demonstrators and vigilantes attacked other civil rights demonstrations. This Protestant escalation of violence led to Catholic riots. The police began using mounted machine guns on armored vehicles with lethal effects, and vigilantes burned Catholic public housing. In response, Catholics formed paramilitary groups in the spring of 1969 to protect Catholic neighborhoods. These disturbances, according to Alfred McClung Lee, author of *Terrorism in Northern Ireland*, "occasioned the resurrection of the IRA and the organization and reorganization of Loyalist vigilante groups."[115] Of course, the issue of housing alone did not create the current conflagration in Ireland, but the issue of housing and the eviction of squatters was a powerful enough cause to form one link in a chain that led to the revival of terrorism.

A housing campaign in the United States also ignited a terrorist organization, the Fuerzas Armadas de Liberación (FALN).[116] In 1973, the courts stymied a predominantly Puerto Rican rent strike in Chicago. When the tenants refused to leave, landlords burned their own buildings down, thus both evicting the rent strikers and allowing the landlords to recoup their losses through the collection of fire insurance remuneration. In one of these buildings, however, nine children and four adult tenants were burned to death. "The adults who died in that fire," said tenant organizer Oscar López Rivera, "were people I had known for years, having practically grown up with them; and the children I had played with. The deaths were a tremendous blow to me."[117] The police made only a cursory investigation and charged nobody with the crime.

In disgust, Rivera gathered several close friends and created the FALN, committed to Marxism and Puerto Rican independence. The FALN was most active between 1974 and 1977. The group bombed a total of 120 buildings, including Citibank, Chase Manhattan, and the U.S. State Department. The FALN deliberately avoided attacks on people, but accidentally killed five persons and wounded scores of others[118] As the case of the FALN illustrates, repression of a housing movement can lead not only to sporadic violent resistance, but to a movement that expands its goals to include the overthrow of the government. When these revolutionary movements succeed, they can cause greater redistribution of land and housing, but they also occasion further cycles of repression.

Effects of Revolution on Land and Housing Movements

Severe repression accompanies any revolutionary movement, including those that arise from land and housing issues. The Germans killed about 75,000 people to temporarily stop the Maji Maji in Tanganyika, while the British killed 11,503 to stop the Mau Mau in Kenya. The massive loss of life inherent to revolutionary movements might have a moral effect on government officials that can provoke land and housing concessions. More pessimistically, the unsustainable loss of profit associated with revolutions might force these concessions. The Maji Maji and the Mau Mau rebellions helped achieve reforms and ultimately national independence.[119]

In Rhodesia, the colonial military hunted down many of the Ndebele and Shona leaders and buried Africans alive in their hiding places to quell the African Risings of 1896. But the colonial government also agreed to several concessions. The proclamation included the abolition of forced labor, a two-year grace period during which no rents were to be paid and no evictions were to take place, and the provision of 33,000 hectares on which about 4,000 people settled. Administrators also assigned more land for African use in the form of reserves.

Concessions in circumstances of revolution, however, usually do not go directly to revolutionaries. Wherever possible, governments seek to act as though revolutionary movements have no effect, and so concessions granted to dampen support of revolution goes to the pool of poor government collaborators or the nonaligned. In the United States, Adam Fortunate Eagle believes the Alcatraz occupation by Indians of All Tribes, though nonviolent, contributed to government fear of a general violent Native American uprising aligning itself with other militant leftist formations such as the Black Panthers and the Weather Underground. "So while the Alcatraz Indians were pressuring the government," he writes, "federal officials were forced to negotiate with other Indian groups to appease the Indian community and stop further criticism from the general liberal population."[120]

Fortunate Eagle interviewed former Commissioner of Indian Affairs Robert Bennett and asked him what effect the Alcatraz invasion had on the condition of Native Americans. "One of the first and direct results of Alcatraz," replied Bennett, "was that the [Bureau of Indian Affairs (BIA)] started working with state employment agencies on a cooperative basis to find jobs for Indians on or near the reservations." This reversed the former BIA policy of termination, which sought the assimilation of Native Americans through dispersal of tribal members to far-flung urban areas. Instead of the old tribal leaders, Bennett continued, "we started to listen more to young Indian leadership."[121]

Other militant actions by Native Americans also forced the U.S. government to make concessions. In 1970, a "fish-in" by Puyallup Indians persuaded the government to bring a fishing-rights suit on behalf of the Indians against the state of Washington. Where previous appeals had failed, the suit was filed nine days after someone firebombed a bridge, Indians shot rifles to ward off police who were attempting to confiscate fishing nets, and police arrested 60 Indians for felony riot. Regarding the effect of the riot on the fishing-rights case, a lawyer from the U.S. Justice Department admitted, "I suppose it may have had some bearing. Maybe we hurried a little bit."[122] While the armed confrontation succeeded for the Puyallup and other Washington tribes on a judicial level, it also helped positive national legislation. Senator Edward Kennedy immediately used the incident to push for a bill that gave better representation to Native Americans doing legal battle with state and federal agencies.[123]

In addition to these isolated Native victories, the repeated, consistent, and armed occupations of the early '70s probably eased passage of the relatively positive federal Indian legislation and reform of the late '70s. These reforms included the Indian Self-Determination Act of 1975, the Indian Freedom of Religion Act of 1978, more generous federal funding of social programs, the change in Department of Interior policy that ended programs of relocation and termination, and various courtroom victories.[124] Even in the early '70s, the general unrest may have helped influence President Nixon to order 45,000 acres (18,000 hectares) of the Sacred Blue Lakes returned to the Taos Pueblo people and more than 160,000 acres (65,000 hectares) returned to the Warm Springs tribes of Oregon.[125]

While revolutionary tactics can help obtain concessions, they also create an atmosphere in which officials become wary of repressing land occupations for fear of fueling further violence. Peasants in and around Chiapas, for example, immediately took advantage of the 1994 Zapatista rebellion with agrarian agitation and land occupations. On February 1, 1994, 4,000 indigenous people in southern Oaxaca occupied nine government buildings and demanded a settlement of agrarian reform land claims. That same week, 3,000 campesinos occupied several banks in Tapachula, calling for an end to farm and house foreclosures and the cancellation of peasant debts.[126] Within nine months of the Zapatistas' initial offensive, landless peasants occupied more than 500 ranches and estates. During an occupation of the German-owned Liquidambar hacienda, peasants of the Francisco Villa Popular Peasants Union wore masks and, according to Latinamerica Press, affected "the style and the militancy — if not the weapons — of the Zapatistas."[127]

The state of Chiapas offered coastal agricultural land to the squatters of Liquidambar, but the squatters told a Latinamerica reporter, "We don't want their crumbs. We want this ranch."[128] Zapatistas have also created the conditions for a better quality of life for Chiapenecos: both the national government of Mexico and international groups have increased humanitarian and development aid to the area. In peace talks with the government, Zapatista negotiators have been pushing hard for a redistribution of land in Chiapas and the creation of a special office for resolving Indian land disputes, in addition to many civil rights advances for Indians.[129]

With the 1996 offenses by the army, however, which paved roads into the jungle, retook the towns, replaced police power, and weakened the Zapatistas, landlords have returned to the region. In March 1996, armed landlords engineered a mass eviction that left at least two peasants dead. How much of the land will be retaken by landowners is still unknown.

In past land occupations supported by leftist governments or revolutionaries, squatters have successfully defended at least a portion of their occupied land after an adversarial government returns to power. Following the 1974 leftist coup in Portugal, for example, squatters orchestrated the largest popular land seizures in European history. They took 35,000 houses and occupied 23% of the nation's agricultural land, a total of more than 1.2 million hectares.

After the rightist reversal of the revolution in November 1975, landlords launched a counter-offensive against the occupations; but in a year and a half they could evict agricultural workers from only 2% of the occupied acreage. Even after a 1977 law allowed landowners to evict many more occupiers, they had to leave a significant number in peace. As noted earlier, government officials and union leaders estimated in 1986 that between one-third and one-half of the cooperatives would survive implementation of the law.[130]

As in Portugal, most concessions due to a revolution are made to land and housing movements within the region of a struggle. Important exceptions have occurred. The Cuban revolution in 1959 changed the attitude of governments throughout Latin America toward land reform. Whereas previously they granted land reforms only when pressured by local agrarian rebellions, "In the aftermath of the Castro revolution, many Latin American countries implemented land reforms to *avert* revolution," writes researcher of Latin American social movements Susan Eckstein.[131] Revolutionary movements can have an effect far outside the region of their direct control, both in encouraging revolutions in other countries and encouraging reforms to avert those revolutions.

Similar pressures can induce rent control. During the Bolshevik scare, New York City rent strikes in the winter of 1907-08 and from 1917 through 1920 achieved some success. As with an earlier 1904 strike, rent increases triggered the successes; after 1904, however, the Socialist Party was increasingly involved. In the context of the 1917 Bolshevik revolution in Russia, an alarmed New York business community interpreted this Socialist involvement as a threat not only to rents but to the "fabric of political and economic organization." The state legislature introduced rent controls quickly in 1920 to defuse the discontent over housing, and though landlords and police evicted many, according to figures printed by the *Jewish Daily Forward,* 3,000 families won rent reductions.[132]

Revolutions help land and housing movements, and these movements help revolution. Even when squatters and landless persons did not directly join in combat operations, according to Eckstein, they played a critical role in the Mexican, Bolivian, and Cuban revolutions, often aiding locally by "seizing lands, disrupting production, and creating disorder."[133] Land occupations help revolutionary movements because they provide an agricultural base from which many guerrilla units receive food donations. Since squatters know their land tenure depends on the victory of the revolution, they understand that they have every material advantage to seeing that revolution succeed. Four days before the Sandinista victory on July 19, 1979, "1,000 dispossessed *campesino* families occupied 22,600 acres [9,150 hectares] of Somocista-owned farmland ... and started bringing it back into production," according to Joseph Collins. "These land seizures were not only a matter of just vindication (*revindicación*) of the wrongful actions of the bigger landlords. Just as important was the need to provide food in the liberated areas."[134]

As Eckstein noted, such occupations of vacant land and land devoted to export agriculture also deprive government and large landowners of wage laborers, taxes, and rent. This weakens the regime's economic strength and makes the payment of military wages and the procurement of military hardware more difficult. The symbiotic relationship between squatters and revolutionaries causes the two groups to effect mutual aid and, in many instances, to become indistinguishable.

South Africa's Rent Strike

Perhaps the best example of a land or housing movement that aided a revolution is the massive rent-strike-*cum*-squatter movement in apartheid-era South Africa. Beginning in September 1984, African residents refused to pay rents on their government-owned homes in the townships. The rent boycotts spread rapidly due to growth in nationalist sentiment, loss of confidence in township officials, a lack of alternative political channels, falling African family real income, and a simultaneous rise in rental costs. Between 1980 and 1985 in the Pretoria-Witwatersrand-Val region, the average proportion of household income demanded for rent rose from 25% to 88%.

While boycotters primarily sought subsidized housing, rent control, and rent cuts, they also used the rent boycott as a tactic for eroding government power. Strikers demanded traditional leadership on a local level, as opposed to town councilors imposed by Pretoria, and deprived the national government of extensive revenue. By 1988, 90% of renters in South Africa's townships had joined the boycotts. They sustained the boycott for the longest period in South Africa since the early 1950s, costing the state an estimated revenue loss of $400 million between 1985 and 1988.[135]

Government attempts to repress the strike largely failed. The government initially attempted to force employers and town councils to deduct rental arrears from wages, but most employers refused to do so, not wanting to transfer the struggle from the government onto factory floors. The government then declared a state of emergency and resorted to ruthless arrests and evictions that included extensive violence and even killings. In just one of these many evictions, on August 26, 1986, in Soweto, police attacked 400 demonstrators protesting against eviction attempts and, according to the Soweto Civic Association, killed 30 and wounded at least 200.[136] Despite heavy repression in this and many other instances, the government failed to force the majority of township residents to pay rent.

This sustained resistance and the transfer of finances from the Pretoria government to the lowest socioeconomic strata of Africans provided tremendous political power to the African National Congress (ANC) in the early '90s. But once Nelson Mandela became president of South Africa in 1994, he was not able to satisfy the land and housing demands of these poorest sectors. At the time of this writing, the ANC government is making futile attempts at rent collection, just as the apartheid government had done for years. The rent strikers, however, have not changed their refusal to pay. The ANC finds itself bucking what South Africans call a "culture of nonpayment," the same noncooperation with authority that bankrupted local apartheid governments and helped bring the ANC to power.[137] In Soweto, only 25% of residents paid taxes, utility fees, and rents to the government in 1997, while the rate of payment has remained at only 3% in Alexandria. Between 1994 and 1997, poor South Africans withheld $1.2 billion in payments.[138]

South African squatters erected 200,000 new shanties every year in the early '90s, with about 250,000 squatters in Johannesburg alone. The Mandela government placed a moratorium on land occupations in July 1995, but the rate of occupation only rose.[139] Unfortunately, the ANC has used repressive tactics similar to those of the apartheid government. According to a May 3, 1996, article in the *New York Times*, "courts have ordered evictions, shacks have been burned, and groups of poor families have fought pitched battles over who will get housing, if it is ever built."[140] Instead of providing places for the poor to live near the city where they can work, Mandela created "reception areas" for evictees in remote areas. Many squatters are not told until just a few days beforehand that they will be evicted; one group of evictees were told only that their new home would be "Plot 139." Where Plot 139 was located, nobody knew until they arrived. "When they came for us," said Paulina Mashebe, mother of six, "I said, no, we could not move. But they said we had to. There was no choice."[141] In February 1997, when the government attempted to raise electricity and water rates in mixed-race neighborhoods around Johannesburg, residents once again blocked roads, burned tires, threw rocks, and looted stores. Mandela's police used tear gas and live ammunition to quell the riots, killing four and wounding thirty.[142]

Cooptation

The common goal of landlords and governments faced with land and housing agitation is to reestablish rent payments by tenants or coerce squatters into moving. To do this, they offer incentives for squatter cooperation and/or alter laws to accommodate the settlements.

The reliance of government and propertied interests on squatter settlements as a form of cheap housing and as a space from which the informal sector of the economy can operate heightens the need to coopt instead of evict. As in any large development of inadequate housing, whether a squatter settlement or slum, government and employers cannot afford to evict mass numbers of people and thereby risk social disorder or irregularities in the ability of laborers to attend work.

In the last 30 years, many Third World governments and international agencies have recognized that the eviction of urban squatter settlements actually harms their economies and creates unmanageable social unrest. They have generally moved away from the policy of eviction and toward a policy of cooptation. Evidence of revision, at least on the level of propaganda, is increasingly visible since the first "Habitat: United Nations Conference on Human Settlements" held in Vancouver in 1976. Government participants in that conference officially recognized the need to provide security of tenure, improve infrastructure, increase low-income housing, and integrate squatters into the national development process. By 1982, the United Nations could argue forcefully in its *Survey of Slum and Squatter Settlements* for positive policies:

> It has been common practice to keep squatters in an illegal state of land occupation to prevent and curb further squatting. There is a fear that granting any form of security of tenure, be it freehold or a form of leasehold, will be tantamount to legitimizing an illegal act and will encourage further squatting and continued migration to the cities.... The benefits accruing from security of tenure can be used as a counter argument. The sheer magnitude of the problem calls for action by society as a whole.[143]

A change of names given to settlements in Peru by President Juan Velasco Alvarado illustrates the new policy. When the Peruvian government no longer seeks eviction of a particular occupation, it changes the area's name from "squatter settlement" to the more upbeat *pueblo joven,* or "young town."[144] This shift of terminology and ideology around the world indicates a victory for squatters, who have used community organizing and protest to push policy from immediate eviction to the provision of skeletal services. But most of what is considered success in these pages is only partial. Government tolerance comes with a condition: squatters usually must surrender their autonomy and cede local power over community decision-making.

The United Nations hints at cooptation with an almost Machiavellian tone in its *Survey of Slum and Squatter Settlements,* which promises reluctant governments that security of tenure will soften, weaken, and divide squatter movements. "The transition from a militant leadership to a moderate one is characteristic of squatter settlements that win acceptance by the authorities. This change in leadership is accompanied by a weakening of community solidarity. As security of tenure increases, unity becomes less important for survival, and latent divisions emerge."[145]

Even though reform and cooptation have become more common during the last 20 years, it goes without saying that most governments freely mix major doses of repression with any forms of cooptation they may adopt. In Puerto Rico, a wave of squatting began in 1968, peaked in 1972, and ended in 1976. During this wave, squatters built approximately 16,800 structures, established 186 communities, and mobilized a population of 84,000 individuals. To resolve these squatter challenges, the government began with anti-squatter legislation, arrests, criminal charges, injunctions, police surveillance, and violent razings. This roused the ire of public opinion, so the government adopted seemingly positive measures: legalizing settlements; encouraging squatters to litigate; and providing partial land distribution, construction, and loan programs.

But these somewhat helpful steps had a negative side. While most of the settlements achieved acceptance by the government, thus safeguarding homes and community, the tactic of cooptation eventually re-enveloped squatters in a dependent relationship with the government, making them vulnerable to government dictates. "The constant pressure of government agencies to re-establish a social-welfare relationship with the mobilized masses," researcher of Puerto Rican squatter movements Liliana Cotto writes, "reduced the space for autonomous action on the part of [squatter] committees."[146]

Beyond the reduction of autonomy, government concessions usually pave the way for a gradual reabsorption of squatter land tenure into mainstream housing and its attendant problems of inequitable distribution. After the intense squatting and violent resistance of West German squatters in the early 1980s,[147] the German government used institutional recognition not only for deradicalization (massive riots receded after cooptation), but to slowly raise rents to market value. After the city of Berlin purchased some of the squatted buildings from the former owners, squatters signed long-term leases at low rents and with extensive self-management rights. A similar process took place in Hamburg in 1984, in other German cities over the next few years, and again in Hamburg in January 1996.[148]

The problem with these negotiated settlements arose when local governments gradually raised the rents of the former squats to near-market levels, absorbing the free labor of self-help squatters in the process and slowly forcing the poorest of the former squatters to vacate.

The eventual dispossession of the squatters on a small scale was mirrored on a neighborhood level as the rehabilitation of old buildings encouraged gentrification. Ironically, the early '80s wave of German squatting began as a protest against redevelopment and gentrification. This cooptation of original squatter goals led the most radical squatting elements in the '90s, the *autonomia*, to attack, sometimes violently, the government housing programs chartered to administer the former squats.[149] By 1995, all except one of the West Berlin squats that signed leases in the mid-'80s became "yuppified"; the former squatters became more affluent and joined mainstream society.

Perhaps the crux of cooptation is the transfer of legal title not to the activists themselves, but to an institutional entity. Because mainstream groups have greater legal liability and connection to governments, or even differing political loyalties, their use of the newly acquired property may contradict or void the original spirit of the activists. In Gresham, Wisconsin, on January 1, 1975, the Menominee Warrior Society occupied a Roman Catholic abbey owned by the Alexian Brothers and called for its use as a cultural center. Eight hundred National Guard troops with several armored vehicles laid siege to the abbey for a month, and a huge group of armed and angry whites called for vigilante violence. To end the tense situation, the Alexian Brothers transferred ownership of the 84-room novitiate, valued at $750,000.[150] They did not transfer the property to the young and radical occupiers, who wanted to create a health and education center, however, but to the U.S.-recognized tribal council that opposed the Warrior Society and the occupation. This ended the occupation, but the tribal council refused to administer the property shortly afterwards, citing fiscal reasons. Amid much controversy between the Warrior Society and the tribal council, the Alexian Brothers repossessed the building in July.[151] Thus the transfer of property to a supposedly benign third party evaporated the direct action and yielded no benefits to the activists or to their community.

The problems attendant to conditional, partial, and self-interested concessions have encouraged many squatters and land activists to reject cooperation with government programs. Half the inhabitants of the Las Colinas squatter settlement in Bogotá, Colombia, formed the Oposicionistas and took a position against reliance upon outside assistance. Likewise, squatters in the north of Mexico and on the periphery of Mexico City deliberately rejected government provision of services to resist cooptation. They preferred to steal materials and illegally obtain water, electricity, and other urban necessities.[152]

"Oposicionistas" exist in the rich nations, as well. One Homes Not Jails squatter infuriated other squatters because he blocked a consensus decision to rent a dumpster. He felt that paying money for a dumpster would place the squatters in a dependent position on the city and instead advocated that they illegally throw the massive amounts of construction trash into other dumpsters or small municipal trash bins they could find on street corners around San Francisco.

In another instance, an African American group called the National Economic Growth and Reconstruction Organization (NEGRO) visited the Indian occupiers on Alcatraz Island in September 1970 to encourage a deal with the government. NEGRO had occupied Ellis Island and successfully attained a government contract and funds to operate a drug-rehabilitation and welfare-recipient training center on the island. They offered to use their channels with the federal government to obtain a five-year lease and a government contract for the Indians to operate the lighthouse, but guessed the occupiers would have to drop their insistence on gaining permanent title to the island. Indians of All Tribes rejected the proposal as giving away too much and were evicted nine months later.

Reform

Movement resistance to cooptation brings activists closer to ultimate goals and ideals, but struggles that make no compromise usually fall to repression. To end conflicts favorably, bargaining with the adversary becomes an essential aspect of direct action. Bargaining (without forgetting the pitfalls of cooptation) becomes the way in which land and housing activists can parlay their struggle into tangible and long-term improvements in community life. Peruvian writer Carolina Carlessi writes that squatters in Lima, Peru, "develop the power to question the state, even as they wrangle concessions, to escape party strictures, and to transcend the limits of Peru's official system of representative democracy."[153]

During a campaign, activists may proclaim the most idyllic, utopian goals possible, and it suits their purpose to do so. But when they tire of the fight, they must negotiate their reemergence into legality. This negotiation is not necessarily the abdication of struggle, but its next phase. Convincing a government to decriminalize a squatter settlement, initiate land reform, or decrease the rent moves society toward an egalitarian ideal. Taking collective action with neighbors, even if only for a short period, is a step toward understanding community and creating new economic relationships.

Not all activists in a movement will agree on when to compromise for concessions. For different sectors of a movement, the costs and benefits of further struggle may differ. This leads to conflict over when the struggle should end. At Co-op City, rent strikers voted to end the strike after 13 months and accept the concessions offered by the state of New York. Some of the strike's lawyers and a few leftist newspaper reporters criticized the settlement as giving away too much. The reason for the discrepancy may stem from the primary costs and risks of the strike falling on the strikers, while a major benefit of the strike — a revolutionary example of people refusing to pay rent — would have been reaped by leftists and society in general.

The Co-op City Rent Strike, 1975-1976

The Co-op City rent strike, which took place in the Bronx between 1975 and 1976, was the largest rent strike in U.S. history. The biggest publicly funded housing project in the world, Co-op City has 60,000 residents in 35 high-rise buildings, six townhouse clusters, three shopping centers, and six schools. The Riverbay Corporation, which administers the housing for the state of New York, gave priority to low-income residents (who were roughly 60% Jewish and 25% African American and Latino) and promised in 1965 to keep monthly carrying charges at $23 per room.[154]

This attractive arrangement quickly collapsed when Riverbay reneged on its promises and increased rent payments by over 125% in ten years.[155] With even larger increases looming in the future, tenants decided to take action in 1975. Represented by a series of steering committees, tenants initiated legal tactics such as a fraud suit, a lobby of the state legislature for aid to public housing, and a gubernatorial electoral campaign for Hugh Carey, who promised $10 million to cover the Co-op City budget deficit.

The fraud suit yielded nothing, the legislation failed, and, following a long tradition of illustrious politicians, Hugh Carey broke his campaign promise after he was elected. Tensions built among Co-op City residents, and, in May 1975, tenants dumped 80% of Co-op City's rent checks on Governor Carey's desk in black garbage bags.

These subtle tactics having failed to bring the message home, tenants began withholding their rent in June 1975. They placed nearly $3 million in escrow the first month, and so began the largest rent strike in U.S. history. Both in the number of people participating and in the amount of money withheld, the strike has not yet been equaled. It lasted 13 months, gained 85% participation, and, by the end in 1976, held an astounding $27 million in escrow.

To administer the strike, tenants printed and distributed 16,000 leaflets a day, carried out building patrols, and facilitated tenant meetings twice weekly in every lobby. Volunteers ran a communications center with a printing press, moving loudspeaker system, and 24-hour hotline. On the first ten nights of each month, 1,500 volunteers collected rents in 75 building lobbies from 7 to 9 p.m. Volunteers then processed, recorded, boxed, and gave the checks to organizer Charles Rosen, who hid them from state housing officials in his friend's attic.

Although the state threatened mass eviction, Rosen called the bluff. "We said we'd like to know which politician was prepared to hire the army necessary to evict 60,000 people," he said. "If they tried to do it legally through the landlord-tenant court … it would take them six years to process the evictions."[156]

Faced with these difficulties, the state of New York used every other tactic at its disposal. Officials reduced maintenance, security personnel, hot water, corridor lighting, and heat. They fired 200 of the 500 Co-op City employees. Tenants expressed solidarity with those who had been laid off and offered to give the state $675,000 out of the escrow fund to rehire the employees, but the state refused. The attempted isolation of Co-op City had a ripple effect. Because the state refused to pay the utility bills, Consolidated Edison announced that it would cut off electricity. Although the state court forbade the transaction, tenants offered Consolidated Edison payment from the escrow account. Con Ed accepted the $1.2 million.

With the failure of these low-intensity forms of repression, the state targeted leaders. It fined the steering committee as a whole $5,000 and individual leaders $1,000 for every day tenants withheld rent. In addition, the judge sentenced ten individual leaders, including Charles Rosen, to jail time. But organizers refused to pay the fines, and threats of imprisonment failed to intimidate them. "They really believe that if they put Charlie in jail that's the end of the strike," one striker told the *Village Voice*. "They don't understand that it's all of us, that we are organized to go on replacing each other forever, that this strike has changed our lives, and that nothing will make us give up."[157] The government never carried out its threat of fines or jail.

In June 1976, the solidarity and economic strength of the tenants finally induced the state to offer concessions. State Commissioner of Housing Lee Goodwin, who opposed the concessions and whose removal tenants demanded, resigned in protest. The agreement provided for six months of tenant rule in which the directorship of the Riverbay Corporation was turned over to the steering committee, the dropping of charges and fines against strike leaders, and the transfer of all Riverbay Corporation books to the new board of directors for use in the initiation of fraud lawsuits relating to the 125% rent increases.

The agreement seemed great at the time, and the tenants voted for its adoption. But there was one big catch. Upon assuming control over the Corporation, tenants agreed to repay the largest mortgage in U.S. history at $436 million. The size of the mortgage formed a major stumbling block for lowering rents. With bank foreclosure, personal financial ruin, and renewed state directorship looming on the horizon, the mortgage coerced former strikers into taking the role of administrators of austerity, procurers of development, and raisers of rent. The agreement resembled the debt crisis facing nations such as Mexico, Brazil, Russia, and elsewhere. By the end of July, Citicorp and other banks had convinced Co-op City residents to cooperate and raise the rent another 20% themselves.

Some of the outside radicals who supported the strike considered the settlement a sell-out. In a somewhat bitter article, *In These Times* reported that middle-income residents voted against lower-income tenants for the rental increase, many tenants were "disturbed by the large salaries the leaders began paying themselves," decision-making was centralized to save money, and Charles Rosen welcomed the construction of an industrial complex on vacant land adjacent to the project to produce income.[158]

An article by Larry Bush in *Shelterforce* printed the opinions of several tenants about the settlement. A comment by one man, according to Bush, represented the most commonly held criticism: "I'm sure a lot of people are glad it's over," he said,

> but I don't think anything's been solved. I heard some people saying that before they had the strike, 80% of the carrying charges [rent] was going for the mortgage, and the cost of maintenance ... is still the same. I don't see much change.... I think it's something good they've started, and I still think they have good intentions.... I don't know, maybe I was expecting too much.

Bush maintained that many outsiders and certain housing lawyers, while "respectful of the basic achievements of the settlement, still feel that because the bank mortgage was not confronted head-on, the long-term effects of the rent strike are not significant."[159]

On the other hand, tenants gained important concessions. For the 13 months of struggle, tenants successfully stabilized rents by placing them in escrow: the state of New York dared not raise rents during a rent strike. Each tenant gained interest on the rent they held in the bank, because their checks went uncashed. After the strike, services and maintenance improved as a result of tenant directorship, and the prospects for legal success in fraud suits increased with the acquisition of access to Riverbay accounting books. Previously, tenants held only five of 15 seats on the Riverbay board of directors, while financial institutions and the state filled the other ten. Afterwards, tenants elected the entire board. This democratization included a tremendous amount of education and empowerment related to the financial issues at stake. Strike leader Rosen supported the settlement and defended the tenants' choice against leftist critics:

> The victory of a reformist struggle is in fact a victory.... But it is not revolution.... All we are hoping to do now is to develop a program of reform to guarantee, on a longer-range basis, an accommodation with the

system. If anyone on the left thinks the Bolsheviks of the Bronx are look-ing to make a Soviet up here in the northeast, they are sadly mistaken.[160]

Thus the conflict between promoters of settlement and promoters of further struggle was resolved by an almost economic equation. For promoters of immediate resolution, costs of further struggle outweigh the benefits. For promoters of further struggle, benefits outweigh the costs. But only the activists involved can make the decision of when to settle. They have something to lose and will bear the costs.

The Continuum of Struggle

The movement at Co-op City was unique, but many campaigns share common trajectories as they leap parallel obstacles that some social movement theorists have called a "continuum of struggle."[161] In the cases studied here, movements begin when one or just a handful of activists do educational work with their neighbors and friends, who might not feel an urgency for action. The movement stays small until an authority raises the rent beyond an acceptable point, announces a mass eviction, or adopts particularly brutal tactics of repression. This string of incidents falls upon the community prepared by the original activists, and so begins a movement.

Initially, most campaigns try legal tactics such as petitions, demonstrations, lobbying, and deputations to the landowner or government. These tactics succeed to a greater or lesser extent. At the very least, they educate the community as to the configuration of power responsible for the problem. At best, they cause major changes that nullify the need for direct action. Sometimes success is only a small reform that deflates community struggle or a concession to particular individuals that divides the campaign.

If insufficient concessions are made during the lobbying stage of a movement and the adversary seems to stop listening, activists usually choose the path of nonviolent direct action. This heightens the conflict so it cannot be ignored by the adversary, demonstrates the strength and determination of the activists, and dramatizes the problem so the media can bring it to a wider audience.

Repression almost always follows organized illegal action by nonviolent organizations. Some campaigns overcome this repression through endurance and other nonviolent tactics. Nonviolence limits the total amount of repression, though it requires a large amount of disciplined self-sacrifice by activists. Other times, movements or individuals choose to augment nonviolent tactics with violence. This violence is usually defensive, but it can bring the most brutal forms of repression and can sometimes escalate into an explicitly revolutionary movement. Although the majority of land and housing movements reported in the national and international media are those few that use violence or the threat of violence, most land and housing movements are nonviolent. These include huge numbers of urban squatters and land occupiers that purposely reject the use of violence and therefore never gain coverage in the local, much less the international, media. Instead, they induce small concessions and reforms through an assiduous use of nonviolent tactics and mass organizing.

Both violent and nonviolent movements cease temporarily when repression causes enough fear or when landowners or governments make concessions. But these struggles consistently return to begin where they left off, to learn from their mistakes, or to fight for even broader goals.

CHAPTER 6

Tactics and Mobilization

The Primacy of Power

The risk of violence and eviction looms for anyone that occupies land, squats a house, or goes on rent strike. But communities worldwide continually take these risks to create affordable housing or to survive in the face of widespread hunger and unemployment. They risk so much in the hope that persistence, mass organizing, and creativity will give them a fighting chance to win. "Initially, most tenant groups fear their own power or are not really convinced that they can actually beat their landlord," wrote activists from the East Orange Tenants Association and the New Jersey Tenants Organization in 1976. "Most of us suffer from the 'you can't beat City Hall' syndrome. This feeling of powerlessness must be overcome."[1]

This chapter explores a few of the many successful land and housing direct actions and campaigns that faced their fears and proved they *could* beat City Hall. Gene Sharp's thesis, that nonviolent political movements have tremendous power to change structural injustice and improve social conditions,[2] is supported by the campaigns explored here. In the only study of its kind on land and housing movements, research conducted during the 1980s by the United Nations Food and Agriculture Organization found that squatter families in Brazil had much higher levels of education and life expectancy and almost double the income of other small rural producers.[3] The campaigns studied here illustrate and specify exactly how participants gain these higher standards of living compared to their unorganized counterparts.

Beyond showing that organization creates success, this chapter delineates the specific tactics that made those struggles successful. While repression and chance make the outcome of direct action unpredictable, careful consideration of past tactics and their outcomes increases the possibility of success.

Mass Organization, Individual Power, and Reoccupation

Of all social movement tactics, the most successful and powerful is mass organization. Not only does mass organization improve the chances for success, it multiplies success by the number of participants. Large movements grow most easily where large sectors of the population feel an identical, pressing need. In 1989, Brazil carried a housing deficit of 10 million homes. Brazil has between 5 and 8 million landless people and 80 million hectares of vacant agricultural land (not including the Amazon region). The Movement of Landless Rural Workers (MST) in Brazil is the largest and most successful land occupation movement in the world; it also claims the most participants of any social movement within Latin America.[4] Between 1990 and 1996, the MST organized a total of 518 land occupations, and it is still going strong. In 1997, 25,000 people affiliated with the MST marched in the capital, and 42,000 MST families camped in plastic tents waiting for the right moment to invade vacant estates.[5]

In addition to instigating almost daily broadcasts regarding the MST in the Brazilian media, the size and success of the MST has allowed the organization to operate 30 radio stations and a monthly newspaper with national distribution. The MST has hosted an "Agrarian Reform Olympics" since 1995 that has included 1,500 athletes from 23 squatted settlements.[6] The squatter Olympics build culture and pride within the movement and present a positive and humanizing image, readily accessible to the mass media. The MST's size has also facilitated a diverse array of services and industry to benefit members. According to the *San Francisco Chronicle*, "the MST has offices in 22 of 26 states, operates ... three banks, ... a school for leadership training, and 47 cooperatives — including a blue-jeans factory, two meat-storage plants, a milk-packing facility, and a coffee-roasting company." The MST is currently exploring the possibility of starting a publishing company. The organization gets 80% of its funding in small amounts from each member cooperative, 15% from progressive organizations and trade unions within Brazil, and only 5% from international agencies.[7] The MST's success and broad base of support within Brazil have won it several international awards, including a UNICEF prize. According to Maria Luisa Mendonça of Global Exchange, "polls show the group to be more popular than President Fernando Henrique Cardoso."[8]

Through this strategy of mass organizing and popularization of its program, the MST has won land for some 150,000 families between 1984, when it began, and 1997. The government, fearing the MST's intense popularity and growth, has initiated massive concessions. Between 1994 and 1998, the Cardoso government provided land to 60,000 families through land reform, more than any previous Brazilian government, and opened a $150 million credit line for infrastructure and the purchase of land for settlements in the northeast.[9]

The MST illustrates how numbers command public attention, provide security for individual members, and threaten unrest if government fails to wrangle concessions from landowner interests. Previous chapters have already examined the successes of other mass movements, like the New York City rent strike of 1963-64, the Co-op City rent strike of 1976, squatting in Berlin in the '80s, and squatting in London and Amsterdam from the '70s to the present. In all these cases, mass organization was the key to success.

For smaller campaigns, as well, organization is important. In the winter of 1976, tenants of Mission Plaza Apartments in Los Angeles could no longer endure corroded pipes, seven days of freezing weather without heat or hot water, fly infestation due to inadequate screening, sewage overflows, and broken balcony railings. One three-year-old child fell from the second story and spent three days in the hospital. Outraged, a few tenants organized 700 tenants to create a rent strike. Though the strike was puny compared to Brazil's landless movement, California media, government, and real estate interests considered its size threatening. After four months, the rent strikers won repairs, one month's free rent, no rent increases for one year, and recognition of the tenant association as a bargaining agent. "We learned that united, we can win," said tenant committee member Theodora Rolette. "Many told us that we couldn't fight four millionaires, but we did it."[10]

Although mass organization is best for pressuring governments and landlords, in a pinch just one or two activists can make a world of difference. In 1969, public housing officials in England refused to rehouse Maggie O'Shannon from her basement apartment, even though a sewage pipe had been leaking into her kitchen for the last five years. With people from her entire neighborhood in similar predicaments, she organized delegations to elected officials and polite news conferences to draw attention to the horrible conditions. The tenants had asked earlier for rehousing, but these lobbying tactics came to nothing. In disgust, O'Shannon and another woman, Bridie Matthews, decided to squat a vacant, publicly owned house across the street. It was in far better condition than their own public housing. After squatting for several months and engaging in civil disobedience at City Hall, the council members reversed their decision; after a year, the entire neighborhood received new housing.[11]

In this case, two individuals spear-headed change, but even then a mass movement applied the necessary pressure. In Boston, an elderly Puerto Rican woman named Doña Julia Diaz also spear-headed change with the support of her community. She used the tactic of reoccupation to snatch success from the jaws of defeat. Originally she had struck in June 1975 to demand repairs and the extermination of rats in her Boston apartment. The court ordered her eviction, and 50 neighbors defended the apartment with a blockade the next day. Six days later, eight squad cars and a busload of tactical police staged "an incredible dawn raid," according to *Shelterforce*.[12] In addition to evicting Diaz, the police arrested five supporters. But the house remained vacant for only a few hours. That evening, 100 people moved Diaz's furniture back into the apartment and guarded the place for five days, until they considered it safe.[13]

Reoccupation is especially effective when additional evictions require time-consuming legal action. Chicago tenant groups in the early '70s routinely moved evicted families back into their homes after police evictions. This forced a renewal of litigation, and each reoccupation lasted many months before coming to trial. The lengthy waiting and repeated legal expenses made many exasperated landlords drop their cases.[14]

Homes Not Jails and Religious Witness in San Francisco also have used reoccupation to great effect. As the housing market has tightened in recent years, reoccupation usually has been the only route through which covert squatters have succeeded. The two homeless advocacy groups have reoccupied the vacant housing at the Presidio Army base half a dozen times to press for its use as affordable housing, and have succeeded in saving nearly all the housing from demolition.

Reoccupation has worked at other military bases, as well. On March 8, 1970, a group of Native Americans scaled the chain-link fence surrounding Fort Lawson, an abandoned military installation in Seattle. The police removed them, but the occupiers returned with other activists, including some from the Alcatraz occupation in San Francisco. Police evicted them again, but the Native occupiers returned to carry out a third, three-month occupation. This persistence finally convinced the authorities to negotiate a 99-year lease of 8 hectares. The occupiers founded a successful cultural center, which remains active to this day.[15]

Peasant squatters have also used reoccupation to good effect, although they face more severe consequences and play a higher-stakes game than the average tenant or homeless person in the United States. Given that few other opportunities exist, reoccupation of farmland becomes a nutritional necessity, and the test of wills between landowner and squatters becomes the deciding factor of success. One especially grueling reoccupation was that by 15 families just south of Santo Antônio in Brazil. After occupying some unused land for between 10 and 15 years, the community was threatened with eviction by the owners of a nearby cattle ranch. The ranchers offered gunmen half the land if they evicted the squatters. Eighteen gunmen arrived at the community in August 1981, tied everyone up, burned their huts, destroyed stocks of food and crops, sent possessions that could not be burned floating down the river, and dropped off the peasants at a distant stretch of highway. The peasants returned to their land, rebuilt their huts to the extent possible, and salvaged their crops. When the gunmen returned, the peasants drove them off with gunfire. At this point, the land reform agency in Brazil began offering deals to the peasants, all of which they refused. Finally, in October 1983, the agency expropriated the land and gave title to the community.[16]

In the case of Santo Antônio, reoccupation worked because the hired gunmen lacked resolve in the face of determined farmer resistance and because this resistance caught the attention of the land reform agency. In this case, the goal of land reform was to avoid revolution by oiling those parts of the agrarian machine that chafed, sparked, and threatened to explode into broader violence. When government forces have only a meager grip on social order or when direct action entails a large proportion of the population, the tactic of reoccupation has a broader level of success.

During the Barcelona rent strike of June 1931, the scale of reoccupation in response to eviction left landlords and governments relatively powerless to repress the movement. In a city of just over 1 million people, the strike grew from 45,000 in July to 100,000 in August. Women, organized in a city-wide rent strike commission, carried out most of the reoccupations. According to Nick Rider,

> The Commission had local committees in many districts, and it was made known that one could go to the local union halls and libertarian clubs to find people to help in resisting evictions. Often, though, this was not really necessary: "When something was going to happen we knew by word of mouth.... All the kids used to go," one woman remembers. The resistance was based in a strong sense of community solidarity. The Commission recommended that people should insult and remonstrate the workers who carried out evictions, and on 26 August a crowd nearly lynched two men who had obeyed the orders of a judge to help in clearing a house in Hospitalet.... [E]ven when evictions were carried out without problems the authorities did not have sufficient forces to mount a permanent guard on each vacant house, so there was nothing to prevent tenants being re-installed at a later time.[17]

Despite intense solidarity and tight organization among rent strikers, the Barcelona government and local landlord organization eventually broke what might be called a "general rent strike" by increasing the frequency of evictions, destroying personal belongings of strikers, and jailing organizers. But, as one organizer pointed out, strikers succeeded in saving themselves four months' rent, a city-wide total of 12 million pesetas.

Timing, Surprise, and Affinity

Another effective method in land and housing struggles is the tactic of surprise. Devaki Jain's essay "India: A Condition Across Caste and Class" describes the story of how unexpected action by women saved their squatter community in Kumarikatta, India, from eviction. The authorities brought a herd of elephants to trample the huts, but while social workers and the rest of the village waited helplessly for the destruction to begin, the women surprised everyone:

> Suddenly, with no discussion and without the advice of any so-called organizers, village women rushed out of the crowd and started to embrace the elephants' trunks and legs, chanting the prayers that they usually sang on a particular *pooja* [sacred] day. This *pooja* was devoted to the elephant god and it was customary for these women to stroke the elephants and rub sandal paste, *kumkum,* and flowers on them with devotion and love. These women started to imitate the same ritual, with full devotion. The elephants responded in turn by accepting this with their conventional grace. They refused to move further. No one — the authorities, the social workers, or even the men squatters — could do anything. The elephants turned back — and the women, men, and children returned to their huts.[18]

As in Kumarikatta, the goal of almost every land and housing direct action is to avoid eviction. Activists can improve their chances against eviction by acting on the fact that governments find eviction extremely embarrassing. Timing an occupation to coincide with holidays, for instance, can make the official sense of embarrassment great enough to at least forestall eviction. San Francisco Homes Not Jails occupied a warehouse on Christmas Day 1995. The next day, police decided against an immediate eviction. Sgt. Steve Howard of the California Highway Patrol told the *San Francisco Examiner*, "We didn't want to walk in there the day after Christmas and look like the Grinch." The police did eventually evict the squatters, but their holiday tactic bought some time.[19]

Widely publicized international events also provide the perfect audience to deter embarrassing evictions, especially when the events relate to social welfare. On April 29, 1971, 4,000 homeless families (all refugees from an earthquake) took advantage of an international development conference hosted by Peru to occupy public land. Fearing adverse coverage at the moment when the international media was focused on Peru and its development, the government left the squatters in peace for the time being. In less than two weeks, the occupation grew to 9,000 families and spread to neighboring private property.

Squatters' successful resistance to a later attempt at eviction by police convinced the government to bargain. Instead of staying at the original site, squatters were given an alternative site suitable for 40,000 families.[20] In 1989, the new settlement, called Villa El Salvador, had a population of 300,000 and boasted title as the largest continuously squatted area in the world. The community has street lighting; children's playgrounds; a network of libraries, health clinics, and community centers; and 34 educational facilities. Brick construction provides solid shelter for most, and nearly 80% of houses have running water, sewer connections, and electricity. Paved streets and sidewalks allow easy access, and 500,000 trees have transformed a former desert into a pleasant neighborhood. Residents even began construction of an industrial park in 1988 with a $3 million grant from the United Nations. A municipal exhibition center opened in 1989.[21]

The timing of the Villa El Salvador occupation to coincide with an internationally publicized event determined its success. But the choice of location, Peruvian government property, also helped. Carefully picking a landowner less likely to evict improves the chances of squatting immensely. On March 19, 1987, in Brazil, 1,000 families organized by the MST squatted an empty wasteland called Jardim São Carlos. All night families measured plots of 125 square meters and erected tents, shanties, and even light wooden buildings.[22] Private landowners can usually get a quicker eviction order than the government, so, by choosing public land, the MST occupiers gained crucial time. They used this time to construct a headquarters to distribute food, water, and medical assistance. Over the next few months, they made dwellings more permanent, built latrines, installed water systems, established a broom-making factory, and formed church groups. Rather than evicting just another new occupation, the government would have had to uproot a fully functioning neighborhood. Instead, within one year, the squatters had convinced the government to begin building permanent homes on the site; by 1989, 1,341 had been completed.[23]

Choosing a particular landlord against whom to take direct action can help to organize direct action against the same landlord by others. This applies to squatting, but rent strikes have found focused campaigns against individual landlords especially useful. Organizing tenants against a common landlord heightens solidarity among tenants and increases income loss for the landlord. Landlords have less money with which to cushion deficits from rent strikers, and the common adversary can facilitate collective bargaining and mutual aid in case of eviction. Targeting particular landlords, rather than landlords in general, utilizes the divide-and-conquer technique in favor of the tenant. Non-target landlords will have less immediate incentive to help the targeted landlord when they think the rent strike campaign will have no effect on their own assets.

In larger rent strikes that encompass more than one landlord, basing "affinity groups" on a common landlord makes for a practical decision-making structure. Affinity groups are collections of people having some similarity to each other that make collective decisions and engage in mutual support during a direct action.

Landlords act differently from each other and require flexible responses by tenants. In Ann Arbor, Michigan, a primarily student-based rent strike between 1969 and 1971 organized tenants according to their landlords. The Ann Arbor Tenants Union targeted the town's 16 largest landlords, who owned from 50 to 450 units apiece. With almost 2,000 rent strike pledges on February 15, 1969, representatives voted to commence the action. Six weeks later, at the end of April, the escrow account held over $150,000, and organizers calculated participation at 1,200 people. After a long struggle and numerous legal battles (including conspiracy charges against 91 activists), nearly all the tenants won rent reductions in court, and, according to the *Sun*, "landlords all over town were scared into making needed repairs."[24]

Mobilizing Support and the Ripple Effect

Squatting and rent strikes may seem self-interested on the surface: participants seek lower rents, better living conditions, or free land for themselves and their families. But these forms of direct action have major benefits for communities and society as a whole. They create a history from which future movements can learn, they act as a constant check on society's increasingly skewed distribution of wealth, and they demonstrate the power of united action. When successful, they inspire new movements and encourage landlords and governments into earlier or even preemptive concessions.

Even when they fail, land and housing movements can have a positive effect on their surrounding community by decreasing the profits associated with land speculation and rack-renting (raising rents to the highest possible market value with little regard to the rate of tenant turnover). In the Ann Arbor campaign mentioned above, landlords other than those confronted with rent strikes improved conditions for their tenants. Just as violent resistance has a deterrent effect on repression, rent strikes and squatting deter irresponsible landlords. In addition to the Ann Arbor example, a rent strike in Vancouver, British Columbia, illustrates this ripple effect, or expanding concession principle. Direct action tends to spread. The more a landowner thinks direct action by tenants is imminent, the more likely he or she is to make preemptive concessions.

The Vancouver rent strike failed for strikers but yielded a success for many other tenants. It targeted buildings managed by Wall and Redekop for five months and began with a high degree of participation. After Wall and Redekop announced 9 to 10% rental increases for all units inhabited for over a year, 195 tenants collectively deposited their rents into a Vancouver Tenants Council (VTC) escrow account on April 1, 1971. By August of the same year, only 18 tenants remained on strike, against all of whom the court ordered eviction. Tenants failed to achieve the main VTC goal, a legal right to collective bargaining where voted for by a majority of tenants. In an illustration of the ripple effect, however, the strike did yield victories for other tenants in Vancouver.

According to the VTC, "Scores of individual tenants had their increases 'voluntarily' reduced by Wall and Redekop in an attempt to dissuade them from joining the strike.... [N]o tenant who was legally 'eligible' for a rent increase commencing on May 1st has subsequently received a notice of an increase from Wall and Redekop."

Even tenants in Vancouver not under management by Wall and Redekop benefited by the strike. "Corporate landlords in the city," states the VTC, "did not raise rent arbitrarily during the course of the strike." In an atmosphere charged with the idea of rent strike, almost all landlords perceived the danger of providing provocation for further strikes. Even those considering the purchase of rental property in Vancouver may have paused for a short period before buying. In this way, the strike's atmosphere of tenant resistance slowed the rate of rent increases for the average Vancouver tenant.[25]

The ripple effect creates positive spillover benefits for the non-striker from the work and risks of the striker, but strikers can use the effect to their advantage. By showing how the rent strike benefits non-strikers, they win non-striker support. Supporters see the success of squatting and rent strikes as movement toward a solution to their own housing problems.

The housing collective of the West Side Women's Liberation Center spoke of its support for housing struggles in New York City in 1970 as an improvement of all women's housing, not as a form of philanthropy. "We must understand our support for the squatting movement in terms of our own very real and immediate housing needs, not as a gesture of sympathy towards others we consider more oppressed than ourselves."[26]

Squatting and rent strikes benefit society as a whole, but they also depend upon society for success. From the very beginning of a land and housing movement to its growth into a mass phenomenon, it utilizes an existing matrix of social connections. Organizing within one's own community at the beginning works because it mobilizes already existing networks of people connected by word of mouth. They know each other from current or past neighborhoods, workplaces, social connections, and cultural or political organizations. This style of community organizing uses to best advantage the trust already existing from long-time membership in an organization or group of friends.[27]

Before an occupation in Lima, Peru, on July 27, 1954, a restaurant worker invited several of the waiters to take part. In turn, one of the waiters recruited a neighbor and a family from his provincial club, the Sons of Paucartambo. The club was a group of recent rural-to-urban immigrants from the province of Paucartambo. These provincial clubs are common organizers of urban squatting in the Third World. Because each new member of the squatter organization had additional contacts in other communities, the group could expand its action to include many different supporter communities at once.[28]

The stronger and more diverse the social movements from which a squatting or rent strike campaign emerges, the more likely it is to succeed. At its height, on January 1, 1964, the New York City rent strike of 1963-64 claimed participation by 525 buildings and 50,000 inhabitants, making it the second largest rent strike in U.S. history. The New York University Congress of Racial Equality (CORE) chapter and a small organization called the Northern Students Movement began this massive struggle by organizing six buildings on the Lower East Side to withhold rent.[29]

What began on this small level grew at an extremely rapid pace because it used already existing organizations to multiply the number of activists and participants. The strike drew on the momentum generated by the burgeoning Civil Rights movement after the March on Washington in the summer of 1963. According to Ronald Lawson, the Civil Rights movement "not only allowed Jesse Gray to find response to his organizing among Harlem's tenants (he worked with them with little success for ten years prior to that), but it also prepared third parties to enter as 'conscience constituents.'"[30] Fifteen Harlem organizations joined a coordinating committee initiated by the Community Council on Housing in early December, and many others aided in an unofficial capacity. They included block associations, church groups, Democratic Party clubs, the local NAACP, local CORE chapters, and a labor union (Local 1199 of the Drug and Hospital Workers), all of which publicized the movement in their communities. The Harlem, Downtown, Columbia, Bronx, and East River CORE chapters went further and "dropped their reformist approach" to become involved in the actual organization of rent strikes in their districts.[31]

At a meeting in January 1964, a broad and cross-cultural coalition calling itself the Lower East Side Rent Strike formed to help spread and provide support for the movement.[32] The height of excitement occurred at a January 11 mass meeting attended by 800 people and composed of Harlem tenants and representatives of almost every Civil Rights group and tenants' organization in the city. Prominent speakers included James Baldwin, William Fitts Ryan, and John Lewis. The rent strike first found its support in the Civil Rights movement and then in housing clinics, which had previously concentrated on isolated buildings.[33] Mark Naison identified several factors that led to success in New York City during 1963-64:

> There were three main qualities of the rent strike that contributed to its
> political effectiveness. First, its *size*. The larger the rent strike grew, the
> more politicians perceived in it a threat to the public order, or the danger

of a broadly based radical movement arising to undermine established political relationships. Second, *militancy*. The more the rent strike broke laws, or massed large numbers of people together in volatile situations, the more politicians felt the danger of a contagion of civil disorder to other groups and other issues — a breakdown of the peaceful "rules of the game" in which they were used to operating. Third, *rapport between leaders and followers*. The more stable the movement's organization was, and the more closely its participants were linked to its leaders, the more politicians grew afraid that agitation would be lengthy and would spread to other issues when the rent strike ended.[34]

Size is the first important aspect of successful movements mentioned by Naison; it plays a role in the other factors mentioned, militancy and rapport between leaders and followers. The addition of new elements from different communities provides the critical mass needed for success. During the St. Louis public housing rent strike of 1969, community support for tenants tipped the balance in their favor and helped win the strike. On February 1, 1969, with 700 rent strike pledges out of 1,300 tenants, the strike against rent increases began in only one housing project. Seven other projects rapidly joined; at the peak, 35 to 40% of St. Louis' 8,000 public housing tenants participated.

Meanwhile, tenants held demonstrations, gained allies, and sent delegations to government authorities. Like the New York City strike of 1963-64, the tenants used their strong ties to the local Black community to gain massive support. Many organizations and individuals lent a hand, including the Southern Christian Leadership Conference, the Black Coalition, CORE, Action, the Zulu 1200s, the Black Liberators, and African American politicians, churches, fraternities, and sororities. Primarily white groups also supported the strike, including church groups, politicians, the *St. Louis Post Dispatch*, the National Tenants Organization, and the New Democratic Party.

When the 58,000-member Joint Council 13 of the Teamsters union met with the strikers in October, endorsed their demands, and organized the Civil Alliance for Housing with 70 members from the ranks of religious, labor, civic, tenant, and business groups, the strike reached critical mass. The alliance supplied the necessary political weight in a meeting with the mayor and other city officials to gain concessions. Three weeks after the discussions on October 29, officials signed an agreement that conceded most tenant demands, including rent reductions for all (to as low as 25% of income for welfare recipients), a new five-member housing authority (two of them tenants, the other three sympathetic to the strike), a program to advance tenants into project management, and a Tenant Affairs Board with one elected representative from each project to hear grievances and set policy.

Two months later, Congress passed the Brooke amendment to the 1969 Housing Act. It provided federal subsidies to reduce rents for public housing tenants across the nation. In addition to Black ghetto riots and the massive Civil Rights, anti-war, and countercultural movements, the St. Louis strike pushed Congress to pass the Brooke amendment.[35]

Many of the most famous land occupations had only a few hundred visible participants but, in fact, utilized massive support structures. Without these structures, most large land occupations would find it difficult to maintain themselves against repressive forces. At Wounded Knee in 1973, the American Indian Movement (AIM) received a steady flow of material goods, people, and written support from groups across the United States. According to the police historian of the occupation, Ronald Dewing, "Demonstrations, speeches, telegrams, letters, editorials, and the like urging the government to use restraint blossomed forth from an imposing number of sources in North America and even Western Europe."[36] These sources included 21 different socialist, prisoner aid, African American, peace, and Asian American groups across the United States.[37] On just one day, the FBI recorded the following numbers of people at demonstrations: Cleveland, 25; Tulsa, 150; Los Angeles, 300-500; Buffalo, 125-150; Milwaukee, 150; Eugene, 25; Salt Lake City, 120; Seattle, 200; Las Vegas, 30; Shawnee, 23; Sioux City, 35-40; and San Antonio, 150.[38] When Dennis Banks and Russell Means went to trial after the occupation in 1974, supporters held further rallies across the nation, including one in Philadelphia that featured speakers from the Women's International League for Peace and Freedom and the United Farm Workers.[39]

Organizations that actually helped occupy Wounded Knee included members from 64 different Native American tribes;[40] the Black Panthers; the Student Non-violent Coordinating Committee (Angela Davis and Stokely Carmichael visited the area); Vietnam Veterans Against the War; and Venceremos, a Cuban support group. The Asian Movement for Military Outreach (AMMO), a Japanese-American anti-Vietnam War group, delivered 5,000 rounds of assorted ammunition.[41]

It is chilling that the FBI should have assembled such an exhaustive list of organizations that supported the occupiers at Wounded Knee, but it shows how diverse movements can identify their interests with an occupation by a relatively small number of people. Chicanas and Chicanos devoted themselves with particular ardor at the Wounded Knee occupation. The Alianza Federal de Mercedes from New Mexico and the newspaper *El Grito del Norte* both sent representatives. An article in *La Raza Magazine* stated that "Chicanos all over the Southwest who have a knowledge of their own history and their cultural ties with Indians (not to mention their identity with the oppression suffered by these class allies) have manifested support for the Indians at Wounded Knee." A Chicano named Graciano Jauregui was killed by police on his way to the occupation, and the Chicano medic Rocky Madrid was grazed by a federal bullet at the site.[42]

People from a wide variety of backgrounds supported Wounded Knee because they saw their own oppression addressed by the struggle. An Asian American group called the Manzanar Committee compared the repression of the occupation to the relocation of Japanese-Americans during World War II. It noted that the struggles surrounding Manzanar and Wounded Knee symbolized the many oppressions of Native Americans, Asian Americans, African Americans, Chicanos, Latinos, women, and "other oppressed people here and around the world." Comparing the internment of Japanese-Americans during World War II with the methods of the Bureau of Indian Affairs, the Manzanar Committee noticed that the federal policies and even the federal personnel were sometimes the same.

> Today, the person in charge of the BIA is the same person who was in charge of the "relocation centers" for Japanese during World War II. He must know, as we do, that it doesn't matter whether you call it a reservation or a "relocation center," it is in reality, a concentration camp. And today, we must realize that Manzanar is, right this minute, our Wounded Knee. If we support one, we must support the other. It is the SAME STRUGGLE WITH MANY FRONTS.[43]

Leaders of the Wounded Knee occupation, in an organization called the Independent Oglala Nation, encouraged cross-cultural coalition by including Native Americans of other tribes, Chicanos, African Americans, Asians, and whites as citizens. They granted three different kinds of citizenship to all Wounded Knee occupiers: Oglala citizenship, dual citizenship for Indians of other tribes (including Chicanos), and naturalization for non-Indians.[44] Had the occupation succeeded in resisting eviction, a multi-ethnic institution might have emerged. Coalition molds the settlement reached and conditions the new type of social organization that it creates. When multicultural coalition succeeds, it can create multicultural solutions.

At another occupation, a multi-ethnic community did emerge. In 1968, the U.S. Army abandoned a communications center in Davis, California. About 75 Chicanos and Native Americans (many of whom had come from Alcatraz) occupied the building on November 3, 1970. After several rounds of eviction and reoccupation, the government legalized the occupation, and it became known as the Deganawidah-Quetzal (D-Q) University, especially oriented toward both Indian and Chicano studies.[45]

Those who occupy land, such as the D-Q University or Wounded Knee, receive broad community support because, by risking imprisonment or even their lives, they demonstrate commitment to something bigger than themselves. Several

years before Wounded Knee, at the Pit River Tribe's occupation of Lassen National Forest in 1970, tribal vice-chair Ross Montgomery explained the altruism of
direct action: "Our fight is not just for the Pit River people, but for all people.
What we're fighting for here is the life of the little people."[46] Much of the best direct action is based on such broad altruistic sentiments, inspiring others to lend
support, identify with movement goals, and join the campaign.

In large coalitions, this concept of a fight for all can help overcome the differences between component movements. Each sees its own goal woven into one
direct action. In the early 1980s, an expanding military base threatened farmers in
Larzac, France, with eviction from 5,600 hectares of land. The army had begun
eminent domain proceedings to remove this entire farming community. To resist,
the farmers organized demonstrations of up to 100,000 people. Activists in atten-
dance represented an unpredictable mixture of peace, environmental, left-wing,
worker, religious, political, Breton, Basque, and even conservative forces.[47]
Farmer Léon Maille said in an interview:

> All types of struggle meet together on the Larzac. There are the ecologists
> who see the Larzac as a land which is rather clean, unpolluted, and which
> has an original character, rather beautiful. This is why there are ecologists
> who are not at all anti-militarist but who defend the Larzac nevertheless.
> There are many people who do not agree with each other … but who are
> in agreement over the Larzac because each recognizes the Larzac struggle
> as representing in part their own ideas.… This is why on demonstrations
> you are likely to find Religious Sisters, for example, side by side with
> left-wingers, communists.[48]

The normally parochial Larzac farmers even got international support. In
many instances, land and housing struggles have crossed borders to form international alliances. Activists in the Sanrizuka farmer struggle against the building of
the Tokyo International Airport, which began during the Vietnam War, envisioned
themselves in a common fight against "the same octopus" with anti-imperialist
movements that addressed land issues, such as the Vietnamese guerrillas, the Pal-
estine Liberation Organization, the Black Panthers, and land movements against
military bases in Okinawa.[49] In 1981, a member of Sanrizuka visited the Larzac
farmers' movement in France, which in turn sent a contingent to Sanrizuka in
1982.[50]

The Larzac struggle, Wounded Knee occupation, and St. Louis rent strike of
1969 show how successful activists garner support from many sources to
strengthen their movements. Movements grow the largest and win the biggest concessions when they form coalitions with the broadest interests possible. Activists
must constantly look in not only the most likely communities of support, but also
the most unlikely. Between riots at People's Park in 1969, demonstrators distrib-

uted leaflets addressed directly to the National Guard. "We really can't offer you an easy way out, you have families and jobs to protect. But when you go home think what it means, as those of us who were in 'Nam or some other place wondered why we had to burn that village down, or shoot that peasant woman in the back. Think about it."[51]

Former military personnel active in the fight for People's Park counseled demonstrators that many in the National Guard felt sympathetic to movement goals. "When a man in the National Guard wishes you 'good luck,'" wrote one person in the *People's Park Outcry,* "when he flashes you the 'V,' and especially when he raises his fist, he means it. He means it because he is in a regimented situation not of his own choosing." The writer instructed demonstrators to offer discussion to small groups of soldiers with no superior officers around or in recreation areas the National Guard frequented. The writer pointed out that the individuality of demonstrators contradicted the stereotypes erected by the media and officers to condition the troops, and should be used to clear avenues of communication.[52]

These tactics seemed to have some success, for the National Guard command felt the need to counter these philosophical assaults by periodically shifting Guard units. The leadership hoped to counterbalance the growing inclination to disobey orders, which actually took place on several occasions. One off-duty guardsman was shot while demonstrating, the same day his unit called him to duty, and, on May 18, an entire unit of Guardsmen refused an order to put on their gas-masks.[53]

An even more unlikely coalition formed in the spring of 1986, when a small-town Georgia bank and rural sheriff attempted to evict Oscar Lorick, an African American farmer. Because he was unable to repay his mortgage, like so many other American farmers in the mid-'80s, the bank had begun foreclosure on Lorick's land near Cochran, Georgia. "They didn't want a colored man to have anything," said Lorick.[54] The case garnered national media attention, with a full article in *People* magazine. What made this episode so different from other Black farm foreclosures was that a group of Posse Comitatus/Christian Identity-style racists offered to defend the property and held several meetings with Lorick. According to James Coates, a historian of right-wing militants, "Other than the fact that he was a Black man, Lorick was in a fix identical to that of so many heartlanders who have adopted the Posse Comitatus/Christian Identity solution to their woes." Larry Humphreys, who was running for Congress on a "Republican/Populist" platform at the time and who had called on banks to declare a "land Sabbath," gathered 50 of his Posse Comitatus/Christian Identity followers. Wearing camouflage clothing and outfitted with semiautomatic weapons, the small militia staked

themselves out at the farm, which they covered with anti-Semitic posters denounc-
ing the "Zionist Occupation Government."

> When the sheriff arrived with a badly outnumbered contingent of depu-
> ties, Humphreys' group began firing their semiautomatics into Lorick's
> haystack to dramatize their firepower. One of the shooters declared, "We
> won't fire until fired upon, but if we are fired upon, heaven help the men
> on the other side." The sheriff and his deputies left the farm without serv-
> ing papers, and that evening the lawman held a press conference to an-
> nounce that a deal had been made between Lorick and the bank to allow
> the embattled farmer more time to raise money to pay off the loan.[55]

It may be that Humphreys used the plight of Lorick to pursue his own anti-
Semitic agenda and garner positive media attention. According to Dave Ostendorf,
who was the executive director during the '80s of PrairieFire (sic) Rural Action, a
nonviolent direct action group dedicated to defending family farmers from eviction, the Posse Comitatus in this case used Lorick to "foment their peculiar anti-
Semitic and anti-government views." The Posse Comitatus was much more active
in these radical right issues than in farm issues, though the desperation of the farm
crisis strengthened its organization.[56]

Despite their politics, Lorick remained grateful and retained a good opinion
of the group that defended his farm. "They came and helped me to keep my farm,
and I appreciated it. I asked them for help, because when you are just one person,
whether you are right or wrong, there is nothing you can do.... They were up for
the right thing. They said I was being mistreated." This unlikely coalition illustrates the benefits of seeking support wherever available. Lorick remains on his
farm to this day.

The left in the United States needs to think deeply about ways to eradicate
the racism of right-wing militants, but it must also provide an alternative. Right-
wing militancy often springs from real grievances understandable to progressives.
For several months in 1996, the "Freemen" standoff in Montana dominated the
news. The media focused on the group's racist, anti-government, Biblically based
philosophies, but rarely covered the bank foreclosure that started the actual conflict. Ralph Clark, the leader of the Freemen, lived on his ranch for 20 years, a
ranch that his family had owned since 1913. But hard times hit the homestead several years in a row. In 1979, interest rates had risen to 21%, a drought struck in
1980, hail flattened Clark's wheat and barley crops in 1981, and in 1982, when
Clark was unable to continue making payments on his mortgage, the Farmers
Home Administration recalled his entire debt of $825,000. Over the next ten years,
Clark labored to keep the farm through litigation and federal subsidies, but it was
sold for $50,000 in 1994 to an out-of-state bank, which re-sold the property the

very next year for $493,000. In 1996, Clark refused to leave the farm, and an 81-day armed stand-off with the FBI began.[57]

However racist they may be, many radical right movements in rural areas of the United States have similar reasonable grievances and similarly provide militant support for farmers who have exhausted legal channels to save their farms. According to the Southern Poverty Law Center, more than 800 militant racist groups operate in all 50 states. To keep these groups from embedding their racism even deeper into rural America, progressive urban groups need to understand, support, and form coalitions with progressive rural groups such as PrairieFire.

Like Lorick, every member of a farmer, tenant, or landless group will have several connections to the community around them. By approaching these groups, they expand the action and increase participation. The rest of this chapter details some of the more progressive sources of support for land and housing movements.

Labor Unions

Labor unions have for a long time had symbiotic relations with tenant and landless groups. In Mexico, according to Saiz Ramirez' *El Movimiento Urbano Popular en Mexico*, the neighborhood organizations "accompany almost systematically in the city the independent workers', peasants', and teachers' marches, making class consciousness grow in the process."[58] The fact that most low-paid workers also rent — and that most renters get low wages — places renters and low-paid workers in coalition simply because the two groups are largely one and the same.

The direct action tactics of the two movements — the labor strike and squatting or rent strikes — complement their common goal to improve members' living standards. The Cambridge Tenants Organizing Committee published the following in 1972 during their rent strike:

> We see our stand as part of a fundamental struggle among classes in our society, not as an isolated fight.... The housing problem can never be solved by itself; in the final analysis it depends on the distribution of wealth in society.[59]

With a higher standard of living as the goal, rent strikers can see their adversary as the same one that labor unions fight. At a rally during the massive 1975-76 Co-op City rent strike in the Bronx, spokesperson Charles Rosen read a message of solidarity from the United Farm Workers in California. He then declared, "Everything is related.... It's the same struggle, the same fight, against the same people."[60]

A conceptual relation of land, housing, and labor struggles has provided the atmosphere in which many labor and rent strike movements give tactical support to each other. British rent strikes enjoy a history of successful coalition with trade unions, which often stage sympathy strikes in their work-places. During World War I, crucial munitions workers in Glasgow walked off the job in support of a massive 1915 rent strike against rent increases. This formidable coalition forced the government, which worried about a possible shortage of ammunition and internal unrest during the war, to pass the first Rent Restriction Act, making the 1915 Glasgow rent strike the most famous in Great Britain's history.[61]

Holding sympathy strikes poses a large risk for unions. But when bosses have fired sympathy strikers, rent strikers can come to their aid. In October 1972, 24 workers from the Birds Eye frozen food factory in Kirkby, England, held a one-day strike to attend a demonstration against the Housing Finance Act rent increases. When they returned to work, management locked them out and suspended their contracts. Upon learning of this, rent-striking Kirkby children and mothers with baby carriages mounted a massive picket of the main gate, stopping production. Adverse media coverage and the prospect of a larger labor strike convinced the Birds Eye chairman to reinstate the workers.[62]

Intellectuals

Activists can also marshal radical academics and intellectuals, an important source of support. The public expression of sympathy for squatters and rent strikers by academics serves to legitimize the struggle for the mainstream press and public and to provide a theoretical basis and tactical gameplan for further action.

Classical Marxists denigrated squatting and tenant drives for owner-occupation as a historical regression to individualized production. They favored labor strikes and the capture of state power, which they saw as promoting a communitarian ideal.[63] But recent developments in academia show support for more diverse types of class action. In the last 20 years, many intellectuals have become more willing and even excited about supporting land and housing struggles. The Soviet, postcolonial nationalist, and Social-Democratic nations have disillusioned many with the state as sole tool for the radical redistribution of property. In Africa, the Lancaster House Agreement that preceded Zimbabwe's independence in 1980 forced the nationalists to abandon plans for land redistribution. Margaret Dongo, a former guerrilla and the only independent member of Zimbabwe's parliament, said in May 1996, "We didn't fight to remove white skin. We fought discrimination against Blacks in land distribution, education, employment. If we are being exploited again by our Black leaders, then what did we fight for?"[64] In post-apartheid South Africa, as well, amid growing African National Congress support for business interests and the consequent rallying of the South African stock market, radical economists doubt the likelihood of anything but surface change in ownership patterns.[65] Third World revolutions in other countries face similar problems. "Illusions about the state as the tribune of the people have faded," writes Muto Ichiyo of the Pacific-Asia Resource Center in Tokyo. "Almost all Third World states — including China — have made a definite shift to the position of promoter of the logic of multinational capital and mediator of capital globalization within their own territories."[66]

The rejection of the state as a tool of social change by many academics has precipitated a rediscovery of social movements such as squatting and rent strikes. "The forms of organization built on the dominant 'traditional' conception of power (power-state) are doomed to lose a good part of their legitimacy as the peoples come to appreciate the nature of the conservative state," writes Samir Amin in his essay "Social Movements in the Periphery: An End to National Liberation?" He continues, "Conversely, the forms of organizations that stress the many-sided social content of the power that has to be developed should experience growing successes."[67] In other words, social movements (like rent strikes and land occupations) that stress the many-sidedness of power are likely to establish justice where the conservative state cannot. Amin and his co-authors write in the introduction to *Transforming the Revolution: Social Movements and the World System*, "we have written this book today on the antisystemic, social, popular movements because we believe that today these movements represent the key lever, and even the key locus, of social transformation."[68]

No longer do radical academics uncategorically condemn landless peasant agitation for land ownership or workers' movements for housing rights as a distraction from the "primary struggle," as did Friedrich Engels and Karl Kautsky. Rather, the academic quest for new sources of social agitation, according to Frans Schuurman in his and Ton van Naerssen's book on squatting in the Third World, "has resulted in (re)discovering the new social movements, whereby the urban social movements in developed and underdeveloped countries alike are considered of prime interest."[69] Activists can turn this interest into concrete support by building alliances that tap the substantial respect accorded to academics by other power elites and by utilizing the resources of the academy to educate people about the work of land and housing struggle.

Religious Groups

The tremendous political power of religious ideology and organization has been used to persuade the media to publicize — and mobilize large numbers of people to lend support to — land and housing campaigns. Activists have used Hindu, Animist, Buddhist, Islamic, Christian, and Judaic theology as powerful additions to their other philosophical and tactical tools. Vinoba Bhave cited Hindu scripture to advance his *Bodhgaya* land movement; the Palestinians used Islamic *fatwas* in their resistance to dispossession; the Sanrizuka farmers in Japan formed coalitions with traditional Buddhist monks; and the Land and Freedom Army in Kenya made Animist oaths and gained the support of medicine men during the Mau Mau war.

In the Americas, progressive Christian organizations have formed the base from which many radical land and housing movements have grown. In Brazil, the Christian Base Communities formed by the Catholic Church during the '60s became one of the most radical segments of the country. They united poor people previously atomized from each other, enabling easier collective action. As soon as the poor formed organizations, they began taking militant action in their own interests.

Elvia Alvarado in Honduras described her Christian-inspired radicalization in *Don't Be Afraid Gringo*. The Catholic church organized programs for women in different communities, which the women themselves led. The church wanted them to distribute food and medicine to malnourished children, but the women began questioning the reasons children had no food in the first place. Alvarado and her *campesina* friends came to the conclusion that landowners, factory owners, and politicians exploited women and therefore caused children's malnutrition. When they began organizing on these issues, the church stopped funding the women's group. Participants then changed the group's name to the Federation of Campesina Women, or FEHMUC.

> I worked many years with FEHMUC, setting up cooperatives, trying to
> raise women's income. But I still kept coming up against what I thought
> was our biggest obstacle: the fact that we *campesinos* didn't have any
> land; some families had small plots but not big enough to feed them-
> selves. I felt that without land we'd never get out of our poverty. I also
> knew some of the other *campesino* organizations, the ones the men were
> in, were trying to regain land for the poor. I decided to join the UNC [the
> National Campesino Union] and later the CNTC [National Congress of
> Rural Workers] so I could participate in the struggle for land.[70]

In Nicaragua, a similar process of radicalization developed in 1968. The bishops of Nicaragua started the Educational Center for Agrarian Advancement (CEPA), envisioned as an organization for preachers and lay volunteers to teach farming skills to *campesinos*. Limited to disbursing technical expertise, the organization had no political agenda. But faced with maldistribution of land and the exploitation of laborers, many CEPA workers began teaching that poor people have a right to the land and organized land occupations. Some even became guerrillas in the Sandinista army.

Eventually, the Catholic hierarchy tried to restrict the activities of CEPA, which in the late 1970s ended its official affiliation with the church to become an independent Christian organization closely allied with the Sandinistas.[71]

From this mass radicalization in Latin America has grown liberation theology. Increasingly, churches are portraying the skewed distribution of land, once considered divinely ordained, as an injustice that the poor can alter through collective action.[72] Elda Broilo has found the Bible an important tool in her organizing with the MST in Brazil:

> There is a profound belief that the struggle is a divine project, that God intends that the land be taken from the landowners who hold it unjustly, and that it be returned to the people who work it so that it can give food, life, and dignity.... In Exodus, chapter 3, verses 7-10, God makes very clear that He has made a choice. "I have seen the oppression of the people, I have heard their cries, I know their suffering, and I have come down to liberate them, and to lead them to a fertile, and spacious land. Go! It is I who send you."[73]

Christian support does not come easily, as a strong trend in Christianity has supported landlords against tenants for hundreds of years. At least from Pius IX to Pius XII, papal social teaching laid a principal emphasis on the sanctity of private property and condemned expropriation without compensation. Radical Christian peasants refute this interpretation. Rigoberta Menchú, a former Guatemalan squatter and the winner of a Nobel Peace Prize, explains that, when she first joined the church, she believed the landlord interpretation of Christianity:

> I thought God was up there and that he had a kingdom for the poor. But we realized that it is not God's will that we should live in suffering, that God did not give us that destiny, but that men on earth have imposed this suffering, poverty, misery and discrimination on us.[74]

Passages throughout the Bible support the argument against landlords, probably because of the oppressive agricultural practices used against the ancient Israelites. All land in theory belonged equally to all non-slave families of Israel, but in reality some families gained the upper hand. According to economic historians Herman Daly and John Cobb,

> The maintenance of this widely distributed system of land rights proved extremely difficult, for some extended their holdings by buying up the neighbors' "inheritance," especially in times of crisis. Climaxing in the eighth century B.C.E., the urban elite turned agriculture from village subsistence to mono-cropping for export, forcing peasants to become day laborers on large estates instead of independent farmers. Much of the prophetic denunciation is directed against this violation of the covenant.[75]

During this period of what amounts to Biblical agribusiness in 730 B.C.E., Micah sets the tone with a critical verse against violent dispossession: "And they covet fields, and take them by violence; and houses, and take them away: so they oppress a man and his house, even a man and his heritage" (Micah 2: 2). Amos must have spoken about similar landlords in 787 B.C.E., "that pant after the dust of the earth on the head of the poor" (Amos 2: 7). Biblical scholars have interpreted this statement to mean that landlords are not satisfied with their own land, but "desire even the dust which rests on the poor man's head."[76]

Ezekiel, likewise, in 587 B.C.E., praises security of tenure:

> They shall be secure in their land; and they shall know that I am the Lord,
> when I have broken the bars of their yoke, and have delivered them out of
> the hand of those that made bondmen of them. And they shall no more be
> a prey to the heathen, neither shall the beast of the earth devour them; but
> they shall dwell securely and none shall make them afraid. (Ezekiel 34:
> 27-28)

Isaiah concurs: "And my people shall abide in a peaceable habitation, and in sure dwellings, and in quiet resting places" (Isaiah 32: 18).

Several hundred years earlier, in 1490 B.C.E., Leviticus put form to these sentiments by providing for a periodic redistribution of all land and slaves in the Hebrew law. Every 50 years in the jubilee year, "Ye shall return every man unto his possession, and ye shall return every man unto his family" (Leviticus 25: 10). John Eagleson and Philip Scharper analyze the jubilee in *The Radical Bible:*

> Behind the law concerning the jubilee year lies the conviction that God
> has bestowed the land and its riches on all the people. Each family had re-
> ceived a just portion in the partitioning of the land. But the original equal-
> ity did not prevent in time the rise of inequality due to debt or reverses.
> The jubilee year was meant to re-establish equality of opportunity and to
> make a new beginning possible for all.[77]

Taking their cue from the Bible, many of the early Christian Fathers in Rome, including Clement of Alexandria, Basil the Great, John Chrysostom, and Saint Augustine, interpreted its meaning to be a denunciation of concentration of land ownership. In the context of severe absentee ownership by town-dwelling Roman landlords, Ambrose of Milan quotes Isaiah 5: 8 in this denunciation of eviction and call for common property: "How far, O ye rich, do you push your mad desires? 'Shall ye alone dwell upon the earth?' Why do you cast out the fellow sharers of nature, and claim it all for yourselves? The earth was made in common for all.... Why do you arrogate to yourselves, ye rich, exclusive right to the soil?"[78]

One could even interpret writings by the Vatican Council II as advocating squatting: "God intended the earth and all that it contains for the use of every human being and people.... The right to have a share of earthly goods sufficient for oneself and one's family belongs to everyone.... If a person is in extreme necessity, he has the right to take from the riches of others what he himself needs."[79]

While the writings of some Christian authorities may justify squatting, very few have sanctioned the violent resistance that squatting often entails. After landowners destroyed Menchú's indigenous squatter community and tortured her father, along with others, she sought guidance from the Christian priests and nuns whom she respected.

> Their religion told us it was a sin to kill while we were being killed.... I tried to get rid of my doubts by asking the nuns: "What would happen if we rose up against the rich?" The nuns tried to avoid the question. I don't know if it was intentional or not, but in any case no-one answered the question.[80]

Menchú's community answered the question themselves after studying the Bible. They found that the stories of Moses, Judith (who beheaded Holofernes), and David (the boy who defeated King Goliath) provided role models for everyone in the community to fight the landowners. "This gave us a vision, a stronger idea of how we Christians must defend ourselves. It made us think that a people could not be victorious without a just war."[81]

Pacifists and Anti-Nuclear Activists

In addition to Christians, pacifists and anti-militarists often support land and housing movements, especially those that are nonviolent. While promoting a decrease in the military budget, most pacifists also promote an increase in government spending on social services, such as housing. Pacifists and anti-militarists especially supported housing movements during the 1990s in the United States, when the fear of nuclear war had receded somewhat due to improved relations with Russia following the changes introduced by President Mikhail Gorbachev. In order to stage a demonstration of sufficient size, pacifists often had to think about how their agitation against nuclear weapons related to other social movements with strong membership bases. A similar diversification of issues followed the general decline of the movement for nuclear disarmament in England after the Partial Test Ban Treaty of 1963. According to nonviolence theorist April Carter, the Committee of 100 (the primary organizers of anti-nuclear civil disobedience in England in the early '60s)

began consciously to broaden its objectives to include action for radical
social change at many levels — it undertook, for example, an early demonstration about the problem of homeless families.... In fact, some of the
most active members of the Committee of 100 moved on to become
prominent in the squatters' campaigns and in community organizing.[82]

The English squatting movement grew exponentially and achieved several successes
in the late '60s and early '70s that formed the base of the massive London squatting
movement of the '80s and '90s.[83]

Following the same trend in the United States, in June 1993, I marched in an
action co-organized by Dignity Housing West, a homeless squatting organization,
and the Livermore Conversion Project, an anti-nuclear weapons group. From the
start the main slogan, "Take Action for Housing, Jobs, and a Nuclear-Free Future," broadcast the connection of nuclear weapons to affordable housing. The first
day, demonstrators cut the locks from two vacant buildings in Oakland and housed
homeless people. The next day, demonstrators blockaded the road to Lawrence
Livermore Laboratories, one of the top designers of nuclear weaponry. By taking
action, people wanted to redirect spending from nuclear weapons to human needs
such as housing. Demands included a 50% cut in the military budget and "$50 bil-
lion to add 8 million units of permanent, affordable, nonprofit housing to the nation's housing stock."

By combining the aggressive and concerted direct action of housing activists with the public relations savvy and independent media sources of pacifists,
both groups multiplied the possibility of success. In 1982, the Southeast Project on
Human Needs and Peace, a coalition of the War Resisters League, the Southern
Organizing Committee for Economic and Social Justice, and the Institute for
Southern Studies, supported a rent strike over utility increases and maintenance
problems by 450 families in a New Orleans public housing complex. By providing
the strike with technical help, leadership training, and information that facilitated
organizing, the coalition met their goal of linking peace and economic justice
movements. After six months of rent strike, tenants won the right to negotiate with
the landlord over utility costs and had maintenance work done on their apartments.[84]

Native American land struggles and anti-nuclear groups have particularly
compelling reasons to coalesce, as Winona LaDuke and Ward Churchill have argued. Churchill writes in *Struggle for the Land*:

> The key to a strategic vision for anti-nuclear activism is and has always
> been in finding ways to sever nuclear weapons and reactors from their
> roots. This means ... focusing everyone's primary energy and attention
> not on places like Seabrook and Diablo Canyon, inhabited though they
> may be by "important" population sectors (i.e., Euroamericans), but upon

places peopled by "mere Indians": Key Lake and Cigar Lake in Canada, for example, or Navajo, Laguna, and a number of other reservations in the United States.[85]

Following the strategy of coalition between Native and anti-nuclear campaigns, Clergy and Laity Concerned wrote in 1985 of their intention to draw on the anti-nuclear movement to resist eviction of Native Americans from Big Mountain: "We expect to tap into the loose federation of nonviolent activists who have committed themselves to ending the proliferation of nuclear technology, which begins with uranium mining, and to opposing U.S. [military] intervention."[86] Bringing their political weight to bear on new issues by concentrating on how peace and justice movements overlap, Clergy and Laity Concerned strengthened not only other movements, but the long-term viability of their own.

Nevada has seen the growth of another strong coalition between native and anti-nuclear interests. As opposition to the Cold War became less overt in the beginning of the '90s, activists who had focused on ending nuclear testing in Nevada increasingly entered into coalition with the Shoshone nation of Newe Segobia, other Native nations, and environmentalists in a bid for the return of land rights to the Shoshone. Shoshone direct action has focused on support of Carrie and Mary Dann, who since 1974 have fought against the Bureau of Land Management's attempt to start extracting grazing fees for land the Dann family has used for dozens of years. Because they refuse to pay fees, the Bureau has confiscated the Dann's livestock; in response, the Dann family and other nonviolent activists have disabled federal vehicles and nonviolently blocked cattle trucks. In one emergency action to keep police from driving away with 40 confiscated horses, Clifford Dann soaked himself with gasoline, stood on his pick-up truck in the middle of the road, and threatened self-immolation. To arrest him, federal police sprayed fire extinguishers on him before he could ignite the lighter. If the Shoshone can reassert land rights secured by the Treaty of Ruby Valley, they pledge to evict the U.S. Department of Energy, which tests nuclear weapons on the vast area of traditional land making up most of Nevada. Working together, both native land activists and anti-nuclear activists may achieve their separate, but interconnected, policy goals.

As the coalitions above suggest, native land activism, squatting, rent strikes, and anti-militarism are interconnected on multiple levels. Land ownership historically grew from violence, conquest, and militarism. If pacifists hope to combat militarism, they must also combat the glaring inequities that militarism is designed to perpetuate. To achieve pacifist goals, activists of all stripes will have to simultaneously work against militarism and for a fair international distribution of economic resources, including land and housing.

The concept of the nation, that modern motor of militarism, comes from a territorial consolidation of war. While land clearance depended on genocide and military force, Europeans organized this violence within the ideology of owner-ship. The expanding use of cartographic representation (the drawing of maps to represent land) subjected the world to European lines of property and nationhood. Maps are the technology necessary to expand the ideology of property from a small farm to the drawing of international boundaries, from the micro level of land ownership to the macro level of nationhood.

In its grossest forms, this expansion of inequitable property manifested itself when the Pope divided the world and continents between Portugal and Spain as spheres of influence, much like when the Monroe Doctrine of 1823 claimed Cen-tral and South America for the United States. In the case of Africa, extensive mili-tary invasion occurred only after the laying of a possessional gridwork embodied by the Berlin Conference (1884-85) and subsequent European treaties.[87] Milita-rism created the conditions for this unequal territorial dominance of the world. To eradicate militarism and war, one must also eradicate its indispensable condition, the right to claim inequitable property by force both on an individual and a na-tional level. Without the prospect of booty embodied by inequitable property, war is unworthy of the expense.

Other Land and Housing Campaigns

Perhaps the population that will ultimately provide the most solid support to any particular housing or land campaign is that of other similar campaigns. These campaigns will have the greatest commitment to the success of their neighbors, for when the government evicts one group or individual, it paves the way for the evic-tion of others. Likewise, when one campaign wins a victory, it provides a model and a precedent for the success of future struggles.

Along these lines, squatters have organized broad federations that encom-pass many different squatter settlements. Widespread squatting in Latin America began after post-World War II industrialization and rural-to-urban migration. For decades, squatter movements remained largely isolated from each other, their struggles exclusively local. But from the late '60s in Puerto Rico, regional organi-zations such as the Committee for the Rescue of Land, the Movement of Res-catadores of the Western Zone, the Federation of Land Rescatadores, the Committee for Property Titles, and the Communal Union, Inc., formed spaces in which a fragmented squatter movement communicated, took collective measures for mutual defense, put pressure on municipalities for land titles and services, gave legal assistance, and promoted squatter participation in national electoral politics. The Communal Union organized a 66-day Washington, D.C., picket and over-night occupation beginning on May 14, 1975. The Communal Union condemned discrimination against the homeless and demanded that the governor of Puerto Rico drop eviction orders.[88]

Throughout Latin America, squatters became more militant, sophisticated, and effective when the depression of the '80s weakened the governments' capacity to repress. This allowed already existing local struggles to form powerful national and city-wide grass-roots coalitions. Squatter federations demonstrated in capitals, demanded the impeachment of presidents, and planned joint actions with national trade unions. Governments and political parties could no longer evict squatters without considering the political consequences and generalized unrest, and so began negotiated concessions in the form of land titles and public services.[89]

In Peru, broad squatter coalitions have had a particularly strong effect on national policy. Peru contains one of the most active squatter movements in the world, including 30% of the capital's 2 million inhabitants.[90] In 1979, squatters tested their strength when conservative President Francisco Morales Bermúdez abolished the independent juridical status of all settlements and rescinded recognition of their popularly elected governing organizations. Over popular disapproval, Bermúdez replaced these with government appointees.

Squatter organizations from throughout the metropolitan area of Lima-Callao responded by forming the Federation of Young Towns and People's Settlements and the General Confederation of City-Dwellers of Peru. These organizations allowed squatters to lend strong support to the United Left political party and take a hand in national politics.[91]

Even in the Northern, rich nations, whose police have forced squatting underground and splintered it into fragments, squatting has become a mass movement that practices mutual aid and can have a powerful voice in local and national politics. Homeless, anarchist, and *autonomia* conferences frequently hold squatting workshops, and radical newspapers print articles on both the theory and practice of squatting. Several small magazines and newspapers specifically target squatters as an audience, including Philadelphia*'s Squat Beautiful,* London's *Squall,* and New York City's *Squatter Comics, The Shadow,* and *Piss Bucket.* Squatter organizations, such as London's Advisory Service for Squatters and San Francisco's Homes Not Jails, provide legal, technical, and material support for squatters and the homeless generally. European squatters have often held a conference in Hamburg on New Year's Eve. The squatters of France are so organized that every major political party in the 1997 national elections had a plank in its platform addressing the issue.

Some squatter movements have affiliated with international organizations. The Movement of Landless Rural Workers in Brazil is a member of the Latin America Co-ordinating Group of Rural Organizations, as well as Via Campesina, a worldwide network of small farmers.[92] These international groups play a supportive role for squatters and offer an already existing structure within which squatters organize pan-national movements.

Children in the Struggle

Chroniclers of struggle usually overlook the large population of young activists within land and housing campaigns. There is almost no mention of the role children play in land and housing struggle, but children's participation adds an entirely different dimension of dedication and passion to any movement.

In the Sanrizuka struggle against airport expansion onto farmer land in Tokyo, children played a crucial role. Along with the Dare to Die Brigade (composed of senior citizens), teenage boys and girls formed the Young Peasant Defense Committee, and grade-schoolers organized the Children's Unit. Young people took part in almost all the movement's activities, including underground tunnel occupations, battles with the riot police, and acts of chaining themselves to homes in the face of bulldozers. Outsiders criticized the Sanrizuka community for their "cruelty" in using children for political ends, but the children organized rebuttals in internationally publicized exchanges with their teachers and principals.[93]

The inclusion of young people in direct action dramatizes the most important reason that a community undertakes a struggle — to ensure a good life for future generations. Young people link the future to the present, and their participation in activism exemplifies the future struggling for its own liberation. Between 1977 and 1978, several hundred Maoris refused to vacate Bastion Point, a piece of land within the metropolitan area of Auckland, New Zealand. The land was declared inalienable and native-owned in 1869, but was subdivided by the government for sale in 1977. Along with other children, a 14-year-old Maori girl named Sharon participated in the occupation. She moved onto the land in her own cabin and changed schools to take a larger role in the struggle. Sharon told an interviewer several years later, "towards the end of the occupation, my uncle Alex encouraged a lot of the younger nieces, nephews, and cousins to become involved in the meetings. One night he coaxed me and another cousin to co-chair a meeting." Sharon also took part in the land marches and risked arrest. On the final eviction day, in 1978, she defied her mother and joined 222 other protestors who refused to leave and were forcefully evicted. "It was their land," said the mother, "and they felt strongly about it, too."[94]

Young people also squat on their own. The Homes Not Jails takeover of a federal building in San Francisco with homeless street teens was already discussed in chapter one. That occupation reflected the fact that a significant portion of squatters in the West are in their late teens, and many are runaways. Young people have very little economic or political power and, like others in a similar predicament, attempt to increase their power through direct action. In supporting these young people in their attempts to provide shelter for themselves, older activists offer support to one of the primary dispossessed classes of modern liberal democracies.

Double-Edged Swords: Using Mainstream Media

Land and housing struggles that succeed are those that persist in the face of repression, think creatively, take advantage of the media, choose vulnerable landowners, make their decisions democratically, mobilize the support of many different communities, and know the time to fight and the time to compromise. The more tactics and angles a movement tries and the more it struggles, the more likely is victory.

But even if they fail to gain their housing goals, direct action movements win other rewards. As with most activism, land and housing movements generate multiple benefits in addition to their primary goals, benefits that are sometimes more important than any single battle. Land and housing activists educate society, erode their own subservient attitudes, expand land and housing movements to other communities, and even give birth to completely new social movements that are not focused on land and housing.

Most land and housing movements want to educate society. News of squatting and rent strikes reach a general audience that may have formerly felt indifference or antipathy about the underlying issues of inequality. Most activists cannot use normal channels of publicity. Just as the relative poverty of most activists often precludes their use of electoral or judicial channels of social change, their inability to pay for advertisements, extensive mailings, sophisticated printing, or movie and video production often precludes their conventional exploitation of mass communications. In addition to acquiring land and housing, then, direct action usually aims at dramatizing the negative aspects of the current land distribution to such an extent that at least one form of cultural production, the news media, will disseminate activist viewpoints to the world.

The occupation of San Francisco's Alcatraz Island by Sioux Indians in 1964 included dissemination of information as an important goal. For four hours, the Sioux Indians occupied the island. They staked claims in accord with their 1868 treaty, a dramatization that they hoped would publicize the more than 600 other treaties with Native Americans broken by the United States and call attention to the excessively low U.S. offer of 47 cents an acre for lands stolen from Native Americans in California since the Gold Rush. The action garnered positive media coverage; as a result, according to Adam Fortunate Eagle, the interests of "Indian

people in the Bay Area got much more public attention than they could have garnered with yet another protest meeting."[95]

Media coverage generally leads to the growth of direct action. Banner headlines and a high level of television reporting helped create the tremendous level of
excitement necessary for the growth of the 1963-64 New York City rent strike.
According to Jesse Gray, spokesperson for the Community Council on Housing,
the number of rent-strike buildings rose from three in the beginning of November
1963 to 50 in December and 167 by the last day of the year. The number of buildings skyrocketed the next month to 300 buildings (with 30,000 inhabitants) on
January 26, 1964, and 525 buildings on January 31, the peak of participation. With
failure in the courts, however, media coverage turned against the strike and relegated it to the back pages. The *New York Times* printed no further articles on the
front page after February 11. On February 26, Jesse Gray announced that only 519
buildings, six less than the month before, remained on strike, after which the figure
continued to fall.[96] The fall in rent strike activity was probably due primarily to
courtroom failure, but can also be linked to the declining media coverage. While
the media focuses on an issue, the issue seems to the public to be growing. That
perception can, in turn, set the stage for actual growth.

Because all types of media have such a strong capacity to mobilize protest,
activists have paid careful attention to the dynamics of media reporting. Certain
types of land and housing direct action tend to gain more media attention than others. In a society obsessed with violence, the more physical conflict involved in an
action, the more media coverage it is likely to attain. Jeffery Paige, who studied
media reports of land occupations and other agrarian forms of resistance in Peru,
Angola, and Vietnam between 1955 and 1970, said that newspapers do not report
many events "unless there are substantial numbers of deaths, substantial property
damage, or large numbers of participants."[97] Before photographing the Homes Not
Jails occupation of the Presidio I made advance offers to several media outlets, including the local San Francisco office of United Press International. I told the
news editor who answered the phone about the nonviolent action, and he declined
to see the photos. "If they aren't going to blow something up, we're not interested," he told me.

Things that blow up sell papers. When governments attempt to evict an occupation, the threat or show of force by activists creates a media spectacle. Because of the defensive nature of land and housing occupations, even when they use
violent resistance, media attention usually brings political pressure against government repression. Often threats of resistance do not work, however, and the government actually arrives to execute its commands, punish dissenters, and evict the
occupants. In these cases, the casualties can be quite severe.

Nevertheless, the issues activists wish to air get more coverage than they ever would if they submitted peacefully. The 1973 Wounded Knee occupation by AIM activists is the most widely known land occupation to take place in recent U.S. history. Participants demanded the ouster of assimilationist tribal chair Dick Wilson, sovereignty for the occupation, land rights, and adherence by the U.S. government to treaty obligations.

For 71 days, over 100 AIM activists defended themselves with gunfire from an exponentially larger force of U.S. marshals that literally surrounded Wounded Knee. This resulted in several injuries and the death of one occupier and one federal marshal. Over time, the extensive media coverage of the occupation, much of it positive, garnered the occupiers a good deal of support. A mid-March Harris Poll indicated that 93% of the U.S. population had heard of Wounded Knee, 51% sympathized with the ongoing takeover, 28% were undecided, and only 21% sympathized with the federal government.[98]

Mainstream media coverage poses problems, however, in that it tends to distort the demands and methods of the direct action. By concentrating on the violent nature of the conflict, the media plays on prejudices against the disenfranchised and hides the causes that brought the activists to confrontation in the first place. The details of weaponry and casualties rivet public attention to the detriment of almost every other issue. In Berlin, a squatter movement of the early '80s had established 180 houses by its peak in 1982. Over the next few years, squatters resisted repeated eviction attempts with street barricades, Molotov cocktails, and slingshots. According to Werner Sewing, an academic peripherally involved in the movement, "When there is a demonstration a policeman will start chasing some people and then the whole thing erupts. Housing politics are then immediately shifted by the press into the issue of street violence."[99]

Mainstream media coverage also creates a problem in that it tends to portray the struggle with prefabricated ideas. When women lead, the media and scholars depict the movement as led by men. When nobody leads, the media gropes for spokespeople whom they can claim are leaders. News reporters elide instances of female leadership, using nongendered language that allows readers to assume activists are male, or concentrate on male spokespersons as leaders when women make the actual decisions behind the scenes. This was the case in the 1963-64 New York City rent strike, which the *New York Times*, Lipsky, and Naison portray as led by the spokesperson, Jesse Gray. "Though still known as the 'Jesse Gray rent strike,' after the man who acted as spokesperson, it was actually run by two women," wrote Lawson and Barton. "Women also predominated on the citywide Strike Coordinating Committee."[100]

When the media has misrepresented land and housing direct action, activists have countered this bias by compensating accordingly. In 1992, when the Santa Cruz

Union of the Homeless occupied land in California, we encouraged the more high-profile people to redirect reporters to quieter occupiers. In other struggles, when the media focused on the violence of an action to the detriment of issues, activists have downplayed tactical details and stressed the ideas and goals of the organization. By recognizing the media's bias and responding accordingly, activists have successfully publicized the real issues that fuel their movement. To avoid being swallowed by a sea of reporters who concentrate only on the spectacle of violence, for example, movements have concentrated on emphasizing their commitment to nonviolence.[101]

Erosion of Subservience

Important pyschological benefits of direct action are *conscientización* (becoming conscious), empowerment, and the erosion of subservience. Whenever a person breaks away from accepted structures of dominance, whenever she defies orders, her attitude and fundamental relationship with the world shifts. She peels away her own subservience and replaces it with self-reliance, pride, and a sense of agency. Even a thwarted campaign can have positive psychological and educational benefits. If participants lose hope for a particular tactic, at least they have become more realistic and may think of new, creative methods for social change.

Understanding themselves as holding power changes the way in which activists act toward the people they thought held power and the way in which they think about the concept of property. When squatters or rent strikers take action and defy orders, conventional attitudes of deference and submission to landowners and government officials wane. A Co-op City rent strike leader told the *Village Voice* of discussion dynamics at negotiating meetings with state officials and management:

> That we have dared to sit across the table from them and dictate our terms
> to them as they have dictated to us, for that they'd like to cut out our
> hearts and eat them. They have uniformly ignored every proposal we have
> made. They treat us like garbage. Rabble. You should see them at those
> uptown meetings, you wouldn't believe the way they talk to us! But me, I
> don't take that shit from anyone, that's why the people here love me. I
> leaned across that negotiating table and I said, "My mother raised me to
> believe I was a prince of Israel. Who the fuck do you think you're talking
> to?"[102]

This cracking of the subservient veneer, an outward appearance that may have enveloped a person for years, can have an exhilarating effect. It gives demonstrators the psychological edge needed to win. Political scientist James Scott has called this process of breaking from the "hidden transcript" an important form of authentication through defiance.[103] One person involved in a public housing rent strike in Newark during the early '70s attributed his dedication to an inner revolt against decades of discrimination. His statement shows direct action as a transformation of fear-induced passivity into liberatory agency:

> I remember when I was a young man in the South. We couldn't talk to Mr. Charlie, much less protest against him or hold his money. So today, I'm trying to do all I couldn't do to him down South. I've waited 40 years for this day.[104]

Direct action breaks the bonds that bind people to legality and, on a broader level, causes a more general transformation in the community. It creates a reference point for people who identify with the activists, but have not yet taken the step of direct action themselves. It emboldens the general public by showing that at least some people refuse to cooperate with an exploitative system. Ward Churchill maintains that occupations on the Pine Ridge Reservation formed a "tremendously important point of departure for the general rebirth of American Indian pride, and an increasing Indian willingness to stand and attempt to (re)assert their broader rights to genuine self-determination."[105] Thus not only does direct action attain land and housing, it also reinvigorates a sense of self and community. This inner strengthening provides a priceless psychological asset that paves the way for future direct action.

Encouraging Further Direct Action

The Chilean word for squatter settlement, *callampas,* means "fungus" in Spanish. Like fungus, squatters are certainly anathema to landlords and city planners who would make city living the sole prerogative of the rich. *Callampas* also conveys the image of uncontrolled growth and expansion. Direct action encourages direct action in a never-ending and mutually reinforcing double helix that reaches toward the idea of a better society. Whether or not it applies to foreign affairs, the "domino effect" first invoked in 1954 by Eisenhower to warn against the spread of communism makes a good point about direct action.

When the media broadcasts successful land and housing direct action to a large audience, others are inspired to take action themselves. As in the formation of the Peruvian squatter settlement noted earlier, personal connections provide an important pool of individuals particularly amenable to suggestion from friends and family. Squatter settlements and rent strikes spread like wildfire when they succeed in their objectives. This expansion strengthens the particular land or housing movement because it provides a larger surface of resisters to diffuse the burden of repression. While a government can easily evict an individual squat or small settlement, it is more difficult to evict a national squatter movement composed of a dozen settlements that practice mutual aid.

The benefits of mutual aid make concerted efforts to expand the movement a worthwhile tactical goal. "We hoped that our action would spark off a squatting campaign on a mass scale," Ron Bailey wrote of the goals that motivated his London squatter group in 1968, "and that homeless people and slum dwellers would be inspired to squat in large numbers by small but successful actions."[106]

Beyond displaying their action as a good example for emulation, many land and housing activists transform their squatted houses or fields into a tangible source of support for others' struggles. While the obstruction of urban renewal formed the primary goal of the first squatters in West Germany during the early '70s, the squatted houses also "served as organizational bases for further squats" and rent strikes, according to Margit Mayer.[107] In Brazil, during the early '90s, successful squatters tithed 8% of their production to support further land occupations. In addition to financial contributions, according to MST organizer Elda Broilo, "From each collective, someone is designated to do training on how to do land occupation resistance and technical training on up-to-date farming methods."[108] Mutual aid makes sense for movements that want to win and ensure their gains for the future.

Whether or not a direct action community dedicates resources to the growth of other movements, the goal of expansion almost always succeeds when the general public can see an improvement in the living standards of activists. Here movements can use the self-interest of the public to everyone's advantage. In 1975, an extremely tight rental market plagued Ann Arbor, Michigan. Compared to a national average of 22%, tenants paid as much as 33% of their income as rent. With a vacancy rate of 0.46% (the U.S. President's Committee on Urban Housing in 1967 called anything below 3.5% unhealthy), landlords held near-monopoly power over tenants, depriving them of alternative housing choices and keeping rents extraordinarily high.[109]

On December 1, tenants struck back, targeting one of Ann Arbor's largest landlords, R. Dewey Black of Trony-Sunrise Associates. By the end of the four-month strike, tenants in over half of Black's 120 units had joined the strike and withheld a total of $40,000. They won a one-month rent abatement for all Ann Arbor Tenants Union members, no rent increase for those who re-rented, an 8% maximum rent increase for new tenants in 1977, maintenance repairs, rights to use rent money to contract for future repairs when managers were negligent, and a collective bargaining agreement with the Ann Arbor Tenant Union as the sole agent for all tenants. News of the Trony-Sunrise success spread quickly, encouraging about 50 other tenants in Ann Arbor to strike as well.[110]

On the same date that the Ann Arbor strike began (December 1, 1975), nine families ignited a huge public housing strike about 20 miles away in Detroit. Within ten months, it had spread to every one of the seven Detroit housing projects, growing at a rate of 30 to 40 apartments per day. Tenants complained of broken windows, leaky siding, flooding, bad plumbing, mildew, cockroaches, rats, and rent increases. Tenants quickly squelched the housing authority's recourse to eviction by organizing physical resistance to four or five attempts. Shortly thereafter, court rulings won rent reductions of 25 to 35%.[111]

The principle of rent strike expansion closely mirrors that of squatter expansion. When squatter settlements succeed, they encourage rapid growth through the addition of new squatter families. A settlement called George Compound in Lusaka, Zambia, began in 1957 after an owner of an eight-hectare plot allowed migrant families to build dwellings for a small payment of rent. Through invasions of surrounding private land, the settlement grew to an area of 250 hectares, with a population of 56,000, by 1976. Likewise, in Bogotá, Colombia, a group of families affiliated with a leftist political party invaded a public park to create Las Colinas in 1976. After successfully squatting their land, the population doubled in ten years.

Successful squatter settlements also encourage the creation of completely new settlements. The government of Sumatra conferred legal status on all squatters already occupying land in 1954. The section that called for the removal of those who took land after the law went into effect had little impact, so a wave of new squatters took over estates in 1956. Within just a few years, in the late '50s, the government had lost control of the squatter movement to such a degree that even the most powerful property owners' organizations held little sway. Changing agricultural techniques on squatted estates revealed the success of the movement. Permanent irrigation systems were installed on formerly dry farms.[112]

In Yugoslavia, squatters' successful evasion of repression in the early '70s encouraged the movement to balloon. Repressive legislation went largely unenforced, and the government instead undertook social welfare measures. Faced with political difficulties and a lack of alternative housing, the government could not implement its plans for massive demolition except for road construction and in some of the poorest shantytowns. Even so, evictions engendered strong organization and militant tactics by squatters, friends, neighbors, and sometimes even the demolition workers. Widespread public support for squatters substantially frustrated government goals. While the government targeted a total of 39% of illegally constructed dwellings for demolition in 1972, it actually demolished only 3%.[113]

Even when governments have successfully completed evictions, land and housing movements cause an increase of militant consciousness and thus in direct action. The 1964 occupation of Alcatraz served as the seed of inspiration for the influential "Indians of All Tribes" occupation in 1969. In turn, the second occupation inspired further movement. While U.S. government marshals eventually evicted Native Americans from Alcatraz in 1971, the Bay Area Native American

Council and Richard Oakes, an Indians of All Tribes leader, maintain that the oc-cupation gave Indians a public voice and formed a catalyst for other takeovers.[114] Kirke Kickingbird and Karen Ducheneaux write of the 1969 Alcatraz occupation,

> Its primary significance lay in awakening the Indian people, particularly the urban Indians, to what was happening on the national scene.... It gave birth to numerous other invasions of federal property in areas in which there was a desperate need by the local Indian people for services and pro-grams. Most of all, Alcatraz gave birth to the idea among Indian people that no more Indian lands should be surrendered to the federal govern-ment. In this sense, Alcatraz became the most important event in the twentieth century for American Indian people.[115]

Even with the mellowing of history, the influence of Alcatraz continues to be felt. "We educated an entire country about Indian life," Fortunate Eagle wrote in 1993 at the end of his book on Alcatraz, "and the experience of the occupation educated many Indians who went on to become leaders and spokespeople in the Indian movement. The spirit and the lessons of Alcatraz became part of history and can never be lost."[116]

Diversification of Issues

Successful land and housing action expands not only land and housing movements, but social movements generally. Just as Christian organization of poor people for band-aid goals in Latin America quickly led to self-organization for more fundamental change, activists who struggle for egalitarian solutions on one level quickly see the power that organizing and resistance can have on other levels. This leads to new forms of resistance and the organization of new constitu-encies. Expansion of issues strengthens the support base for the original movement and also conditions the ultimate settlement.

The process of expansion into multiple issues begins with education. In in-terviews with several tenants who became active in the Co-op City rent strike in New York (1975-77), Marc Weiss found that the public's view of strikers as "radi-cals" and recurring contact of strikers with leftist organizers affected the politics of participants. "Ten years ago, I was a real flag-waver," said one resident. But as a result of strike participation, "[I] had discussions with people I never would have talked to otherwise. Before, whatever the government said was OK with me. Now I can understand the views of people who oppose it."[117]

As land and housing activists gain confidence in their ability to resist, they bring that confidence into other aspects of their lives. During rent strikes against the 1972 Housing Finance Act in England, women did the primary organizing af-ter male politicians abandoned the cause; their new political voice strengthened their personal politics within the family. "Whatever the action women get in-volved in, it always modifies, sometimes transforms, personal relationships at home," Cynthia Cockburn writes of the strike. "When they feel that they are in a struggle they share with other women, and that it is not just for themselves, they are prepared to 'take on' their husbands or menfolk in a way they would not other-wise do."[118] According to one woman Cockburn interviewed, involvement in the tenants' association expanded her familial independence and assertiveness: "When you start getting involved, you find you're not a cabbage any more," Jan Kirk said: "You've got a mind and can do things. I don't think men like that idea."

The new-found political agency of individuals manifests itself in collective movements. Land struggles of peasants in Maharashtra, India, during the early '70s created the environment within which women organized on issues of drunk-enness, wife-beating, and women's self-defense. Mira Savara and Sujatha Got-hoskar write of women's changing response to the "first night" tradition, which allows a man of high status to demand sex from a betrothed woman before the consummation of her marriage.

> In Piplod village, for example, the rich peasants had the right of the "first night." After the women began participating in the [land] struggle, they refused to be so used. Rape and sexual harassment of women by rich peasants and landlords had been regular occurrences. Now, the rapists were given an organized beating up, as in Kurangi village in 1973. The incidence of rape consequently declined.[119]

The birth of new movements actually strengthens land and housing struggle. Their diversification and the cross-networking of the organized population make it tremendously difficult to carry out repression with any lasting effect. Even when the government or landlords decimate a squatter movement, the other movements that squatters set in motion form the basis from which squatting can reappear. "By the mid-1970s in most German cities," Margit Mayer writes, squatting produced "a new political actor — a self-confident urban counterculture with its own infra-structure of newspapers, self-managed collectives and housing cooperatives, femi-nist groups, and so on, which was prepared to intervene in local and broader politics." This new counterculture outlasted the West German squats of 1973'74 that had given birth to it. After the squats were evicted, the counterculture pro-vided "an organizational basis for another massive [squatter] mobilization during the early 1980s."[120]

In addition to providing the impetus for resurrection, spin-off movements have an egalitarian effect on the land and housing struggle itself, which, like the rest of society, has its own internal hierarchies. The Bodhgaya land struggle in In-dia began with a focus on land but started a separate women's movement that forced the land struggle to call for land redistribution in women's names.

From the beginning, discrimination against Bodhgaya women incited them to seek a separate forum for expression. Though women took a leading role in actions, walking in front at volatile demonstrations and doing the dangerous work of reaping crops against the commands of armed police, men often ignored issues of particular importance to women. In a founding conference attended by 48 men and only two women, the strategy and focus decided upon foreshadowed future gender conflicts. One active participant named Manimala says the meeting

> concluded that it was enough to begin with a broad consensus that the focus of our organization would be the landless poor and their struggle for their rights over the land. The issue of women's exploitation was passed over. Since, in creating the organization and deciding on the main issues, we overlooked the specific nature of the exploitation of women, it was inevitable that both the organization and the struggle came to be dominated by men.[121]

Though the male-dominated conference recognized the need to lend women support in "their" struggle, the conference prioritized the issue of land. Other issues, the men said, would ultimately be linked to land, leading to a "movement for total change." Because the movement did not clearly and systematically analyze women's specific needs from the beginning, however, the land struggle became *the* struggle, with very little action on gender inequality and violence against women.[122]

In response to this stonewalling of their issues, women in the Bodhgaya land campaign organized themselves and began agitating against wife-beating, alcoholism, rape, wife-abandonment, and arranged marriages. Women activists showed the connections between these problems and the land concerns of the men. Drunkenness made land struggle meetings impossible to conduct when men arrived inebriated and talked nonsense. "If they free themselves from this cruelty and addiction to liquor and establish in their homes relationships based on justice and equality," wrote Manimala, "will this not strengthen them in their struggle against the Math [landowner]?"[123]

This solidarity of women on issues other than the land struggle provided the basis from which to demand the allocation of land to women. Though, at first, women's activism led some to think that it detracted from the land movement, in fact, it only broadened the land movement from one that demanded equality of land distribution among men to one that demanded equal distribution to women, as well. Thus thorough and consistent activists have viewed campaigns that branch off from land or housing movements not as adversarial, but as beneficial, especially to aims of an egalitarian distribution of land and housing.

As with the Bodhgaya struggle, land and housing campaigns have unintended benefits that equal, if not exceed, the stated goals. Campaigns educate society about hidden inequalities and the ways in which they can be overcome. Campaigns erode the culture of subservience that afflicts society as a whole. Campaigns encourage people, both on a societal and individual level, to free themselves of what are ultimately self-imposed psychological strictures. Campaigns, especially when they win concessions for participants, encourage other social movements to grow and expand movement goals beyond land and housing issues. Finally, when well-organized and intelligently orchestrated, campaigns prove that regular folks can join together and beat City Hall.

Conclusion

The Future of
Land and Housing Movements

Throughout history people have struggled to improve their access to economic resources, including land and housing. These movements have succeeded in some places and at some times in slowing and even reversing the trends toward greater and greater concentration of wealth. But will these movements continue in the future? Will they become more or less frequent, larger or smaller? Can we hope that these and other social movements might one day turn the tide and grow into more permanent, egalitarian institutions?

Squatting and rent strikes, at least, tend to expand exponentially under certain social and economic circumstances. One of those circumstances is a pro-land reform government. Jeffery Paige's research in Peru counted 463 land occupations between 1955 and 1970. However, *campesinos* and indigenous farmers initiated 75% of these during just two years after 1962, when a pro-land reform government won election. At its peak, in 1963, the Peruvian land occupation movement involved as many as 300,000 individuals from over 100 distinct communities. Occupiers correctly guessed that the new government would have less interest in repressing land occupations than the previous conservative government.[1]

Squatting in Great Britain reached its broadest levels of participation during the juxtaposition of three factors: a rapid influx of people to urban areas, a feeling of militancy, and a feeling of indignation and entitlement. When soldiers returned from World War I in 1919 and from World War II in 1945, the government failed to provide housing. In both cases, returning soldiers organized squatting movements to house their families. On October 11, 1946, the government announced that 39,535 people had squatted in 1,038 camps in England and Wales and that another 4,000 had squatted in Scotland. Returning soldiers easily transferred their experience of the general upheaval and sense of crisis occasioned by war to a powerful feeling of militancy during their campaign for housing; their rapid demobilization and need for immediate living accommodations required immediate action; and their sense of having sacrificed all for a country that would now make them homeless gave them the indignation required for radical action.[2]

As in Great Britain, a rapid influx of people to Puerto Rican cities in the 1940s caused an increase in squatter activity. Industrialization had caused rural-to-urban migration, and the new migrants had nowhere to live. In their drive to shelter themselves, they created a wave of squatter settlements that began in 1942 and peaked in 1950. For similar reasons, another squatter wave washed over Puerto Rico between 1968 and 1976.[3] Both the Puerto Rican and British struggles suggest that squatting movements tend to develop when major social change occasions mass migration to areas with insufficient housing.

In the United States, the frequency of rent strikes seems to have increased substantially during the late '60s. One way to measure the frequency of social movements is to count the number of articles devoted to them over time. Few mainstream newspapers cover rent strikes, but some alternative periodicals have done so: the Alternative Press Index listed 58 articles on U.S. rent strikes in 1970, but the figure declined to 33 in 1971 and eight in 1972. The latter figure, plus or minus a few, remained constant into the late '90s. The declining number of articles covering rent strikes could be explained by lower interest among readers of the alternative press. But if these figures are indeed indicative of a national trend away from the rent strike strategy, it seems likely that rent strike activity peaked in the United States when the new social movements of the late '60s were at their maximum level of power and when the real standard of living first began to fall. The coincidence of the two trends sparked an expanded level of economic direct action. As the social movement network of the late '60s and the initial shock of falling living standards ebbed, so did the most intense forms of indignation and organizational basis for rent strikes.

Squatting and rent strikes increase because of greater economic hardship or political crisis, the expectation of success due to the reluctance of leftist governments to evict or repress, the lack of available housing due to sudden changes in population, and the strength of local social movements that provide an already existing social network from which to organize.

How do these general guidelines fit the circumstances of the near- and long-term future? In predicting the wave-like rise of land and housing direct action, one must account for circumstances that differ from region to region. If the standard of living continues to fall and labor unions in the manufacturing sector continue to weaken, we will see an increase in new forms of economic direct action in the Northern, rich nations, including Japan. While the shift of the U.S. economy toward the service sector has given service workers some victories (for example, the success of the 1997 United Parcel Service strike and the new militancy and growth of the Service Employees International Union), manufacturing workers and welfare recipients have experienced no such luck. Rising unemployment, anti-labor legislation, and the relocation of industrial capital to Southern, unindustrialized countries have caused falling real wages for the lower 30 to 50% of the population since the late '60s, weakening the labor movements in the manufacturing sector.[4] In the Netherlands, membership in unions fell from 39% in 1978 to 24% in 1991. In 1998, only 14% of U.S. workers were unionized, compared with 24% three decades ago, and labor unions have only mustered about 35 major strikes annually — down from 400 in the mid-1970s.[5]

As capital increasingly migrates to Third World nations for cheaper wages and as the standard of living in the West decreases, relatively more people will turn to new forms of direct action as a remedy. Although most people in the Western nations are nowhere near the poverty level that generates a massive movement like that in Brazil, the increasing gap between rich and poor will increase the numbers of people who seriously consider more radical tactics. If manufacturing wages and government supports continue to decline, unions may shift some of their economic demands from the production of income (the employer) to the expenditure of income (the market, including the housing market). Because people have less money when labor unions are repressed, their ability to pay high rents deteriorates, and their relationship to housing becomes stressed. In other words, if people are living below the level they feel is economically acceptable, and their attempts to rectify the situation through labor unions or lobbying for a reasonable level of government support are thwarted, they increasingly turn to other forms of economic direct action, such as squatting and rent strikes. This need not be a massive shift to create a significant growth in housing movements.

The nature of the deindustrializing, Southward shift of capital may change the focus of some economic direct action targets onto nonmovable assets and industries, such as service and real estate, that wealthy sectors cannot relocate to the South. To direct labor's attention toward movable assets such as industry is essential, but if done without legislation or broad international coalition efforts to limit capital flight, it may cost more jobs. Increased loss of jobs due to capital flight means greater poverty and a greater proportion of nonunionized workers, both of which lead the most marginalized workers (including youth) to seek other forms of economic direct action.

In the United States, housing has increasingly moved beyond the reach of the poor. Since 1970, real wages have fallen, and the cost of residential real estate has increased much faster than the rate of inflation. The availability of affordable housing has decreased from a surplus of 300,000 units in 1970 to a deficit of 4.4 million units in 1995, when about 60% of poor renters paid more than half of their income on rent. Rather than moving to provide relief for those falling into this widening gap, the federal government has cut housing subsidies. In the late '70s, 260,000 additional family homes were subsidized each year, but this number steadily fell to zero between 1977 and 1995.[6] As the affordable housing stock shrinks and the proportion of household income paid in rent or mortgage by the Northern poor continues to increase, the focus on housing direct action can only intensify.

One can predict the rise of squatting in Northern, rich nations because of its common occurrence throughout history when labor unions have been repressed. When unions were at a low level in the '30s, rent strikes and Hoovervilles (squatter settlements named after President Herbert Hoover) proliferated around the country. In Chile, mobilizations shifted from the organized, work-based sectors to the economically marginal neighborhood associations when a large proportion of workers lost jobs under the Pinochet government and union power declined.[7] In Sumatra, squatting accelerated with unprecedented vigor in the late '50s when labor unions faded.[8] The growth of squatter movements in various German cities during the early '80s also resulted in part from the period's growing unemployment, higher poverty rates, and federal austerity measures.[9]

When activists can't organize at work, they look elsewhere. While the weakening of labor unions by capital flight and union-busting depletes the resources for working people, activists attempting to arrest the fall in standards of living can augment their labor organizing by diversifying tactics to utilize the "home court advantage," that is, fighting for assets that cannot be shipped South.

With this rising poverty and diversification of strategy may come the disintegration of the relative social quiescence that characterizes the industrialized North. As Samir Amin points out:

> The West's stability rests on a double consensus: on the one hand, the acceptance by all social classes and political forces of right and left of the rules of the economic game which define capitalism (private property, the market, etc.), and on the other hand, acceptance of the rules of the political game of electoral pluralist democracy, which functions precisely because a consensus exists which does not call capitalism into question.[10]

While we can expect a growth in Northern social movements that transgress property, we must, at the same time, expect the greater amount of repression that will surely follow these tactics.

Trends in the Third World are taking a different form, but similarly indicate increased land and housing struggle. Most of the 15 squatter settlements studied by the United Nations in its *Survey of Slum and Squatter Settlements* were founded shortly after the Second World War during the rapid growth of cities in the Third World. The study found that, in the '70s, squatting gained among the poor as a source of housing; while slums (low-rent areas) grew at a slower rate than the surrounding urban areas, squatter settlements grew faster.[11] We can expect this trend to continue its acceleration in the early 21st century. In rural areas, home to 63% of the Third World's population in 1991,[12] the expansion of agricultural mechanization and the consolidation of small farms into large, export-oriented plantations worked by wage labor continually lead to agrarian unrest.[13] Mechanization dispossesses small farmers, exacerbates inequality, and erodes peasant economic security, a process partially driven by international creditors such as the IMF and World Bank, as well as local elites eager for export earnings.[14]

Other communities faced with dispossession by industrial society include those who find their lands flooded by massive dam projects, especially in China, and Pacific Islanders displaced by tourism, golf courses, forced land purchase, and militarization. The incursion of ranchers, plantations, and desertification on 200 million forest dwellers in Africa, Latin America, and Southeast Asia at the annual rate of 1.1% (20 million hectares) also continues,[15] but faces increasingly consistent and often violent resistance.

Urbanization will also increase Third World urban squatting in the 21st century. Displaced rural populations and increasingly high rates of population growth, especially in Asia and Africa, combine to cause extensive rural-to-urban migration and require a rapid expansion of housing facilities. In 1991, 37% of the developing countries' population lived in cities; by the year 2000, the United Nations Development Programme estimates the urbanized population will be 45%, contributing to an urban population increase of approximately 2 billion in 15 years.[16]

Because governments and landowners on the periphery of existing urban areas almost never willingly cede land cheaply for construction, the majority of new urban migrants will likely continue initiating land takeovers. Indeed, during the early '80s, according to the United Nations Development Programme, nine out of ten housing units added to the total urban housing stock of Third World countries was illegal.[17]

Factors that encourage land and housing direct action are the increase of poverty, hunger, socio-economic polarization, and unemployment. The lower strata in sub-Saharan Africa, Latin America, and some Asian nations face this economic degradation,[18] a trend expected to continue into the 21st century. Worsening conditions are traceable, in part, to an aggregate net flow of financial resources from the South to Northern banks starting in 1983 and reaching $242 billion by the end of 1989. In spite of this massive transfer, the balance owed is not declining. Total debt contracted by local Southern elites and multinational corporations grew by over 100% during the '80s.[19] In order to extract these large sums from the relatively impoverished Southern economies, institutions such as the World Bank and IMF continue to impose austerity measures that cause consumer prices to rise, real wages to fall, and social services to be cut.

World Bank and IMF conditions hit small-scale agriculturists and laborers particularly hard. Former IMF economist Davison Budhoo writes that IMF policies "led to the devastation of traditional agriculture and to the emergence of hordes of landless farmers in virtually every country in which the World Bank and IMF operate."[20] Scholars have linked a rise in protest movement to this '80s trend of debtor impoverishment.[21] Despite meager attempts by these institutions to reform their lending practices and the crushing debt load of the Third World, living conditions continue to deteriorate, and economic unrest and urban social movement, an already "fast growing phenomenon," according to analysts Schuurman and van Naerssen,[22] will probably increase at an even quicker rate.

Another region seeing the growth of incipient squatting and rent strike movements is Eastern Europe, including the former Soviet republics. While hierarchical land and housing relationships thoroughly differed from the Western model of ownership prior to the disintegration of the Soviet Union, these former communist countries are rapidly reorganizing themselves on a model of individual property. Before Russian President Boris Yeltsin's decrees of December 1991 facilitated decollectivization and the legalization of private land ownership in Russia (which contains 57% of all cultivated land in the former USSR), only about 4,400 privately owned peasant farms existed. By July 1, 1992, however, 127,000 peasant farms covered nearly 5.2 million hectares, and analysts expect the number of such farms to reach 1 million around the year 2000.[23]

Policies that allow farmers to choose between individual and collective farming do allow greater freedom for many well-off farmers, but Russia and the Eastern republics that have adopted quick privatization schemes have made themselves vulnerable to greater concentration of wealth. One can see awareness of this stratification in differing opinions regarding privatization. The government and urban electorate push decollectivization and individual land ownership, but rural support is weaker. While mandatory decollectivization is the exception to the rule, the government forced around 1,000 of the poorest collective farms in Russia to "reorganize" against their will in 1992.[24]

Many rural Russians have voiced their distaste for decollectivization. A survey of 1,400 rural dwellers indicated that four out of five felt that land should be state property. Rural residents expressed apprehension about private ownership of land because they see privatization as linked to possible falls in productivity, standards of living, and security and to a rise in wage labor for agriculture (which has been legal since the 1990 Russian Law on the Peasant Farm took effect). Many Russian farmers also dislike speculation, which has led to the popularizing of Georgist proposals. Georgism is a radical economic philosophy that amounts to the nationalization of land, not improvements, by taxing the entirety of land rent. In the context of Russia, the state would lease land to private farmers, rather than grant them ownership. Georgism benefits from some of the allocative efficiency aspects of the market economy, but retains the egalitarian benefits of social ownership.[25] When another survey questioned more than 2,500 urban and rural dwellers as to which form of farming would best provide the country with food, the Georgist solution received significant support. A relatively small 26% answered "individual peasant farming," while the left-leaning respondents split between farming on land leased from the state (25%), and collective farming (33%).[26] Despite strong rural sentiment in favor of non-capitalist systems of land tenure, powerful local and international interests, including the IMF, resolutely opposed Georgism and stopped it in Russia and almost all of the emerging Eastern European countries by threatening to withdraw loans and capital investments.

Privatization of land and housing in the new republics tends to favor the richer elements of society, such as former black marketeers and the professional and managerial elite. This wealthy class is known as the *nomenklaturnaia*, and the privatization process is known as the *nomenklaturnaia privatizatsiia*. Though not representative of Russia as a whole, urban reform in Moscow illustrates how the elite can skim the cream from the privatization process. During the early stages, high Moscow officials made arrangements with joint ventures and other commercial structures that they co-owned to purchase and lease prime residential property and land in the city center. By the time poorer Muscovites attempted to buy the lands with state-distributed privatization vouchers, speculators with inside information had snatched up all the best properties.

In Latvia, Lithuania, Estonia, Czechoslovakia, and other Eastern European countries, all integrated into the Soviet bloc after World War II, the process is even more skewed. Their respective governments, especially in Estonia and Lithuania, are taking nationalized land and housing from residents and farmers to return it to '40s- and '50s-era landlords.[27] This threatens to dispossess large numbers of residents, cost the financially strapped governments large sums of money, and cause further cuts in already butchered social services and wages. In May 1995, Poland estimated that its program of returning land to landlords had cost $237 million.[28]

The poor in Eastern Europe must ultimately pay the costs of privatization, both through taxes and the loss of land. These policies will further force impoverished Eastern Europeans into destitution and increase the need to seek routes of economic direct action. As initial shocks of economic "liberalization" urged by organizations such as the World Bank, IMF, and GATT have caused social services to be cut, living standards to fall, and inequitable distribution and unemployment to increase, people become more desperate. Xabier Gorostiaga at the Central American University in Managua predicts a rapid "Latin Americanization" of Eastern Europe, which "could easily be transformed into an area of natural resources and cheap labor for further development in Western Europe and the rest of the North."[29] Thus a class hierarchy is emerging from Eastern European real estate deals, composed of new entrepreneurs and *nomenklatura*, sharpening divisions between rich and poor.[30] If the social movements in Eastern Europe react to the trends of privatization and future conglomeration of land and housing assets as they have in Latin America, we can expect an incipient squatting and possibly even land occupation movement to emerge.

Already in the early '90s, the main locale of German squatting shifted from West to East Berlin, where about 1,500 squatters occupied more than 100 large tenement buildings in the fall of 1990.[31] In Moscow, a campaign flourished in 1996 to save a squatted apartment called Bulgakov House from eviction by a development company that wanted to build luxury offices. Estimates of the number of homeless in Moscow, an unknown phenomenon prior to privatization, sometimes exceed 300,000, including about 30,000 children.[32] Compared with 25,000 government shelter beds in New York City, Moscow has only 25. In 1996, the city government of Moscow spent $4.5 million to deport 6,000 homeless rural immigrants back to their rural and privatized homelands.[33] If the supposed economic benefits of privatization in Russia do not reach the lower economic strata soon, their extreme situation will likely lead to increasing unrest.

In Albania, a militant squatting movement has begun to emerge. On February 1, 1996, police in the capital city of Tirana evicted 30 families from apartments they had occupied for four years. Two protesters and two police were injured during the battle, which pitted protesters on rooftops, throwing bricks and rocks against assaulting police, who pelted demonstrators with water cannons.[34] Squatter settlements similar to the Third World are also beginning to emerge in ever-widening rings around Tirana. In one squatter campaign for running water and electricity reported in July 1997, squatters fought police and then kidnapped a prominent politician. This led to a settlement that now provides electricity and sporadic infusions of public water.[35] The massive "ethnic cleansing" of Kosovo in 1999 and the resulting exodus of first Albanians and then Serbians has drastically increased the housing pressures, as well as the development of squatter settlements in neighboring regions.

Another factor leading to greater conflict in almost every region of the world is increasing concentration of wealth. As wealth to a large extent determines political power, concentration of wealth has an exponential impact not only on the pocketbooks of poor people, but on their ability to regain that wealth through normal channels of political change. The concentration of wealth and capital makes it more difficult than ever to lift oneself up by the traditional bootstraps of hard work and populist political parties. So, on a very broad level, since the concentration of wealth is increasing worldwide, we can expect a renewed search for alternative routes to subsistence. With traditional routes of electoral change increasingly blocked by campaign donations and other forms of influence by the wealthy, we can expect an increasing intensity and frequency of economic direct action in general.

As these social movements grow and thereby experience increased success, they can also expect increased repression. The loss of international influence from the Soviet Union, Eastern Bloc, and, to a lesser extent, the non-aligned movement, has meant the collapse of a "counterbalance of sorts," according to Gorostiaga, "that permitted a geopolitical space and a rear guard of support for changes in the South."[36] This "geopolitical space" meant pro-land reform governments had breathing room to a greater or lesser extent. For example, Allende in Chile, Echeverría in Mexico, and the Sandinistas in Nicaragua all tacitly approved peasant land occupations. Allende and Echeverría fell during the Cold War stalemate, but the end of any Soviet protection or trade privileges to pro-land reform governments such as Nicaragua and Cuba, and the increasing influence of World Bank and IMF economics on almost all Third World governments, means greater repression for land struggles in the South. Neoliberal economics and centrist governments may enhance development of direct action movements in the North. But as noted in chapter five, repression in response to greater agitation could lead activists to take up other, and possibly more violent, methods of struggle. The better alternative is to immediately improve the access of people around the world to employment and housing through the organization of strong and strictly nonviolent movements.

Components of Change

Regardless of repression and setbacks, the landless and homeless continue to struggle. Cycles of occupation, repression, and reoccupation in the most highly active land occupation zones, such as Central and South America, recur every five or ten years, indicating an incredible willingness on the part of movement participants to face adversity and the strong pressure they feel for changing their situations. This continual struggle shows that the current inequitable distribution of land and housing, though widely accepted by elected governments and even public opinion worldwide, is strongly disputed on an operational level by people with the short end of the stick. Yet the power that large nations possess jointly with local elites to support right-wing coups and counter-revolutionary forces, to withhold economic assistance through structural adjustment plans, and to embargo leftist countries, threatens the ability of even elected socialist governments to support large movements for resource redistribution.

How can movements overcome this international dynamic that seems to guarantee repression? Is it possible, distant as it may seem, for land and housing campaigns to organize viable, joint international coalitions? Surely such coalitions would have to include more than just land and housing movements. To fight effectively, alliances would have to include many types of social movements drawn from around the globe.

Perhaps the small percentage of land that the counter-reforms in Chile, Portugal, and Nicaragua have left to original occupiers indicates a two-steps-forward, one-step-back model of social change. Such a model would dispense with the need to create broad international alliances and concentrate social movement efforts on making local connections with people in their neighborhoods. Each struggle, though repressed and forced into tactical retreat, leaves a core concession. Adding these concessions over time amounts to significant social change over long historical periods.

Social movements have chosen from past successful models of social change, created new indigenous forms unique to their environment, and combined models to suit their particular circumstances. This book presents some of the creative strategies of land and housing activists and some of the reasons that squatters and rent strikers break the law to better their living conditions. It suggests the vast extent of land and housing direct action and reviews the history of failure and success. It examines some of the basic arguments in favor of squatting that past movements have developed for hundreds of years. In sum, it shows how squatting and rent strikes have succeeded in their goals.

Many of the activists featured in this book want a world with a more egalitarian distribution of wealth, where society has compassion for the hungry and homeless, where an economic system saves rather than condemns 60,000 people a day to death by starvation and malnutrition-related disease. They see direct action as one of the most effective ways to make change, not only for land and housing movements, but for all social movements. Ultimately change comes not from single activists, but from people working together, not in one movement, but in the combination of many movements into a coalition.

The statistics on the distribution of land and housing make it clear that the current ownership and market structures that govern the distribution of land and housing do not achieve the goals of allocative efficiency and egalitarian distribution. Exactly how a more efficient structure might look and the particular reforms required to move society toward that structure have not been a primary part of this book. For housing in the Northern, rich nations, these reforms will include a strengthening of rent control, public housing provision, rent vouchers and certificates, and nonprofit, low-income housing providers. Third World nations will also need a greater public role for housing provision: the transfer of ownership of squatted lands from owners to squatters through purchase or otherwise, increased security of tenure, utility service provision to squatter settlements, and slum improvement measures. Rural areas of the Third World also require major legislation to halt the erosion of small farming and slow the increase in landlessness and rural-to-urban migration. This will require an end to takeovers of agricultural markets in Third World countries by subsidized Western exports, a reinvigoration of lapsed redistributive land reform, and enforcement of land reforms that already have workable laws, such as those in Brazil. Strengthening the small farmer will require increased provision of microcredit schemes, as in Bangladesh, and increased technical support for farmers. A rational agricultural system will require a strengthening of the agrarian "social function" concept: land use must have a function, whether for environmental, food security, or other purposes. If the market is not allocating land to its best function, for example, if agricultural land is left vacant beyond the time it should be left fallow, it should be reassigned to owners who will use it most efficiently for production.

The details of these broad policy goals are beyond the scope of this book, but political strategies for achieving them have been central to its analysis. Compared to the broad goals outlined above, the goals and strategies of land and housing campaigns may, at first glance, seem immediate, local, and sporadic. Peasants fight for a particular 400 hectares, tenants fight their landlord for heating in Pittsburgh, or an indigenous tribe resists cattle interests from polluting a particular stream that runs through a particular forest in Colombia. However immediate and localized these campaigns may seem, even when they involve only a few dozen people and do not articulate broad policy goals, together they bring tremendous pressure for changes in national and international policies. These changes in policy were clearly apparent in response to urban riots and rent strikes during the '60s and to militant Native American activism in the '70s. Effective agrarian reform policies from the '60s until the '80s also had as a primary cause militant land occupations and broader unrest. Institutionalization of radical reforms through positive legislation caused the solidification of many grass-roots demands, but also created a power vacuum where the radical popular movements used to be. As these movements institutionalized their demands, their grass-roots base disappeared to some extent. By the '80s and '90s, neoliberal policy advocates were able to take advantage of a lack of grass-roots opposition to begin a reversal of many progressive gains of the previous decades. Advocates of progressive policy have begun to recognize this need to focus on regaining a mass and militant political base. As Harold Simon, Executive Director of the National Institute for Housing, puts it, "We have the resources to provide housing for everybody in this nation, now we need the political will."[37]

To gain this political will, grass-roots activists and non-governmental organizations that promote progressive policy need to reconnect their efforts. In particular, policy advocates need to make a conscious effort to advocate for and support nascent forms of direct action. Likewise, activist groups can multiply the power of their actions tremendously by synchronizing their direct action move-

ments with non-governmental organizations and policy advocates who are attempting to change the broad laws and international economic structures that will
significantly improve the position not just of those in a particular campaign, but of
all those in a similar class that would benefit from making that campaign symbol-
ize a broader movement.

Martin Wolpold, Latin America coordinator for FIAN-International, notes
that the 1996 World Food Summit in Rome produced a plan of action that included a commitment by the international community to promote agrarian reform
policy and access to productive resources for sectors of society at risk of malnutrition. But there has been little or no response in practical policy. "That is why we
have to globalize the national struggles of many peasant movements and human
rights advocates," argues Wolpold, using the example of Via Campesina, an international coalition of 73 peasant movements that includes the largest movements in
Brazil, the Philippines, and India. "We have to strengthen social movements, civil
society actors, and non-governmental organizations all over the world who are
struggling for the goal of agrarian reform," Wolpold explains. "We must start with
the ongoing processes because we can observe that in many countries there are
strong movements for a different agricultural policy." Actually putting agrarian reforms into place will also require coalition with broader progressive campaigns.
"Movements regarding gender, the environment, human rights, and other public
interests reach other sectors of society than the peasants," according to Wolpold.
"Peasants need the solidarity of the whole society, and need to explain that the
agrarian issue is a problem of the whole society as such."[38]

What is true for agrarian reform movements is also true for indigenous and
housing movements. To attain the political power necessary for the institution of
massive and effective reforms will require the coalition of numerous direct action
and public policy groups, as well as their unification behind a cogent set of reform
proposals. Only with such a unified and activist approach will progressives actually begin to see government making the necessary reforms.

The actions that individuals and movements take now will determine
whether future land and housing movements have the power to instigate government action. As the Honduran land occupation leader Elvia Alvarado reminds us:
"I hate to offend you, but we won't get anywhere by just writing and reading
books.... The important thing is for you to do something."[39]

Notes

Introduction

1. The families occupied a total of 12,800 hectares.

2. Nicaragua Solidarity Network of Greater New York. "Massive Land Occupations in Southern Brazil." *Weekly News Update on the Americas*, no. 423 (3/8/98), p. 2.

3. Kinzer, Stephen. "At 25, the Hippies' 'Free City' Isn't So Carefree." *New York Times*, 5/16/96, p. A4. While I found the *New York Times* coverage of squatter issues better on average than that of other U.S. dailies, the headlines tend to be far more conservative than the articles warrant. This very positive article on Christiania's achievements, accompanied by a photograph of a smiling squatter surrounded by children's tricycles, is in stark contrast to its headline.

4. For a description of "right to roam" movements in Britain, see Rebecca Solnit's forthcoming book on the history of walking.

5. Some of the works that denounce land ownership and promote land and housing direct action are Ambrose of Milan's *De Nabuthe Jezraelita* (386 A.D.), William Ogilvie's *Right of Property in Land* (1781), Thomas Paine's *Agrarian Justice* (1795), the many 18th-century works by the humorous pamphleteer Thomas Spence, Pierre Joseph Proudhon's *What is Property?* (1840), John Stuart Mill's *Principles of Political Economy* (1848), Leo Tolstoy's pamphlet *Slavery of Our Times* (1900), Ralph Waldo Emerson's poem "Hamatreya" (1876), Thomas Ainge Devyr's brilliant and little-known, self-published *Odd Book of the Nineteenth Century* (1882), Alfred Russel Wallace's *Land Nationalisation* (1882), Charles Wicksteed's *Land for the People* (1885), Mark Twain's sarcastic "Archimedes" (1889), Samuel Thackeray's *Land and the Community* (1889), Hamlin Garland's short story "Under the Lion's Paw" (1891), Max Hirsch's *Democracy and Socialism* (1901), Edmund Vance Cooke's poem "Uncivilized" (1903), Robert Frost's "Mending Wall" (1914), Pablo Neruda's *Canto General* (1950), Vinoba Bhave's writings after Mahatma Gandhi's death in 1948, Jeremias Montemayor's *Ours to Share* (1966), and Francisco Julião's *Cambão* (1968). See the suggested reading list for bibliographic information.

6. Pleskovic, Boris. "Squatter Housing in Yugoslavia." In *Spontaneous Shelter: International Perspectives and Prospects*. Carl V. Patton, ed. Philadelphia: Temple University Press, 1988, p. 282.

7. Gullickson, Ted. Interview with the author. San Francisco, 6/12/95.

8. United Nations Development Programme. *Human Development Report 1993*. New York: Oxford University Press, 1993, p. 169.

9. Wilkie, James W., and Carlos Alberto Contreras. *Statistical Abstract of Latin America,* vol. 29, part 1. Los Angeles: UCLA Latin American Center Publications, 1992, p. 34.

10. Paige, Jeffery M. *Agrarian Revolution: Social Movements and Export Agriculture in the Underdeveloped World.* New York: Free Press, 1975, p. 165.

11. Collins, Joseph. *Nicaragua: What Difference Could a Revolution Make? Food and Farming in the New Nicaragua.* New York: Grove Press, 1986, p. 22.

12. Brockett, Charles D. *Land, Power, and Poverty: Agrarian Transformation and Political Conflict in Central America.* Boston: Unwin Hyman, 1990, p. 209.

13. Bermeo, Nancy Gina. *The Revolution within the Revolution: Workers' Control in Rural Portugal.* Princeton: Princeton University Press, 1986, pp. 4, 5, 103.

14. Farnsworth, Clyde H. "Ontario's Indian's Death Is An Issue that Won't Die." *New York Times,* 6/26/96, p. A4.

15. United Nations Department of Economics and Social Affairs. *World Housing Survey 1974: An Overview of the State of Housing, Building and Planning within Human Settlements.* New York: United Nations, 1976, p. 28.

16. United Nations Centre for Human Settlement. *Shelter: From Projects to National Strategies.* New York: United Nations, 1990; Hanley, Charles J. "Urbanized Planet Ahead." San Francisco Examiner, 5/26/96, p. A14. According to the the 1990 report, an estimated 1 billion people either lived under conditions of inadequate shelter or had no shelter at all. Total population growth between 1990 and 1996 was 9.6% (Wright, John W. *The Universal Almanac 1996.* Kansas City, MO: Andrews and McMeel, 1996, pp. 353-354). Compare total population growth with the 10% growth of inadequate shelter between 1990 and 1996, and it becomes evident that the rate of shelterlessness is slowly but surely exceeding the rate of population growth (0.4%). This is a significant percentage considering that it suggests that 400,000 more people became inadequately sheltered between 1990 and 1996 than was attributable to population growth.

17. Crossette, Barbara. "Hope, and Pragmatism, for U.N. Cities Conference." *New York Times,* 6/3/96, p. A3.

18. Pleskovic's essay documents the process of squatter expansion, government response, and squatter success. The appropriateness of Pleskovic's term "squatting" for the phenomenon of *crne gradnje,* or "black housing," in Yugoslavia is debatable, since "squatters" in Yugoslavia usually owned the land on which they built. The laws that they violated were not related to trespass, but rather to building codes and zoning regulations. However, because the common definition of property is "that which belongs exclusively to one" (Black, Henry Campbell. *Black's Law Dictionary,* Fifth Edition. St. Paul, MN: West Publishing, 1979, p. 1095), the imposition of regulations on its use could be considered expropriation of property, a gathering of land unto the state. In the context of environmental regulations, this concept is a much-debated one. If accepted for theoretical purposes in the case of Yugoslavia, then Yugoslavians who defied regulations were in a sense "squatting" public land. Rhetorical convolutions aside, the practical effect of squatting and *crne gradnje* were the same: both were subject to forced eviction and bulldozers.

19. Rohter, Larry. "Cuba's Unwanted Refugees: Squatters in Havana." *New York Times,* 10/20/97, p. A6.

20. Cited in Glasser, Irene. *Homelessness in Global Perspective.* New York: G.K. Hall, 1994, p. 101.

21. Glasser, p. 101.

22. Interview with Werner Sewing. "Alternative Politics in West Germany." *Our Generation,* vol. 16, no. 2, Mar. 1984, p. 49. Also see Mayer, Margit. "The Career of Urban Social Movements in West Germany." In *Mobilizing the Community: Local Politics in the Era of the Global City.* Robert Fisher and Joseph Kling, eds. Urban Affairs Annual Review, vol. 41. Newbury Park, CA: Sage Publications, 1993, pp. 158, 167.

23. Cited in *New Internationalist*, vol. 285, Nov. 1996, p. 12.

24. Widrow, Woody. Letter to the author. 8/19/96.

25. Ichiyo, Muto. "For an Alliance of Hope." In *Global Visions: Beyond the New World Order.* Jeremy Brecher, John Brown Childs, and Jill Cutler, eds. Boston: South End Press, 1993, p. 161.

Chapter 1: Homes Not Jails

1. Freemantle, Tony. "Hoping to Be Home Free: Urban Guerrillas 'Liberate' Abandoned Housing for Use by The Homeless." *Houston Chronicle*, 4/4/93, p. 22A.

2. Freemantle.

3. Graham, Jeremy. Interview with the author. San Francisco. 4/9/97.

4. Boston Emergency Shelter Commission. *City of Boston Homeless Census 1996-1997.*

5. Homes Not Jails, Boston. press release, 5/10/97, p. 2.

6. All quotes from HNJ members in this chapter are from interviews the author conducted in San Francisco on the following dates:
Anonymous: 4/22/97
Cristian: 4/10/97
Whirlwind Dreamer: 4/21/97
Eric: 4/14/97
Jeremy Graham: 4/9/97
Ted Gullickson: 4/14/97 and 7/21/97
Chance Martin: 4/9/97
Connie Morganstern: 4/11/97
Mara Raider: 4/22/97
Miguel Wooding: 7/27/97

7. Voltaire, Philip Stanhope, Earl of Chesterfield, and Tryon Edwards. Cited in Adams, Franklin Pierce, ed. *FPA Book of Quotations.* New York: Funk and Wagnalls, 1952, p. 171.

8. Spence, Jan. "Homes Not Jails Takes Over a Long-Neglected House." *Street Spirit*, Oct. 1995, p. 2.

9. Cothran, George. "Homes Not Jails: Squatters' Group Gets Off Ground." *SF Weekly*, 12/2/92, p. 6.

10. Dietz, David. "S.F. Mayor Says the Homeless Can't Occupy Empty Buildings." *San Francisco Chronicle* (East Bay Edition), 1/5/93, p. A14.

11. "Squatter Takeover of Ben Hur Building Prompts City to Consider Use of Site for Housing." *Polk Street Express*, Jul. 1993, p. 1.

12. Galvin, Sister Bernie, Congregation of Divine Providence. "Position Paper on the Presidio Wherry Housing: Correspondence to Members of the Presidio Trust." San Francisco: Religious Witness with Homeless People, 7/25/97.

13. Hinkle, Warren. *Independent* (San Francisco). 1996.

14. In addition to the national media attention already mentioned, HNJ has gotten coverage in the *New York Times,* 11/28/97, p. A18.

Chapter 2: Battling the Banana Baron

1. Boudreaux, Richard. "Troops Sent to Help End Banana Strike." *Los Angeles Times*, 8/6/90, p. A12; "Honduras Banana Strike." *Wall Street Journal*, 8/1/90, p. A12; "Banana Workers Back on Job." *Wall Street Journal*, 8/8/90, p. A8.

2. "Shutdown at Banana Farms to Result in Quarterly Loss." *Wall Street Journal*, 10/11/94, p. B10; "Chiquita Sees Quarterly Loss." *New York Times*, 10/11/94, p. D16; Rohter, Larry. "Where Banana is King, a Land Revolt." *New York Times*, 7/22/96, p. A4; Owens, Rev. Joseph. Letter to Fathers Leo Klein, Ben Urmston, and Michael Graham. 7/27/95. Reverend Owens is a Jesuit priest and radio journalist who has lived in El Progresso, a town near Tacamiche, for over a dozen years. He ministers to the banana workers.

3. All quotes from Miguel Rodriguez in this chapter are from a telephone interview conducted by the author on 8/16/96.

4. Rohter. "Where Banana is King, a Land Revolt."

5. Owens, Rev. Joseph. Interview with the author. 11/10/96.

6. Harmon, Patrick. Unpublished paper. Harmon was a Cincinnati undergraduate who spent several weeks with the Tacamiches. Cincinnati, OH. 1997. p. 4.

7. *New York Times,* 7/22/96, p. A4.

8. Harmon, Patrick. Personal journal entry. Tacamiche, Honduras. 5/17/96.

9. All quotes from Rev. Joseph Owens in this chapter are from telephone interviews conducted by the author on 11/10/96 and 6/12/98.

10. Alvarado, Elvia. *Don't Be Afraid Gringo: A Honduran Woman Speaks from the Heart.* Medea Benjamin, trans. and ed. New York: Harper and Row, 1989.

11. Windfuhr, Michael. Telephone interview with the author. 11/10/96.

12. "Peasants Ejected From Tacamiche." *Central America UPDATE*, vol. 2, no. 3, 2/1/96.

13. Lindner, Carl H. Letter to Father Benjamin Urmston, S.J. 8/18/95.

14. Wirpsa, Leslie. "Banana Lands Site of Conflict in Honduras: Peasants Face Eviction from Chiquita Farm." National Catholic Reporter. 9/22/95, p. 11

15. "Peasants Ejected From Tacamiche."

16. Lindner.

17. Chiquita Brands International, www.chiquita.com, 8/9/96; Chiquita Brands International. *Shareholder Prospectus.* Cincinnati: Chiquita Brands International, 1996.

18. Karnes, Thomas. "United Fruit in Central America." In *The Central American Crisis Reader.* Robert S. Leiken, ed. New York: Summit Books, 1987, pp. 104-105; McCann, Thomas. *An American Company: The Tragedy of United Fruit.* Henry Scammell, ed. New York: Crown, 1976, p. 15; Mae, Stacy, and Galo Plaza. *The United Fruit Company in Latin America.* New York: National Planning Association, 1958, p. 16.

19. May and Plaza. pp. 10, 16, 19; Barry, Tom. *Roots of Rebellion: Land and Hunger in Central America.* Boston: South End Press, 1987, p. 70.

20. MacCameron, Robert. *Bananas, Labor, and Politics in Honduras, 1954-1963.* Syracuse, NY: Syracuse University Press, 1983.

21. MacCameron, p. 295.

22. Boudreaux.

23. McCann, p. 6; Skidmore, Thomas E., and Peter H. Smith. *Modern Latin America.* New York: Oxford University Press, 1984, p. 308; Barry, pp. 74-76.

24. Chiquita Brands International. *Shareholder Prospectus.*

25. de Cordoba, Jose. "Banana War: Honduras Farm's Sales to a Rival of Chiquita Spark Bitter Struggle." *Wall Street Journal,* 6/7/90, pp. A1, A12; Sanger, David. "Dole at Forefront of Trade Battle to Aid Donor's Banana Empire." *New York Times,* 12/5/95, pp. A1, B9; Schemo, Diana Jean. "U.S. Pesticide Kills Foreign Fruit Pickers' Hopes." *New York Times,* 12/6/95, p. A12; Harrington, Jeff. "A Soldier in the Banana War." *Cincinnati Enquirer.* 12/10/95, pp. H1, H6; Herbert, Bob. "Banana Bully." *New York Times,* 5/13/96, p. A15.

26. Food and Agriculture Organization of the United Nations. *1970 World Census of Agriculture: Analysis and International Comparison of the Results.* Rome: Food and Agriculture Organization of the United Nations, 1981, p. 55.

27. Chiquita Brands International, www.chiquita.com, 8/9/96.

Chapter 3: Philosophy to Squat By

1. Avila, Charles R. *Peasant Theology: Reflections by the Filipino Peasants on their Process of Social Revolution.* Bangkok: World Student Christian Federation Asia Region, 1976, p. 11.

2. Bohlen, Celestine. "Conference on Food Aid Starts in Rome." *New York Times,* 11/13/96, p. A5.

3. Branford, Sue, and Oriel Glock. *The Last Frontier: Fighting Over Land in the Amazon.* London: Zed, 1985, p. 1.

4. Avila, p. 9.

5. Avila, p. 34.

6. "Ganienkeh's 612-Acre Settlement Tiny Compared to Royal Domain of Timber, Mining, Wealthy Interests." *Akwesasne Notes,* Early Spring 1975, p. 39.

7. Associated Press. "McQueen Left Property to Tenants." *San Francisco Chronicle*, 1/1/96, p. E6. McQueen's generosity was similar to that of Leo Tolstoy and his daughter Sonya. In 1912, following Tolstoy's death, Sonya bought the massive Yasnaya Polyana estate from her mother and, per Tolstoy's request, donated it to his former serfs (Asquith, Cynthia. *Married to Tolstoy*. Boston: Houghton Mifflin, 1961, pp. 274-275).

8. Price, Rich, and Jayne Price. "Land Gift Generous." *Santa Cruz Sentinel*, 5/11/96.

9. Sink, Mindy. "Religion and Recreation Clash at Park." *New York Times*, 7/1/96, p. A8.

10. United Nations Development Programme. New York: United Nations, 1992, p. 36; Passell, Peter. "The Rich Are Getting Richer, Etc., and It's Likely to Remain That Way." *New York Times*, 3/28/96, p. C2; Crossette, Barbara. "U.N. Survey Finds World Rich-Poor Gap Widening." *New York Times*, 7/15/96, p. A3.

11. Sinha, Radha. *Landlessness: A Growing Problem*. FAO Economic and Social Development Series, no. 28. Rome: Food and Agriculture Organization of the United Nations, 1984, p. 16. In addition to the rural landless, all those who migrate to urban areas for want of rural employment are also landless, but do not count in the official census because they live in cities. For figures on world homelessness and inadequate shelter, see the introduction.

12. For further information, see *The Tribune: A Women and Development Quarterly*, no. 39 Dec. 1987, a special issue on women, land, and housing.

13. Sinha, p. 20

14. U.S. Congress. *Concentration of Wealth in the United States*. Washington, D.C., 1987.

15. Lewis, James A. *Landownership in the United States, 1978*. Washington, D.C.: United States Department of Agriculture, 1980, p. 15.

16. Comparisons between population and land ownership for races other than Hispanics are less than perfect, since the 1980 population census did not provide figures for non-Hispanic whites, non-Hispanic blacks, or non-Hispanic Indians, and the 1978 land ownership study gave figures for these categories only. However, nearly all Hispanics were included in the white population census category, so one can adjust the population figures to draw a rough comparison.

17. Lewis, p. 18.

18. Fuller, Chet. "I Hear Them Call It the New South." *Black Enterprise*, Nov. 1981, p. 42.

19. United States Department of Commerce. *1990 Census of Housing*. Washington, D.C., 1992.

20. Widener, Mary Lee. "A Hunger for Homeownership." *San Francisco Chronicle*, 7/18/96, p. A21.

21. Geisler, Charles C. "Land and Poverty in the United States: Insights and Oversights." Unpublished paper. Cornell University. 1993

22. Cushman, John. "Ranchers Descend on Capital to Lobby Senate Grazing Bill." *New York Times*, 3/21/96, p. A13.

23. Radin, Margaret Jane. *Reinterpreting Property.* Chicago: University of Chicago Press, 1993, p. 197.

24. See Radin, who made this argument to support rent control and "takings" by the government.

25. Avila, pp. 10-11.

26. Locke, John. *Second Treatise on Civil Government.* Buffalo, NY: Prometheus Books, 1986, p. 20.

27. Radin, p. 112.

28. Branford and Glock, p. 124. Unfortunately, impoverished peasant squatters in Brazil, pushed ever deeper into the Amazon rainforest by expanding cattle ranches, are threatening the livelihood and even the survival of many indigenous communities. The clearing of land by these squatters and the environmental degradation that that entails is being engineered by cattle and land companies that allow the squatters to live on cleared land for a few years, after which the companies evict the squatters, send them to clear more forest, and take the cleared land for company use.

29. Avila, p. 9.

30. Locke, sections 6 and 50. For a critique of Locke's concept of just acquisition in a state of nature, see Radin, p. 48.

31. Nozick, Robert. *Anarchy, State, and Utopia.* New York: Basic Books, 1974, p. 177.

32. Wenke, Robert J. *Patterns in Prehistory: Humankind's First Three Million Years.* New York: Oxford University Press, 1984, p. 443.

33. Cohen, G.A. *Self Ownership, Freedom, and Equality.* Cambridge: Cambridge University Press, 1995, p. 86.

34. Pacari, Nina. "Ecuador: Taking on the Neoliberal Agenda." *NACLA Report on the Americas,* vol. 24, no. 5, Mar./Apr. 1996, p. 25.

35. *Excelsior* (newspaper), 9/835, p. 1. Quoted in Sanderson, Steven E. *Agrarian Populism and the Mexican State: The Struggle for Land in Sonora.* Berkeley: University of California Press, 1981, p. 104.

36. Gray, Charles. "Toward a Nonviolent Economics." Unpublished manuscript. Eugene, Oregon: 1989.

37. Avila, p. 4.

38. Emerson, Ralph Waldo. "Hamatreya" (1876). In *The Norton Anthology of Poetry.* Alexander W. Allison et al., eds. New York: W.W. Norton & Company Inc., 1970.

39. Avila, p. 55.

40. Though some interpreters claim that "Mending Wall" is actually pro-fence, A.R. Coulthard's essay, "Frost's Mending Wall," in *Explicator,* vol. 45, no. 2, Winter 1987, solidly established the critical attitude of the poem to walls and other forms of property.

41. Whitecloud, Jesse John Roe. Interview with the author. Santa Cruz, CA. 7/17/92.

42. Rohter, Larry. "Cuba's Unwanted Refugees: Squatters in Havana." *New York Times,* 10/20/97, p. A6.

43. Ross, John. "Land Battles Continue After Chiapas Uprising." *Latinamerica Press,* 9/29/94, p. 15.

44. Alvarado, p. 69.

45. Abrams, Charles. *Man's Struggle for Shelter in an Urbanizing World.* Cambridge, MA: MIT Press, 1970, pp. 12, 16.

46. Nozick, pp. 149-150.

47. Nozick, p. 293.

48. Nozick, p. 151.

49. Nozick, p. 152.

50. Avila, pp. 9-10.

51. See, for example, Churchill, Ward. *Struggle for the Land: Indigenous Resistance to Genocide, Ecocide and Expropriation in Contemporary North America.* Monroe, ME: Common Courage Press, 1993.

52. Rousseau, Jean-Jacques. *Discourse on the Origin and Foundation of Inequality Among Mankind.* New York: Washington Square Press, 1971, pp. 225-226.

53. Tacamiche plantation worker paraphrased in the journal of Pat Harmon. 5/16/96.

54. George, Henry. *Progress and Poverty: An Inquiry into the Cause of Industrial Depressions and of Increase of Want with Increase of Wealth.* New York: Robert Schalkenbach Foundation, 1948, p. 370.

55. George, p. 372.

56. Epstein, Richard. *Takings: Private Property and the Power of Eminent Domain.* Cambridge, MA: Harvard University Press, 1985, p. 347.

57. Lindner, Carl H. Letter to Father Benjamin Urmston, S.J. 8/18/95. p. 2.

58. Schwartzman, Stephan, Ana Valéria Araújo and Paulo Pankararú. "The Legal Battle Over Indigenous Land Rights." *NACLA Report on the Americas,* vol. 29, no. 5, Mar./Apr. 1996.

59. Epstein, p. 349.

60. Bohlen, Celestine. "Conference on Food Aid Starts in Rome." *New York Times,* 11/13/96, p. A12; "U.N. Report Shows Billion Adults Unemployed or Underemployed." *New York Times,* 11/26/96, p. A6.

61. Radin, p. 232.

62. Avila, p. 10.

63. Nozick, pp. 152-153.

64. Hirsch, Eric, and Peter Wood. "Squatting in New York City: Justification and Strategy." *Review of Law and Social Change,* vol. 16, no. 4, 1987-1988. Reprinted in *The Homeless: Opposing Viewpoints.* Lisa Orr, ed. San Diego: Greenhaven Press, 1990, p 176.

65. Aisha Stone. Interview with the author. San Diego. 7/10/93.

66. Cited in Irene Glasser. *Homelessness in Global Perspective.* New York: G.K. Hall & Co., 1994, p. 86.

67. "Squatters' Rights vs. City Rights." *New York Times,* 7/14/95, p. A10.

68. Weber, Peter. "Scenes from Squatting Life." *National Review,* 2/27/87. Reprinted in Orr, p. 185.

69. Fortunate Eagle, Adam. *Alcatraz! Alcatraz! The Indian Occupation of 1969-1971.* Berkeley: Heyday Books, 1992, p. 38.

70. Van Savage, Rick. "Defending the Indefensible: Thoughts on the Politics of Squatting in New York City." *Free Society,* vol. 2, no. 4, Winter 1995, p. 26.

71. Ogilvie, William. *Birthright in Land: An Essay on the Right of Property in Land.* (1782) New York: Augustus M. Kelley Publishers, 1970, pp. 7-18.

Chapter 4: Tell It to The Judge

1. Domhoff, William. *The Power Elite and the State: How Policy is Made in America.* New York: Aldine de Gruyter, 1990, pp. 260-261.

2. Baird, Vanessa. "Our Earth, Our Home: Land Rights and Wrongs." *New Internationalist,* Nov. 1987, p. 5.

3. Capek, Stella M., and John Gilderbloom. *Community versus Commodity: Tenants and the American City.* Albany: State University of New York Press, 1992, pp. 19-20.

4. Van Savage, Rick. "Defending the Indefensible: Thoughts on the Politics of Squatting in New York City." *Free Society,* vol. 2, no. 4, Winter 1995, p. 26.

5. Singh, Inderjit. World Bank. *Land and Labor in South Asia.* Washington, D.C.: World Bank, 1988, p. ix.

6. Menchú, Rigoberta. *I, Rigoberta Menchú: An Indian Woman in Guatemala.* New York: Verso, 1992, p. 26. Whether or not anthropologist David Stoll's argument that some particulars of Menchú's story are fabricated, her stories roughly describe the experience of thousands of people in Guatemala during its brutal civil war. See Stoll, David. *Rigoberta Menchú and the Story of All Poor Guatemalans.* Boulder: Westview Press, 1999.

7. Menchú, p. 105.

8. Milligan, Amanda. "Bangladesh's Landless Hit Back: The Wretched of the Earth." *Inside Asia,* Apr. 1986, pp. 43-44.

9. Inter-American Development Bank. *Working Women in Latin America.* Economic and Social Progress in Latin America: 1990 Progress Report. Washington, D.C., Oct. 1990, p. 237.

10. MacDonald, Geoffrey. "Mexicano Victory in Tierra Amarilla Land-Rights Struggle." *Guardian,* 3/28/90, p. 7.

11. Chamberlain, C.W., and H.F. Moorhouse. "Lower Class Attitudes Towards the British Political System. *Sociological Review,* Nov. 1974, p. 514.

12. Broilo, Elda. Interview with the author. Santa Cruz, CA, 5/1/91.

13. Union des Campesinos de Queretaro (UCEQ). Letter. *Industrial Worker,* Apr. 1977, p. 2.

14. Neagu, George. "Tenant Power in Public Housing—the East Park Manor Rent Strike." In *Tenants and the Urban Housing Crisis.* Stephan Burghardt, ed. Dexter, Michigan: New Press, 1972, p. 35.

15. Bunster, Ximena. "The Emergence of a Mapuche Leader: Chile." In *Sex and Class in Latin America: Women's Perspectives on Politics, Economics and the Family in the Third World.* June Nash and Helen Icken Safa, eds. South Hadley, Massachusetts: J.E. Bergin, 1980, pp. 310-311.

16. Cited in Blackstock, Nelson. "Villa Sin Miedo: A Village Without Fear." *Militant,* 11/20/81, p. 18.

17. Lawson, Ronald, and Stephen E. Barton. "Sex Roles in Social Movements: A Case Study of the Tenant Movement in New York City." In *Women and Social Protest.* Gwida West and Rhoda Lois Blumberg, eds. New York: Oxford University Press, 1990, pp. 41-56.

18. Lawson and Barton, p. 52.

19. Lawson and Barton, pp. 52-53.

20. Apter, David E. and Nagaya Sawa. *Against the State: Politics and Social Protest in Japan.* Cambridge, MA: Harvard University Press, 1984, p. 191.

21. Apter and Sawa, p. 192.

22. Naison, Mark D. "The Rent Strikes in New York." In Burghardt.

23. Atlas, John, Ron Atlas, and Phyllis Salowe-Kaye. "Negotiating with Landlords, Part 1." *Shelterforce*, Mar. 1976, p. 4.

24. "Mountain-Moving in the Bronx." *Mother Jones,* Apr. 1976, pp. 5-6.

25. Atlas, John.

26. Camacho, Daniel. "Latin America: A Society in Motion." In *New Social Movements in the South: Empowering People.* Ponna Wignaraja, ed. London: Zed Books, 1993, p. 46.

27. Cambridge Tenants Organizing Committee. "Where We Stand." *Vocations for Social Change,* Mar. 1972, p. 26.

28. Sharp, Gene. *Social Power and Political Freedom.* Boston: Porter Sargent, 1980, p. 301.

29. Barton, Stephen E. "The Urban Housing Problem: Marxist Theory and Community Organizing." *Review of Radical Political Economics*, vol. 9, no. 4, Winter 1977, p. 27.

30. Rosenbaum, Linda. "Day We Stopped the Sheriff." *This Magazine,* vol. 14, no. 5, Sept./Oct. 1980, pp. 20-24, 26.

31. Broilo, Elda. Interview with the author. Santa Cruz, CA. 5/1/91.

32. Jaimes, M. Annette. "Pit River Indian Claim Dispute in Northern California." In *Critical Issues in Native North America*, vol. 2. Ward Churchill, ed. IWGIA Document no. 68. Copenhagen: International Work Group for Indigenous Affairs, 1991, p. 82.

33. Churchill, Ward. *Struggle for the Land: Indigenous Resistance to Genocide, Ecocide and Expropriation in Contemporary North America.* Monroe, ME: Common Courage Press, 1993. pp. 129-130.

34. Sharp, Gene. *Politics of Nonviolent Action.* Boston: Porter Sargent, 1973, p. 406.

35. Milligan, pp. 43-44.

36. de Janvry, Alain. *Agrarian Question and Reformism in Latin America.* Baltimore: John Hopkins University Press, 1985, p. 206.

37. "Hondurans Battle Landowners." *Guardian*, 11/26/75, p. 13; "Honduras: Struggle for Land." *Guardian*, 6/23/76, p. 13; Brockett, Charles D. "Structure of Political Opportunities and Peasant Mobilization in Central America." In *Social Movements in Latin America*. Jorge I. Domínguez, ed. New York: Garland Publishing, 1994, pp. 261-262.

38. Komisar, Lucy. "Campesino Land Invasions in Honduras." *Dissent*, vol. 32, no. 1, Winter 1985, p. 114.

39. Komisar, pp. 113-114.

40. Glickman, Paul. "Peasants Orchestrate Nationwide Land Grabs." *In These Times*, 5/22/85, p. 10.

41. Komisar, p. 114.

42. See Elvia Alvarado's *Don't Be Afraid Gringo* for an excellent first-hand account of the '80s Honduran land occupations; Benjamin, Medea. "Campesinos: Between Carrot and Stick." *NACLA Report on the Americas*, Jan. 1988, pp. 22-30.

43. For a similar example of agrarian reform between 1961 and 1965 inspired by land occupation , see de Janvry, p. 208; Reed, Jon. "Hondurans Reap a Harvest of Misery." *Guardian*, 4/15/92, p. 9.

44. Lipsky, Michael. *Protest in City Politics: Rent Strikes, Housing and the Power of the Poor.* Chicago: Rand McNally & Company, 1970, p. 153-55.

45. Quoted in Lipsky, p. 157.

46. Lipsky, p. 159.

47. National Tenants Organization. "Rent Strikes." In Burghardt, p. 174.

48. Lipsky, pp. 63, 66.

49. Naison, pp. 26, 29.

50. Naison, p. 26.

51. Lipsky, p. 143.

52. Naison, p. 27.

53. Naison, p. 28.

54. Lipsky, p. 137.

55. Lipsky, p. 142.

56. Lipsky, p. 139.

57. Lawson, Ronald. "Origins and Evolution of a Social Movement Strategy: The Rent Strike in New York City, 1904-1980." *Urban Affairs Quarterly*, vol. 18, no. 3, Mar. 1983, p. 384.

58. Naison, p. 33.

59. Lipsky, p. 142; Naison, p. 30.

60. Naison, p. 31.

61. Cotto, Liliana. "The Rescate Movement: An Alternative Way of Doing Politics." In *Colonial Dilemma: Critical Perspectives on Contemporary Puerto Rico.* Edwin Meléndez and Edgardo Meléndez, eds. Boston: South End Press, 1993, p. 127.

62. Lawson, pp. 371-395.

63. Lawson and Barton, pp. 43-44.

64. Lawson, p. 378.

65. Neagu, pp. 35-46.

66. National Tenants Organization. p. 173.

67. De La Torre, Alfredo. "Entrevista con Mario Cantu—Interview." [Interview with Mario Cantu.] *Caracol*, Dec. 1978, pp. 11-14.

68. Cotto, p. 125.

69. Klaarhamer, Roel. "The Chilean Squatter Movement and the State." In *Urban Social Movements in the Third World.* Frans Schuurman and Ton van Naerssen, eds. London: Routledge, 1989, pp. 180.

Chapter 5: Violence and Cycles of Reform

1. Goldin, Frances. "Tenants Movement." *Vocations for Social Change*, Mar. 1972, p. 25.

2. "Third Offensive Against Tangwena." *Peace News*, 8/4/72, p. 2.

3. Norris, Alexander. "Patrões and Pistoleiros: Brazil's Land Barons Refine Tactics." *New Internationalist*, Oct. 1992, p. 31.

4. Thomson, Marilyn. *Women of El Salvador: The Price of Freedom.* London: Zed Books, 1986, pp. 55-56. The repression testified to by Susana came when, for the first time in 30 years, many rural trade unions occupied lands in 1977 and 1978. The military was responding to armed insurrection and broad-based civil unrest, not simply land occupation.

5. Alvarado, p. 36.

6. "'Land to the Landless' Convulses India." *People's World*, 8/29/70, p. 6.

7. Fernandez, Ronald. *Prisoners of Colonialism: The Struggle for Justice in Puerto Rico.* Monroe, ME: Common Courage, 1994, pp. 319-320.

8. "Guarani: The Kaiowá Prepare to Die for Their Land Rights." *Nonviolent Activist*, May 1994, p. 17.

9. Churchill, Ward. *Indians Are Us? Culture and Genocide in Native North America.* Monroe, ME: Common Courage Press, 1994, pp. 178, 191.

10. *Indígena,* Spring 1974; Churchill, Ward, and Winona LaDuke. "Native America: The Political Economy of Radioactive Colonialism." *Insurgent Sociologist,* vol. 13, no. 5, Spring 1986, p. 71.

11. "Sovereignty of Ganienkeh." *Indígena,* Winter 1974-75, p. 12.

12. "Indians Ask Protection, Get Clubs, Gassed Instead." *Akwesasne Notes,* Oct. 1970, pp. 1-5; "Revolt in Washington State." *El Grito del Norte,* 9/16/70, pp. 3, 9; *El Grito del Norte,* 12/7/71.

13. Desroches, Leonard. "Oil, Golf Courses and War: Discovering Weapons of the Spirit." *Reconciliation International,* Winter 1991-92, p. 9.

14. "People's Park." *Berkeley Monitor,* 5/3/69, p. 8; "Outcry! An Eight-Page Supplement on the War for People's Park." *Indianapolis Free Press,* 5/30/69; Goldberg, Art. "The Battle of Berkeley." *Guardian,* 6/7/69, pp. 3, 8; La Simpatica. "One Dead, 60 Wounded, 1000 Jailed, City Gassed in Fight for Land." *El Grito del Norte,* 6/14/69, pp. 8, 16; "Police Riot in People's Park Annex." *Berkeley Monitor,* 6/14/69, pp. 1, 4; Funstenberg, Michael. "Springtime in Berkeley: People's Park Revisited." *Berkeley Monitor,* 5/29/71, p. 5; Kehler, Randy. "People's Park 1969." *Win,* 6/1/81, pp. 5-6.

15. People's Park Emergency Bulletin, 8/4/91, flyer; "Defend and Support People's Park." *Uncommon Sense,* Mar. 1992, p. 5; Matzek, Virginia. "People's Park: UC Berkeley's Development Plans Ignite Opposition." Undated flyer, circa 1993.

16. Davidson, Ellen. "N.Y.C. Cops Go Berserk At Park Demo." *Guardian,* 8/17/88, p. 7. The curfew was a city law covering all parks, but activists enjoyed a measure of success when the local Community Board voted to overturn the law for Tompkin's Square Park after the riot. Tompkin's became the only park in the city without a curfew. Until the early '90s, police repeatedly evicted the homeless, who usually returned after a few days (Weinberg, Bill. "New York City's Class War Zone: Police Army Invades Tompkins Square Park." *Guardian,* 7/17/91, pp. 10-11).

17. *Workers World,* 4/20/72.

18. For more on the ways in which geopolitics limit major political and economic change, see Theda Skocpol's structural theories of revolution. "The outcomes of social revolutions have always been powerfully conditioned not only by international politics, but also by the world-economic constraints and opportunities faced by emergent regimes," Skocpol observes in *States and Revolutions: A Comparative Analysis of France, Russia, and China.* Cambridge: Cambridge University Press, 1980, p. 23.

19. Julião, Francisco. *Cambão: The Yoke.* John Butt, trans. Middlesex, England: Penguin Books, 1972. Also see Gene Sharp, *The Politics of Nonviolent Action,* Part II, "The Methods of Nonviolent Action." p. 408.

20. de Janvry, Alain. *Agrarian Question and Reformism in Latin America.* Baltimore: John Hopkins University Press, 1985, p. 219.

21. Bunster, Ximena. "The Emergence of a Mapuche Leader: Chile." In *Sex and Class in Latin America: Women's Perspectives on Politics, Economics and the Family in*

the Third World. June Nash and Helen Icken Safa, eds. South Hadley, Massachusetts: J.E. Bergin, 1980, pp. 308-309.

22. Bermeo, Nancy Gina. "Chile 1970." *The Revolution Within the Revolution: Workers' Control in Rural Portugal*. Princeton: Princeton University Press, 1986, pp. 210-213.

23. Currie, Elliot. "Revolt in Mexico: Peasants Defy Agribusiness." *East Bay Voice*, Feb. 1977, p. 9; Rivas, Cristina. "Mexico: Peasant Land Occupations Shatter Myth of Stability." *Militant*, 12/24/1976, p. 22.

24. The agrarian reform instituted after the Mexican revolution of 1911 ushered in the *ejido* system. Modeled on traditional Indian land tenure, it aimed at communalizing large estates for use by *ejidatarios*. These beneficiaries do not own the land and cannot sell it, but may rent it to others and bequeath it to heirs. President Venustiano Carranza announced the reform in 1915, but, with the exception of President Lázaro Cárdenas in the '30s, it went largely unenforced. The number of *ejidatarios* has declined since the '60s, with fatal cutbacks by the Salinas de Gortari government in the mid-'90s as a condition of the North American Free Trade Agreement (NAFTA). This modern threat to *ejidatarios* helped precipitate the Zapatista rebellion in Chiapas on January 1, 1994, the date on which NAFTA took effect.

25. Townsdin, Carl J. "Peasant Struggles Intensify." *Guardian*, 3/5/75, p. 15.

26. "Armed Mexican Peasants Seize Prime Land." *Guardian*, 10/8/75, p. 12.

27. Gellen, Karen. "Mexico: Peasants Seize Land." *Guardian*, 5/5/76, p. 13.

28. "Mexico: The Rich Inherit the Earth ... But the Poor Are Taking It Back." *Akwesasne Notes*, vol. 8, no. 5, Mid-Winter 76-77, pp. 26-27.

29. "Mexico: The Rich Inherit the Earth ...."

30. "Mexico: The Rich Inherit the Earth ...."

31. *NACLA's Latin America and Empire Report*, Jul. 1976; "Bloody Land War Mounts in Northern Mexico." *Black Panther*, 10/2/76, pp. 19, 22; "Campesinos Continue Agrarian Revolt." *Northwest Passage*, 12/6/76, p. 16; "Mexico: Peasant Land Occupations Shatter Myth of Stability." *Militant*, 12/24/76, p. 22; Wright, Morris. "Mexico Peasant Land Seizures Firm." *Guardian*, 1/12/77, p. 17; "Revolt in Mexico: Peasants Defy Agribusiness." *East Bay Voice*, Feb. 1977, p. 9; Adams, Jane. "Mexico: The Struggle for Land." *Indígena*, Summer 1977, pp. 28, 30; Johnson, Kirsten. "Peasant Struggles in Contemporary Mexico." *Antipode*, vol. 14, no. 3, 1982, pp. 39-50; Skidmore, Thomas E., and Peter H. Smith. *Modern Latin America*. New York: Oxford University Press, 1984, pp. 248-252.

32. van Naerssen, Ton. "Continuity and Change in the Urban Poor Movement of Manila, the Philippines." In *Urban Social Movements in the Third World*. Frans Schuurman and Ton van Naerssen, eds. London: Routledge, 1989, pp. 204-206.

33. Bermeo, pp. 69, 70, 71, 189.

34. Bermeo. p. 78

35. Bermeo, p. 79.

36. Bermeo, p. 199.

37. Bermeo, p. 203.

38. Collins, Joseph. *Nicaragua: What Difference Could a Revolution Make? Food and Farming in the New Nicaragua.* New York: Grove Press, 1986, p. 28.

39. Collins, pp. 32-33.

40. Collins, p. 43.

41. Collins, pp. 70, 76.

42. Collins, p. 81.

43. Collins, p. 247.

44. Collins, p. 147.

45. Collins, pp. 144-147.

46. Collins, p. 148.

47. Collins, p. 206.

48. de Janvry, p. 210.

49. Chomsky, Noam. *Year 501: The Conquest Continues.* Boston: South End Press, 1993, pp. 192, 193.

50. Rohter, Larry. "U.S. Prods Nicaragua on Seized Land." *New York Times*, 7/25/95, p. A4.

51. Preston, Julia. "It's Indians vs. Loggers in Nicaragua." *New York Times*, 6/25/96, p. A8.

52. Caster, Mark. "The Return of Somocismo? The Rise of Arnoldo Alemán." *NACLA Report on the Americas*, vol. 30, no. 2, Sept./Oct. 1996, pp. 6-9; "Nicaragua's New President." *New York Times*, 10/23/96, pp. A3, A18.

53. Sklair, Leslie. "The Struggle Against the Housing Finance Act." *Socialist Register* 1975, p. 273.

54. Sklair, p. 274.

55. According to Sklair, at least in the case of the Tower Hill strike in Kirkby, "the development of solidarity and political education on the estate and outside it" cannot be described as failure (p. 274).

56. Goldberg, p. 8.

57. Gitlin, Todd. *The Sixties: Years of Hope, Days of Rage.* New York: Bantam Books, 1989, p. 358.

58. Freedberg, Louis. "South Africa: Blacks Resist White Force." *Africa News*, 3/12/84, p. 4.

59. Scott, James. *Weapons of the Weak: Everyday Forms of Peasant Resistance.* New Haven: Yale University Press, 1985, p. xvi.

60. Scott, James. *Domination and the Arts of Resistance: Hidden Transcripts.* New Haven: Yale University Press, 1990.

61. Foundation for the Advancement of Illegal Knowledge (ADILKNO). *Cracking the Movement: Squatting Beyond the Media.* Laura Martz, trans. Brooklyn: Autonomedia, 1994, p. 114.

62. Sharp, Gene. *Politics of Nonviolent Action.* Boston: Porter Sargent, 1973, p. 547.

63. "Tenant Organizer Attacked." *Guardian,* 8/11/71, p. 2.

64. "Colombia: Repression in the Cauca." *Indígena,* Summer 1974, p. 1.

65. Mayer, Margit. "The Career of Urban Social Movements in West Germany." In *Mobilizing the Community: Local Politics in the Era of the Global City.* Robert Fisher and Joseph Kling, eds. Urban Affairs Annual Review, vol. 41. Newbury Park, CA: Sage Publications, 1993, p. 154.

66. Guatemala News and Information Bureau. "Guatemala: Peasant Massacre." *NACLA Report on the Americas* Jul. 1978, pp. 44-45; "Guatemala: Peasants, Owners Clash." *Guardian,* 6/14/78, p. 12; Menchú, Rigoberta. *I, Rigoberta Menchú: An Indian Woman in Guatemala.* New York: Verso, 1992.

67. Stoler, Laura Ann. *Capitalism and Confrontation in Sumatra's Plantation Belt, 1870-1979.* New Haven: Yale University Press, 1985, p. 15.

68. V, Hettie. "An Africaner Rebels." In *Lives of Courage: Women for a New South Africa.* Diana E.H. Russell, ed. New York: Basic Books, 1989, pp. 279-295.

69. Schemo, Diana Jean. "Rio Ex-Officer Is Convicted in Massacre of Children." *New York Times,* 5/1/96, p. A5.

70. Weinberg, Bill. "Cops Evict Homeless from 'Dinkinsville' Shantytown." *Guardian.* 10/30/91.

71. Griffin, Nicholas. "Aborigines' Tent Embassy." *Peace News,* 8/4/72, p. 4.

72. Liberation News Service. "Police Assault Rent Strikers in Bridgeport." *Guardian* 6/9/71, p. 7.

73. ADILKNO, p. 114.

74. ADILKNO, p. 121.

75. ADILKNO, p. 123.

76. ADILKNO, p. 123.

77. Branford and Glock, p. 197.

78. "Sovereignty of the Ganienkeh." *Indígena,* Winter 1974-1975, p. 12. Deterrence also allowed the relatively unimpeded growth of London's squatter movement after successful squatter resistance to eviction at Redbridge in 1969. See Bailey, Ron. *The Squatters.* Middlesex: Penguin, 1973, pp. 118-120, 154, 186.

79. Jackson, Frank, ed. *Squatting in West Berlin.* London: Hooligan Press, 1987, p. 8.

80. ADILKNO, p. 68.

81. ADILKNO, p. 70.

82. ADILKNO, p. 78.

83. ADILKNO, pp. 79-100.

84. Liberation News Service. "10,000 Tenants Strike Newark Public Housing." *City Star,* 8/1/73, p. 18.

85. Wolpold, Martin. Telephone interview with the author. 4/6/99.

86. Mayer, pp. 149-170.

87. In 1981, Puerto Rican squatter communities housed a total of 18,000 families (Fauteux, Danielle. "Puerto Rico Squatters Battle Squatters." *Guardian,* 12/16/81, p. 18).

88. Blackstock, Nelson. "Villa Sin Miedo: A Village Without Fear." *Militant,* 11/20/81, p. 18.

89. Fauteux, p. 18

90. Paige, Jeffery M. *Agrarian Revolution: Social Movements and Export Agriculture in the Underdeveloped World.* New York: Free Press, 1975, p. 19.

91. The Zapatistas gain their name from the philosophy of Mexican revolutionary leader Emiliano Zapata who focused his goals on the expropriation of land for indigenous Mexicans.

92. Batt, Kevin. "Violence Erupts in Mexico's Land Wars." *In These Times,* 9/10/80, p. 11.

93. The CNPA named itself after Emiliano Zapata's 1911 land reform decree, the Plan of Ayala (Sanderson, Steven E. *Agrarian Populism and the Mexican State: The Struggle for Land in Sonora.* Berkeley: University of California Press, 1981, p. 62).

94. Fox, Jonathan, and Gustavo Gordillo. "Between State and Market: the Campesinos' Quest for Autonomy." Cornelius, Wayne A., Judith Gentleman, and Peter H. Smith, eds. *Mexico's Alternative Political Futures.* San Diego: Center for U.S.-Mexican Studies, University of California, San Diego, 1989, p. 148.

95. Interview with Subcommander Marcos in *¡Zapatistas! Documents of the New Mexican Revolution.* Brooklyn: Autonomedia, 1994, pp. 150-151.

96. Interview with Major Ana María in *¡Zapatistas!* pp. 228-229. See also Menchú for the description of how an indigenous squatter community turned to guerrilla tactics and hostage-taking in response to repression and hunger.

97. Toledo, Rebecca. "Zapatistas Inspire Strikes, Takeovers." *EZLN E-Mail Reader,* Feb. 1994, p. 3; Antonio García de Léon, lecture at the IberoAmerican University in Mexico City. February 1994. Trans. Centro de Reflexion Teologica. As reprinted in *EZLN E-Mail Reader,* Feb. 1994, pp. 8-11.

98. Lingo, Tracey. "La Lucha Sigue: Understanding the Connections Between Campesino Unions and the Zapatista Rebellion in Chiapas." Unpublished thesis. Reed College, 1997.

99. Thaxton, Ralph. "Mao Zedong, Red *Misérables,* and the Moral Economy of Peasant Rebellion in Modern China." In *Power and Protest in the Countryside: Rural Unrest in Asia, Europe, and Latin America.* Robert P. Weller and Scott E. Guggenheim, eds. Durham, NC: Duke University Press, 1989, p. 149.

100. Boahen, A. Adu. *African Perspectives on Colonialism.* Baltimore: John Hopkins University Press, 1992, p. 65.

101. Palmer, Robin. *Land and Racial Domination in Rhodesia.* Berkeley: University of California Press, 1977, p. 89.

102. Kanogo, Tabitha. *Squatters and the Roots of Mau Mau.* Nairobi: Heinemann, 1987.

103. wa Kinyatti, Maina, ed. Thunder from the Mountains: Mau Mau Patriotic Songs. London: Zed press, 1980, p. 19.

104. Palmer, pp. 70, 244-246.

105. Denoeux, Guilain. *Urban Unrest in the Middle East: A Comparative Study of Informal Networks in Egypt, Iran, and Lebanon.* Albany: State University of New York Press, 1993, p. 211.

106. Rüland, J. "Political Change, Urban Services and Social Movements: Political Participation and Grassroots Politics in Metro Manila." *Public Administration and Development,* vol. 4, pp. 325-333.

107. van Naerssen, Ton. Letter to the author. 7/29/96.

108. Schuurman and van Naerssen, p. 20.

109. Stokes, Susan C. "Politics and Latin America's Urban Poor: Reflections from a Lima Shantytown." *Latin American Research Review,* vol. 26, 1991, pp. 355-35.

110. Capek, Stella M., and John Gilderbloom. *Community versus Commodity: Tenants and the American City.* Albany: State University of New York Press, 1992, pp. 21-22.

111. Vague, Tom. *The Red Army Faction Story, 1963-1993.* Edinburgh: AK Press, 1994, pp. 94, 98.

112. Aust, Stefan. *The Baader-Meinhof Group: The Inside Story of a Phenomenon.* Anthea Bell, trans. London: Bodley Head, 1987, p. 289.

113. Jackson, p. 8.

114. Red Army Faction. "Communiqué on the Assassination of Detlev Rohwedder, President of the Treuhandanstalt, in Düsseldorf on 1 April 1991," and "Communiqué, dated 10 April 1992, Offering to Suspend the RAF's Terrorist Campaign against the German State." Reprinted in Alexander, Yonah, and Dennis A. Pluchinsky. *Europe's Red Terrorists: The Fighting Communist Organizations.* London: Frank Cass and Company, 1992, pp. 83, 88.

115. McClung Lee, Alfred. Terrorism in Northern Ireland. Bayside, NY: General Hall, 1983, p. 94.

116. Some would dispute the use of the term "terrorist group" to identify the FALN, arguing that a term such as "revolutionary group" or "freedom fighters" is more accurate. By using the term "terrorist organization," I do not condemn the FALN, but only differentiate it from revolutionary groups like the FMLN, the Zapatistas, the pre-1979 Sandinistas, and other larger groups that hold territory and can credibly threaten to overthrow the reigning government. In my application of "terrorism" to the FALN, I follow Martha Crenshaw's definition: "the systematic use of unorthodox political violence by small conspiratorial groups with the purpose of manipulating political attitudes rather than physically defeating an enemy.... Terrorism is premeditated and purposeful violence, employed in a struggle for political power" (Crenshaw. *Terrorism, Legitimacy, and Power: The Consequences of Political Violence.* Middletown, Connecticut: Wesleyan University Press, 1983, p. 2). Crenshaw's definition applies to the Boston Tea Party and the French Resistance as much as to the FALN.

117. Fernandez, Ronald. *Prisoners of Colonialism: The Struggle for Justice in Puerto Rico.* Monroe, ME: Common Courage, 1994, p. 174.

118. Fernandez, pp. 173-175.

119. Boahen, pp. 7, 66; Ansprenger, Franz. *The Dissolution of the Colonial Empires.* London: Routledge, 1989, pp. 198-200.

120. Fortunate Eagle, Adam. *Alcatraz! Alcatraz! The Indian Occupation of 1969-1971.* Berkeley: Heyday Books, 1992, p. 147.

121. Fortunate Eagle, p. 150.

122. Greider, William. "U.S. Had Warning of Indian Wrath on Fishing Rights." *Washington Post,* 9/5/70, p. A3

123. Smith, Robert. "Indians Need U.S. Legal Aid, Says Kennedy." *Akwesasne Notes,* Nov. 1970, p. 7.

124. Dewing, Rolland. *Wounded Knee: The Meaning and Significance of the Second Incident.* New York: Irvington Publishers, 1985, p. 350.

125. Fortunate Eagle, p. 150.

126. National Zapatista Liberation Army (Ejército Zapatista Liberación Nacional). "Revolutionary Agrarian Law." *El Despertador Mexicano,* Dec. 1993, reprinted in *Resist,* 1/21/94, pp. 7-10.; Toledo, p. 3.; *Nonviolent Activist,* May 1994.

127. Ross, John. "Land Battles Continue After Chiapas Uprising." *Latinamerica Press,* 9/29/94, p. 15.

128. Ross, p. 15. For a similar example in Bolivia during the 1952 Movimiento Nacional Revolucionaria, see Paige, Jeffery M. *Agrarian Revolution: Social Movements and Export Agriculture in the Underdeveloped World* (New York: Free Press, 1975). According to Paige, "the Bolivian peasantry destroyed the entire system of landed estates in less than a year and a half of concentrated land invasions. Landlords fled to the cities, and most of the countryside passed into the hands of the peasants" (p. 44).

129. Preston, Julia. "Mexico and Insurgent Group Reach Pact on Indian Rights." *New York Times,* 2/15/96, p. A12.

130. Bermeo, p. 9.

131. Eckstein, Susan. "The Impact of Revolution on Social Welfare in Latin America." In *Revolutions: Theoretical, Comparative, and Historical Studies.* Jack A. Gladstone, ed. San Diego: Harcourt Brace Jovanovich, 1986, p. 290.

132. Cited in Joselit, Jenna. "Tenant Strikes of the Early 1900s." *Shelterforce,* Winter 1979, p. 15.

133. Eckstein, Susan. *Power and Popular Protest: Latin American Social Movements.* Berkeley: University of California Press, 1989, p. 15.

134. Collins, p. 27.

135. Claiborne, William. "Officials Act to Break Soweto Rent Boycott." *Washington Post,* 11/19/87, p. A45; Claiborne, William. "Power Cut In Bid to End Rent Strike in Soweto." *Washington Post,* 7/8/88, p. A16. Kraft, Scott. "With Landlord at Door, Strike Becomes Unhinged." *Los Angeles Times,* 7/3/88, pp. 1, 24; Battersby, John D. "Blacks Pressing a Rent Boycott in South Africa." *New York Times* (New York

Late Edition), 2/22/88, pp. A1, A8; Grandino, Marc. "Mass Rent Boycotts." Flyer, Santa Cruz, CA, 1990.

136. Hornsby, Michael. "Inquest to Look at Soweto Violence." *Times* (London), 8/29/86, pp. 1, 5.

137. Chaskelson, Matthew, Karen Jochelson, and Jeremy Seekings. "Rent Boycotts, The State, and the Transformation of the Urban Political Economy in South Africa." *Review of African Political Economy*, vol. 40, Dec. 1987, pp. 47-64; Moeti, Sello. "Resisting the Emergency of Botha's Generals: The Case of Rent Boycotts." *Sechaba*, vol. 21, no. 2, Feb. 1987, pp. 23-28; Press Trust. "A Most Bloody Assault on Soweto Rent Boycott." *Guardian*, 9/10/86, p. 13.

138. Daley, Suzanne. "Country Club in Revolt Over Post-Apartheid Taxes." *New York Times*, 1/8/97, p. A4.

139. Raghavan, Sudarsan. "Rural Black Squatters Battling Homeowners: South Africa's Homeless Problem." *San Francisco Chronicle*, 1/3/96, p. A10.

140. Daley, Suzanne. "South Africa Losing Battle to House Homeless." *New York Times*, 5/3/96, p. A10.

141. Daley.

142. Daley, Suzanne. "Seeing Bias in Their Utility Rates, Mixed-Race South Africans Riot." *New York Times*, 2/7/97, p. A15.

143. United Nations Centre for Human Settlements (Habitat). *Survey of Slum and Squatter Settlements*. Development Studies Series, vol. 1. Nairobi: UNCHS, 1982, p. 186.

144. Carlessi, Carolina. "The Reconquest." *NACLA: Report on the Americas*, vol. 23, no. 4, Nov./Dec. 1989, p. 15.

145. United Nations Centre for Human Settlements, p. 96.

146. Cotto, Liliana. "The Rescate Movement: An Alternative Way of Doing Politics." In *Colonial Dilemma: Critical Perspectives on Contemporary Puerto Rico*. Edwin Meléndez and Edgardo Meléndez, eds. Boston: South End Press, 1993, p. 129.

147. See Jackson for photographs and first person accounts of West Berlin squatting in the 1980s.

148. Mayer, p. 159; *New York Times*, 1/5/96, p. 4

149. Mayer, p. 164.

150. "Indian Occupation Wins Abbey." *Great Speckled Bird*, 2/13/75, p. 9.

151. Dewing, p. 306.

152. Eckstein, *Power and Popular Protest*, p. 23.

153. Carlessi, p. 14.

154. Rosen, Charles. Telephone interview with the author. 8/1/94.

155. Tasker, Mary, and Woody Widrow. "Rent Strikers Withholding $25 Million." *Shelterforce,* Mar. 1976, p. 1.

156. Gornick, Vivian. "The 60,000 Rent Strikers At Coop City." *Liberation*, Spring 1976, p. 37.

157. Quoted in Tasker and Widrow, p. 1.

158. Mattera, Philip, and Donna Demac. "Keeping the Wolf Out of Co-op City." *In These Times,* 8/31/77, p. 4.

159. Bush, Larry. "Co-op City Rent Strike Settled." *Shelterforce,* Fall 1976, p. 10.

160. Bush, p. 10.

161. See Anderson, Leslie. *The Political Ecology of the Modern Peasant.* (Baltimore: John Hopkins University Press, 1994).

Chapter 6: Tactics and Mobilization

1. Tasker, Mary, and Woody Widrow. "Rent Strikers Withholding $25 Million." *Shelterforce,* Mar. 1976, p. 1.

2. Sharp, Gene. *Politics of Nonviolent Action.* Boston: Porter Sargent, 1973.

3. Tautz, Carlos. "Republic of the Landless." *New Internationalist,* no. 285, Nov. 1996, pp. 12-13.

4. Tautz, pp. 12-13.

5. Epstein, Jack. "Land Grabbers Under Fire in Brazil." *San Francisco Chronicle,* 6/28/97, p. A12.

6. *NACLA Report on the Americas,* vol. 30, no. 3, Nov./Dec. 1996, p. 1.

7. Tautz, pp. 12-13.

8. Epstein, Jack, p. A10. Mendonça, Maria Luisa. Interview with the author. San Francisco. 4/3/99. Mendonça heads the Brazil Program at Global Exchange. She has worked with the MST since 1994 and is their primary United States contact.

9. Epstein, Jack, pp. A10, A12.

10. Keta, Miranda. "Rent Strike Battles Slumlords." *People's World,* 3/27/76, p. 4; Keta, Miranda. "Tenants Win in Long Rent Strike." *People's World,* 6/5/76, p. 8.

11. O'Malley, Jan. "The Housing Struggles of Two Women." In *Women in the Community.* Marjorie Mayo, ed. London: Routledge & Kegan Paul, 1977, pp. 52-60.

12. Cited in Tasker and Widrow, p. 1.

13. For a moving fictional account of reoccupation, see Ralph Ellison's *Invisible Man* (New York: Vintage, 1980), written in 1946. Chapter 13 portrays the eviction of an elderly African American grandmother, a former slave, from her Harlem apartment. Her neighbors spontaneously overcome the single policeman sent to evict her and return the elderly woman's belongings to the apartment. Also see chapter 25, in which several tenants torch their own tenement building during a riot because of the rotten conditions. "It's the only way to git [sic] rid of it, man...." Ellison's brief accounts of tenant struggles in Harlem portray the emotional aspects of struggle more accurately than most nonfiction can approximate.

14. National Tenants Organization. "Rent Strikes." In *Tenants and the Urban Housing Crisis.* Stephan Burghardt, ed. Dexter, Michigan: New Press, 1972, p. 175.

15. Kickingbird, Kirke, and Karen Ducheneaux. *One Hundred Million Acres.* New York: Macmillan, 1973, pp. 216-218; Fortunate Eagle, Adam. *Alcatraz! Alcatraz! The Indian Occupation of 1969-1971.* Berkeley: Heyday Books, 1992, p. 147.

16. Branford, Sue, and Oriel Glock. *The Last Frontier: Fighting Over Land in the Amazon.* London: Zed, 1985, pp. 129-131.

17. Rider, Nick. "The Practice of Direct Action: The Barcelona Rent Strike of 1931." In *For Anarchism.* David Goodway, ed. London: Routledge, 1989, p. 95. Reoccupations also took place in the United States during the depression years of the '30s. Jeremy Brecher depicts one such reoccupation in the book *Strike!*, Revised and Updated Edition, Cambridge, MA: South End Press, 1997, pp. 159-160.

18. Jain, Devaki. "India: A Condition Across Caste and Class." In *Sisterhood Is Global: The International Women's Movement Anthology.* Robin Morgan, ed. Garden City, NY: Anchor Press, 1984, p. 309.

19. Raine, George. "Protest Goes on Without Eviction." *San Francisco Examiner,* 12/27/95, p. A4.

20. *New Internationalist,* Nov. 1987

21. Carlessi, pp. 14-21.

22. Rocha, Jan. "Sao Paulo: Acting on Faith." *NACLA Report on the Americas,* Nov. 1989, pp. 36-37.

23. Rocha, p. 37.

24. Denton, Peter, and Nancy Holstrom. "Ann Arbor Rent Strike." *International Socialist,* Oct. 1969, p. 20; *Vocations for Change,* Mar. 1972; Neff, Kathie, and Maureen McDonald. "Rent Strike in Ann Arbor: How to Create a Housing Crisis." *Detroit Sun,* 12/3/75, pp. 6-7.

25. Tongue, Mousey. "Redekop Drops by Flop." *Georgia Straight,* 4/30/71, p. 2; Tugwell, Tony. "Rent Strike Helps Everybody." *Georgia Straight,* 6/11/71, p. 9; Tugwell, Tony. "Wall Redekop Rent Strike." *Georgia Straight,* 6/18/71, p. 2; Tongue, Mousey. "22,000 Withheld: Rent Strike." *Georgia Straight,* 3/31/71, p. 3; Balaclava, Nigel. "Wall and Redekop is No Two-Bit Operation." *Georgia Straight,* 7/30/71, p. 2; Tenants Council. "Tenants Council Statement Re: Wall & Redekop." *Georgia Straight,* 8/20/71, p. 10.

26. "Housing Crimes Trial." *Rat,* 12/17/70, pp. 10-11.

27. For further discussion of the way in which campaign participants succeed through gaining allies from established sectors of their community, see Doug McAdam's discussion of "indigenous movement resources" in the context of African American organizing. McAdam, Doug, John D. McCarthy, and Mayer N. Zald, eds. *Comparative Perspectives on Social Movements: Political Opportunities, Mobilizing Structures, and Cultural Framings.* New York: Cambridge University Press, 1996.

28. Mangin, William. "The Barriaca: A Case History from Peru." *Anarchy,* vol. 4, no. 1, Jan. 1964, p. 20.

29. Naison, Mark D. "The Rent Strikes in New York." In *Tenants and the Urban Housing Crisis.* Stephan Burghardt, ed. Dexter, Michigan: New Press, 1972, p. 19.

30. Lawson, Ronald, and Stephen E. Barton. "Sex Roles in Social Movements: A Case Study of the Tenant Movement in New York City." In *Women and Social Protest.*

Gwida West and Rhoda Lois Blumberg, eds. New York: Oxford University Press, 1990, p. 383

31. Naison, pp. 21-22.

32. A diverse group of housing organizations attended the meeting, including the University Settlement Housing Clinic (housing clinics are tenant legal aid organizations), the East Side Tenants Council, the Educational Alliance Housing Clinic, the Presbyterian Church of the Crossroads Housing Clinic, the Downtown CORE Housing Committee, the Integrated Workers Housing Clinic, the Housing Clinic of the Council of Puerto Rican Organizations, the Stanton Housing Clinic, the Community House Tenants Association Housing Clinic, and the Negro Action Group. Lipsky, Michael. *Protest in City Politics: Rent Strikes, Housing and the Power of the Poor.* Chicago: Rand McNally & Company, 1970, p. 34, n. 8.

33. Naison, p. 23.

34. Naison, p. 33.

35. Thomas, Mary. "Unity Made the Point in St. Louis." *People's World,* 4/11/70, p. M11.

36. Dewing, Rolland. *Wounded Knee: The Meaning and Significance of the Second Incident.* New York: Irvington Publishers, 1985, p. 145.

37. The demonstrating groups included Students for a Democratic Society, Socialist Workers Party, Workers World Party, Youth Against War and Fascism, Young Socialist Alliance, Progressive Labor Party, Republic of New Africa, National Committee for Defense of Political Prisoners, U.S. Committee to Aid the National Liberation Front, Medical Aid for Indochina, the Red Collective, the Black Workers Medical Committee for Human Rights, Pittsburgh Peace and Freedom Center, Kiva Club, Concerned Physicians for Wounded Knee, Committee for Asian American Action, and some prisoners at Attica.

38. Cited in Dewing.

39. Cook, John. "Nationwide Rallies Hit Wounded Knee Trial." *Guardian,* 3/13/74, p. 4.

40. Zimmerman, Bill. "Life in the Occupied Zone." *Akwesasne Notes,* Spring 1977, pp. 11-14; Lyman, Stanley David. *Wounded Knee 1973: A Personal Account.* Floyd A. O'Neil, June K. Lyman, and Susan McKay, eds. Lincoln: University of Nebraska Press, 1993, p. 133.

41. Dewing, pp. 129, 167.

42. "American Indians Struggle to Survive." *La Raza Magazine,* vol. 1, no. 11, May (circa 1973), pp. 14-19.

43. *La Raza Magazine,* Jul. 1973.

44. *El Grito del Norte,* Apr. 1973.

45. Fortunate Eagle, p. 148.

46. Hurst, John. "The Pit River Story: A Century of Genocide." *Akwesasne Notes,* Mar. 1971, p. 44.

47. "Larzac: Bringing It All Back Home." *Peace News,* 1/19/73, p. 1.

48. "Small Farmers Against the Army." *North Country Anvil,* Jul. 1975, p. 46.

49. Rose, Jeanne. "How Peasants Rose up in Japan." *El Grito del Norte,* 12/7/70, pp. 19-20. The land movement in Okinawa, where U.S. military bases in Japan are concentrated, recently won a victory. After the rape of a sixth-grade girl by three U.S. servicemen caused huge protests and the refusal of small landowners to renew their leases to the United States, the United States agreed on April 12, 1996, to relinquish control of up to one-third of its land on the island. This small concession does little to change the U.S. military presence in Japan, however. The U.S. government will most likely redistribute its evicted military activity onto other Japanese bases (Kristof, Nicholas. "U.S. Will Return Base in Okinawa." *New York Times,* 4/13/96, p. A1).

50. Apter, David E., and Nagaya Sawa. *Against the State: Politics and Social Protest in Japan.* Cambridge, MA: Harvard University Press, 1984.

51. "Forgive Them, They Know Not What They Guard." *Indianapolis Free Press,* 5/30/69, p. 5.

52. "Forgive Them, They Know Not What They Guard."

53. "Forgive Them, They Know Not What They Guard."

54. All quotes from Oscar Lorick in this chapter are from a telephone interview conducted by the author on 4/6/98. Another radical right group of about a dozen people attempted to prevent a foreclosure of one of their farms in 1996. Led by Tom Prahl of Yellville, Arkansas, the group subscribes to Christian Identity views, as did the group that defended Lorick's farm. (Janofsky, Michael. "Home-Grown Courts Spring up as Judicial Arm of the Far Right." *New York Times,* 4/17/96, pp. A1, A14).

55. Coates, James. *Armed and Dangerous: The Rise of the Survivalist Right.* New York: Noonday Press, 1988, p. 155.

56. Ostendorf, Dave. Telephone interview with the author. 4/1/99.

57. Brooke, James. "Freeman Depended on Subsidies." *New York Times,* 4/30/96, p. A8.

58. Quoted in Camacho, Daniel. "Latin America: A Society in Motion." In *New Social Movements in the South: Empowering People.* Ponna Wignaraja, ed. London: Zed Books, 1993, p. 47.

59. Cambridge Tenants Organizing Committee. "Where We Stand." *Vocations for Social Change,* Mar. 1972, p. 26.

60. "New York City Tenants Rally in Support of Co-op City Strikers." *Win,* 3/4/76, p. 17.

61. Sklair, Leslie. "The Struggle Against the Housing Finance Act." *Socialist Register* 1975, p. 266.

62. "Kirby [*sic*] Rent Strikers Jailed for 'Contempt.'" *Peace News,* 12/14/73, p. 7. Sklair, p. 273

63. Engels, Frederick. *The Housing Question.* In *Karl Marx and Frederick Engels: Collected Works,* vol. 23. London: Lawrence and Wishart, pp. 317-391; Kautsky, Karl. *The Agrarian Question.* Pete Burgess, trans. London: Zwan Publications, 1988.

64. McNeil Jr., Donald G. "Zimbabwe Opposition: A One-Woman Tempest." *New York Times*, 5/13/96, p. A4.

65. Grovogui, Siba N'Zatioula. "The New World Order and Postcolonialism in Africa." In *Global Visions: Beyond the New World Order*. Jeremy Brecher, John Brown Childs, and Jill Cutler, eds. Boston: South End Press, 1993, p. 96; Seidman, Gay W. "Facing the New International Context of Development." In Brecher, et al., p. 181.

66. Ichiyo, Muto. "For an Alliance of Hope." In Brecher, et al., p. 157.

67. Amin, Samir. "Social Movements in the Periphery: and End to National Liberation?" In *Transforming the Revolution: Social Movements and the World System*. Samir Amin, et al, eds. New York: Monthly Review Press, 1990, p. 125.

68. Amin, et al., p. 11.

69. Schuurman, Frans J., and Ton van Naerssen, eds. *Urban Social Movements in the Third World*. London: Routledge, 1989, p. 11. See also Burbach, Roger, Orlando Nuñez, and Boris Kagarlitsky's *Globalization and Its Discontents: The Rise of Postmodern Socialisms*. London: Pluto Press, 1997.

70. Alvarado, Elvia. *Don't Be Afraid Gringo: A Honduran Woman Speaks from the Heart*. Medea Benjamin, trans. and ed. New York: Harper and Row, 1989, p. 17.

71. Collins, Joseph. *Nicaragua: What Difference Could a Revolution Make? Food and Farming in the New Nicaragua*. New York: Grove Press, 1986, p. 23-25.

72. Levine, Daniel H., and Scott Mainwaring. "Religion and Popular Protest in Latin America: Contrasting Experiences." pp. 203-216. In Eckstein, Susan, ed. *Power and Popular Protest: Latin American Social Movements*. Berkeley: University of California Press, 1989; Banck, Geert A., and Ana Maria Doimo. "Between Utopia and Strategy: A Case Study of a Brazilian Urban Social Movement." In Schuurman and van Naerssen, p. 131.

73. Broilo, Elda. Interview with the author. Santa Cruz, CA, 5/1/91.

74. Menchú, Rigoberta. *I, Rigoberta Menchú: An Indian Woman in Guatemala*. New York: Verso, 1992, p. 132.

75. Daly, Herman, and John B. Cobb, Jr. *For the Common Good: Redirecting the Economy Toward the Community, the Environment, and a Sustainable Future*. Boston: Beacon Press, 1989, pp. 102-103. For more information on the Bible and land, Daly and Cobb cite Martin L. Chaney's "Systematic Study of the Israelite Monarchy." In *Social Scientific Criticism of the Hebrew Bible and Social World*, Gottwald, N.K., ed., Semeia, vol. 37, pp. 53-76; See also, Walter Brueggemann, *The Land*. Philadelphia: Fortress, 1977; Archer Torrey, *The Land and Biblical Economics*. New York: Henry George Institute, 1985.

76. Horton, cited in Verinder, Frederick. *My Neighbor's Landmark*. Cincinnati, OH: Joseph Fels Fund, 1917.

77. Eagleson, John, and Philip Scharper. *The Radical Bible*. Maryknoll, NY: Orbis Books, 1972, pp. 17-18.

78. Ambrose of Milan, *De Nabuthe Jezraelita* (386 A.D.), cited in Charles Avila, *Ownership: Early Christian Teaching*. Maryknoll, NY: Orbis Books, 1983.

79. *The Church in the Modern World*, no. 59. Cited in Eagleson and Scharper, p. 3.

80. Menchú, p. 121.

81. Menchú, p. 132. For further Christian arguments against land concentration, see Isaiah 62: 8-9, Isaiah 65: 21-22, Leviticus 25: 23, Psalms 115: 16; and Verinder. Also see quote by Saint John Chrysostom in Ramsay MacMullen's *Corruption and the Decline of Rome* (New Haven: Yale University Press, 1988), p. 85. For interesting landlord arguments against squatters that draw from Christianity, see Julião, Francisco. *Cambão: The Yoke*. John Butt, trans. Middlesex, England: Penguin Books, 1972, p. 105.

82. Carter, April. *Direct Action and Liberal Democracy*. New York: Harper and Row, 1974, p. 66.

83. Bailey, Ron. *The Squatters*. Middlesex: Penguin, 1973, pp. 118-120, 154, 186.

84. "Rent Strike Backed by Peace and Civil Rights Coalition." *Shelterforce,* Feb. 1983, p. 4.

85. Churchill, Ward. *Struggle for the Land: Indigenous Resistance to Genocide, Ecocide and Expropriation in Contemporary North America*. Monroe, ME: Common Courage Press, 1993, pp. 306-307. See also Churchill and LaDuke. "Native North America: The Political Economy of Radioactive Colonialism." In The State of Native America. M. Annette Jaimes, ed. (Cambridge, MA: South End Press, 1992; Winona LaDuke. All Our Relations: Native Struggles for Land and Life (Cambridge, MA: South End Press, 1999); Al Gedicks. New Resource Wars: Native and Environmental Struggles Against Multinational Corporations. (Cambridge, MA: South End Press, 1993).

86. Clergy and Laity Concerned. "Big Mountain: We Shall Not Be Moved." *Akwesasne Notes,* Winter 1985, p. 7.

87. Boahen, A. Adu. *African Perspectives on Colonialism*. Baltimore: John Hopkins University Press, 1992, p. 33.

88. Cotto, Liliana. "The Rescate Movement: An Alternative Way of Doing Politics." In *Colonial Dilemma: Critical Perspectives on Contemporary Puerto Rico*. Edwin Meléndez and Edgardo Meléndez, eds. Boston: South End Press, 1993.

89. Fox, Geoffrey. "The Homeless Organize." *NACLA Report on the Americas,* vol. 23, no. 4, Nov. 1989, p. 13.

90. Carlessi, p. 14.

91. Carlessi, p. 16.

92. Tautz, pp. 12-13.

93. Inglis, Jean. "Japanese Farmers Dig in under Proposed Airport." *Liberated Guardian,* 3/31/71, p. 24; "How Peasants Rose Up In Japan." *El Grito del Norte,* 12/7/70, pp. 19-20.; In 1966, the Japanese government attempted to use eminent domain against the Sanrizuka community of 1,500 farming families who lived 60 miles outside of Tokyo to build a new international airport. Farmers and tens of thousands of supporters waged militant demonstrations from 1966 until the late '70s, when most of the families were forcibly evicted or sold their farms under pressure. Construction of the Narita International Airport began, and one runway at the airport became operational in 1979. By 1997, it was the world's sixth-largest airport in terms of passenger traffic. During the '80s, militant demonstrations of up to 6,500 people

stopped a second runway from being built on land owned by a handful of farmers who continued to resist. The government finally abandoned attempts to exercise eminent domain and has bought off many of the remaining farmers one by one with large cash settlements. Led by 75-year-old Koji Kitahara, a small group of steadfast farmers has refused to sell, and the second runway remains unbuilt (WuDunn, Sheryl. "Airfield Swallowing Potato Field, In Tiny Bites." *New York Times*, 8/26/97, p. A4).

94. Halkyard, Hilda. "Reclaiming Maori Land." *Spare Rib*, Feb. 1983, p. 8.

95. Fortunate Eagle, p. 16.

96. Lipsky, p. 74; Naison, p. 25. Lipsky refutes Gray's figures of rent strike participation on the basis of court records and interviews with reporters and "individuals with close connections to rent strike operations," implying that actual participation was one-third to one-fifth of that claimed in 1964. While Lipsky may or may not be correct, caution should be taken with the figures given by Gray. As Lipsky points out, inflated reports of rent strike participation is a strategy which, when taken as truth by the public, landlords, and city government, doubtless results in greater rent strike participation (Lipsky, pp. 73-80).

97. Paige, Jeffery M. *Agrarian Revolution: Social Movements and Export Agriculture in the Underdeveloped World.* New York: Free Press, 1975, pp. 88-89.

98. Dewing, p. 200.

99. Interviewed by John Ely. "Alternative Politics in West Germany." *Our Generation*, vol. 16, no. 2, Mar. 1984, p. 50.

100. Lawson, Ronald, and Stephen E. Barton. "Sex Roles in Social Movements: A Case Study of the Tenant Movement in New York City." In *Women and Social Protest.* Gwida West and Rhoda Lois Blumberg, eds. New York: Oxford University Press, 1990, p. 43.

101. For more on activism and the media, see Ryan, Charlotte. *Prime Time Activism: Media Strategies for Grassroots Organizing.* (Boston: South End Press, 1991).

102. Cited in Tasker and Widrow, p. 1.

103. Scott, James. *Domination and the Arts of Resistance: Hidden Transcripts.* New Haven: Yale University Press, 1990, p. 208.

104. Anonymous statement to the Liberation News Service, cited in *City Star,* 8/1/73.

105. Churchill, p. 388.

106. Bailey, p. 34.

107. Mayer, Margit. "The Career of Urban Social Movements in West Germany." In *Mobilizing the Community: Local Politics in the Era of the Global City.* Robert Fisher and Joseph Kling, eds. Urban Affairs Annual Review, vol. 41. Newbury Park, CA: Sage Publications, 1993, p. 154.

108. Broilo, Elda. Interview with the author. Santa Cruz, CA, 5/1/91.

109. President's Committee on Urban Housing. *United States Housing Needs 1968-1978.* Washington: U.S. Government Printing Office, 1967, p. 24. Since the general

fall in real incomes beginning in the early '70s, U.S. tenants have paid a much larger percentage of their incomes, on average, than did Ann Arbor tenants in 1975.

110. Neff, Kathie, and Maureen McDonald. "Rent Strike in Ann Arbor: How to Create a Housing Crisis." *Sun,* 12/3/75, pp. 6-7; Porter, Martin. "Rent Strike Spreads in Ann Arbor." *Sun,* 2/5/76, pp. 4-5; Porter, Martin. "Historic Settlement in A2 Rent Strike." *Sun,* 5/6/76, p. 3.

111. Miller, Robert. "Tenants Strike Projects." *Sun* (Detroit), 9/24/76, pp. 1, 5.

112. Stoler, Laura Ann. *Capitalism and Confrontation in Sumatra's Plantation Belt, 1870-1979.* New Haven: Yale University Press, 1985, p. 156.

113. Pleskovic, Boris. "Squatter Housing in Yugoslavia." In *Spontaneous Shelter: International Perspectives and Prospects.* Carl V. Patton, ed. Philadelphia: Temple University Press, 1988, p. 285.

114. "Seize Land: Red Power on the Warpath." *Ann Arbor Argus,* 7/8/70, pp. 8-9; Dumas, Eleanor. "Richard Oakes Renews Cause in East; Saved by Medicine Men." *Akwesasne Notes,* vol. 2, no. 7, Nov. 1970, p. 18.

115. Kickingbird and Ducheneaux, p. 215.

116. Fortunate Eagle, p. 151.

117. Weiss, Marc. "Co-op City Strike: People Changed." *New Harbinger,* vol. 4, no. 4, Winter 1978, p. 18.

118. Cockburn, Cynthia. "When Women Get Involved in Community Action." In *Women in the Community.* Marjorie Mayo, ed. London: Routledge & Kegan Paul, 1977, p. 64.

119. Savara, Mira, and Sujatha Gothoskar. "An Assertion of Womanpower: Organizing Landless Women in Maharashtra." In *In Search of Answers: Indian Women's Voices from Manushi.* Madhu Kishwar and Ruth Vanita, eds. London: Zed, 1985, pp. 134-148. The "first night" was also practiced in some areas of feudal Europe, where lords demanded the *jus primae noctis* (right of the first night).

120. Mayer, pp. 154-155.

121. Manimala. "Zameen Kenkar? Jote Onkar! The Story of Women's Participation in the Bodhgaya Struggle." In Kishwar and Vanita, pp. 149-176.

122. Manimala, p. 3.

123. Manimala, pp. 8, 10. For another example of land actions leading to women's growing political power, see Kumud Sharma's "Women in Struggle: A Case Study of the Chipko Movement." *Samya Shakti: A Journal of Women's Studies,* vol. 1, no. 2, 1984, p. 61.

Conclusion

1.   Paige, Jeffery M. *Agrarian Revolution: Social Movements and Export Agriculture in the Underdeveloped World.* New York: Free Press, 1975, pp. 165-166, 185. See also *Land or Death* by Hugo Blanco, a leader in the Peruvian land occupation movement in the early '60s (New York: Pathfinder Press, 1972). He named the book after the indigenous battle cry during the occupations, *"Tierra o Muerte."*

2. Bailey, Ron. *The Squatters*. Middlesex: Penguin, 1973, pp. 21-22.

3. Cotto, Liliana. "The Rescate Movement: An Alternative Way of Doing Politics." In *Colonial Dilemma: Critical Perspectives on Contemporary Puerto Rico*. Edwin Meléndez and Edgardo Meléndez, eds. Boston: South End Press, 1993, p. 121.

4. United Nations Development Programme, *Human Development Report 1993*. New York: Oxford University Press, 1993, p. 43; Arrighi, Giovani. "Marxist Century — American Century: The Making and Remaking of the World Labor Movement." In *Transforming the Revolution: Social Movements and the World System*. Samir Amin, et al, eds. New York: Monthly Review Press, 1990, p. 79.

5. McClune, Laura. "Clinton Administration's Labor Policy: Cooperate!" *Z Magazine*, May 1994, pp. 48-52.

6. DeParle, Jason. "In Booming Economy, Poor Still Struggle to Pay the Rent." *New York Times*, 6/16/98, p. A14.

7. Eckstein, Susan. *Power and Popular Protest: Latin American Social Movements*. Berkeley: University of California Press, 1989, p. 15.

8. Stoler, Laura Ann. *Capitalism and Confrontation in Sumatra's Plantation Belt, 1870-1979*. New Haven: Yale University Press, 1985, pp. 153-157.

9. Mayer, Margit. "The Career of Urban Social Movements in West Germany." In *Mobilizing the Community: Local Politics in the Era of the Global City*. Robert Fisher and Joseph Kling, eds. Urban Affairs Annual Review, vol. 41. Newbury Park, CA: Sage Publications, 1993, p. 150.

10. Amin, Samir. "Social Movements in the Periphery: and End to National Liberation?" In *Transforming the Revolution: Social Movements and the World System*. Samir Amin, et al, eds. New York: Monthly Review Press, 1990, p. 119.

11. United Nations Centre for Human Settlements (Habitat). *Survey of Slum and Squatter Settlements*. Development Studies Series, vol. 1. Nairobi: UNCHS, 1982.

12. United Nations Development Programme, p. 155.

13. Scott, James. *Weapons of the Weak: Everyday Forms of Peasant Resistance*. New Haven: Yale University Press, 1985, pp. 248-284; Brockett, Charles D. *Land, Power, and Poverty: Agrarian Transformation and Political Conflict in Central America*. Boston: Unwin Hyman, 1990.

14. Korten, Alicia. "Structural Adjustment and Costa Rican Agriculture." In *50 Years Is Enough: The Case Against the World Bank and the International Monetary Fund*. Kevin Danaher, ed. Boston: South End Press, 1994, pp. 56-61.

15. Aigbokhan, Ben. E. "Peaceful, People-Centered, and Ecologically Sensitive Development: A Mechanism for Promoting a New World Order." In *Global Visions: Beyond the New World Order*. Jeremy Brecher, John Brown Childs, and Jill Cutler, eds. Boston: South End Press, 1993, p. 36; United Nations Development Programme, p. 183.

16. United Nations Centre for Human Settlements. *Shelter: From Projects to National Strategies*, 1990, p. 87; United Nations Development Programme, p. 179

17. United Nations Development Programme, p. 88.

18. United Nations Development Programme.

19. United Nations Development Programme. *Human Development Report 1992*. New York: Oxford University Press, 1992, p. 45.

20. Budhoo, Davison. "IMF/World Bank Wreak Havoc on Third World." In Danaher, p. 20.

21. Walton, John. "Debt, Protest, and the State in Latin America." In Eckstein, ed. *Power and Popular Protest*, pp. 299-328.

22. Schuurman, Frans J., and Ton van Naerssen, eds. *Urban Social Movements in the Third World*. London: Routledge, 1989, p. 7.

23. Wegren, Stephen K. "Political Institutions and Agrarian Reform in Russia." In *The "Farmer Threat": The Political Economy of Agrarian Reform in Post-Soviet Russia*. Don Van·Atta, ed. Boulder: Westview Press, 1993, pp. 136, 137.

24. Prosterman, Roy L., and Timothy Hanstead. "A Fieldwork-Based Appraisal of Individual Peasant Farming in Russia." In *The "Farmer Threat": The Political Economy of Agrarian Reform in Post-Soviet Russia*. Don Van Atta, ed. Boulder: Westview Press, 1993, pp. 184-185.

25. Prosterman and Hanstead, pp. 166, 167, 179.

26. Wegren, pp. 139-140.

27. Van Atta, ed., p. 1; Prosterman and Hanstead, p. 184.

28. "Poland Approves Pay for Seized Property." *New York Times*, 5/17/95, p. A4.

29. Gorostiaga, Xabier. "Latin America in the New World Order." In Brecher, et al., p 70.

30. Feffer, John. "The Lessons of 1989." In Brecher, et al., p. 249.

31. The police used riot troops, tanks, and water cannons to evict the East Berlin squatters in November 1990; Mayer, p. 168.

32. *People's Weekly World*, 4/6/96, p. 15.

33. Swarns, Rachel. "Moscow Sends Homeless to Faraway Places." *New York Times*, 10/15/96, pp. A1, A6.

34. "Albania." *Collective Action Notes,* no. 10, Apr. 1996, p. 1; "Albania Police Evict Families, Arrest Journalist." Reuters News Service, 2/1/96.

35. Perlez, Jane. "In a Land Adrift, the Albanian People Drift, Too." *New York Times*, 7/16/97, p. A4.

36. Gorostiaga, p. 70.

37. Simon, Harold, Executive Director of the National Housing Institute. Telephone interview with the author. 4/5/99.

38. Wolpold, Martin, coordinator for Latin America at FIAN-International. Telephone interview with the author. 4/6/99.

39. Alvarado, Elvia. *Don't Be Afraid Gringo: A Honduran Woman Speaks from the Heart*. Medea Benjamin, trans. and ed. New York: Harper and Row, 1989, p. 146.

Resources

Activist Groups
and Bookstores Associated with Activist Groups

Advisory Service for Squatters, 2 St. Paul's Road, London N1, UK, (171) 359-8814, advice@squat.freeserve.co.uk, www.squat.freeserve.co.uk.

Blackout Books, 50 Avenue B, New York, NY, (212) 777-1967.

Bound Together Books, 1369 Haight St., San Francisco CA 94107, (415) 431-8355.

Federation of Southern Cooperatives/Land Assistance Fund, 2769 Church St., East Point GA 30344, fsc@mindspring.com, www.federationsoutherncoop.com.

FIAN-International (Germany), P.O. Box 102243, D-69012 Heidelberg, 49-6221-830620. In the United States you may call the FIAN office in Oakland, CA, at (510) 654-4400.

Homes Not Jails, 558 Capp St., San Francisco, CA 94110, call (415) 282-5525, fax (415) 282-6622, or visit their web site at iww.org/housing/hnj/.

Homes Not Jail Boston, P.O. Box 390351, Cambridge, MA 02139, (617) 287-9494, red@iww.org, www.geocities.com/CapitolHill/7996/.

Left Bank Books, 92 Pike St., Seattle WA 98101.

Longhall Infoshop, 3124 Shattuck Ave., Berkeley CA 94705, (510) 540-0751.

Missouri Rural Crisis Center, 1108 Rangeline St., Columbia, MO 65201, (573) 449-1336, morural@mail.coin.missouri.edu,www.inmotionmagazine.com/rural.html.

National Family Farm Coalition, 110 Maryland Ave. NE, Washington D.C., 20002, (202) 543-5675, nfsc@nfsc.net, www.nfsc.net.

National Housing Institute, 439 Main St., Orange NJ 07050, (973) 678-9060.

Program on Nonviolent Sanctions and Cultural Survival, Weatherhead Center for International Affairs, Harvard University, 1737 Cambridge St., Cambridge MA 02138, (617) 441-5400, hdc-www.harvard.edu/cfia/pnscs.

Via Campesina, Apt. Postal 3628, Tegucigalpa Honduras, 504-220-1218, viacam@gbm.hn.

Video Resources

Acts of Defiance. Directed by Alec G. Macleod; written, narrated and produced by Mark Zannis. Montreal, Quebec: National Film Board of Canada, 1992. 104 minutes. Discusses Mohawk land and sovereignty claim and the conflict with Canadian armed forces and non-Indian citizens during the summer of 1990 in Kahnawake and Kanesatake near Oka.

Down and Out in America. Directed and narrated by Lee Grant. Joseph Feury Productions. Oak Forest, Illinois: MPI Home Video, 1987. 57 minutes. Presents the family farm crisis as a pattern structured to transform North American agriculture from independent to corporate control, relating this to plant closures, the movement of capital from Northern to Southern hemispheres, homelessness and poverty. Depicts occupations of a Midwest bank by farmers and New York City housing and a Los Angeles vacant lot by the homeless.

Elvia: the Fight for Land and Liberty. Directed and written by Laura Rodriguez. San Francisco, CA: Alturas Films, 1988. 27 minutes. Chronicles the activism of Honduran peasant Elvia Alvarado aimed at occupying land and empowering women in the context of a failed agrarian reform.

The Fall of the I Hotel. Produced and Directed by Curtis Choy. San Francisco, CA: Crosscurrent Media, 1993. 55 minutes. Documents the broad-based movement of senior citizens, churches, labor groups, and community activists to preserve the International Hotel in San Francisco as low-cost housing for the elderly and as an Filipino-American community center. The primary theme of direct action revolves around resistance to an eviction ordered in January 1969 which the owners and police were unable to carry out until August of 1977, when they faced 5,000 blockaders.

Land Rights: The Mayans and the Guatemalan Military. Produced by Johnathan Schwartz and Interlock Media, 1985. Focused on oppression of indigenous Guatamalans, the conflict between the military government and the Indians is viewed in historic, economic, and racial contexts.

Newe Segobia is Not for Sale: the Struggle for Western Shoshone Lands. Produced by Jesse Drew. San Francisco, CA: Mission Creek Video, 1993. Depicts the battle between Western Shoshone activists Mary and Carrie Dann and the United States Bureau of Land Management over control of lands in North-eastern Nevada.

Books and Periodicals

Indigenous Occupations and Eviction Resistance

Branford, Sue and Oriel Glock. *The Last Frontier: Fighting Over Land in the Amazon.* London: Zed Books, 1985.

Churchill, Ward. *Struggle for the Land: Indigenous Resistance to Genocide, Ecocide and Expropriation in Contemporary North America.* Monroe, Maine: Common Courage Press, 1993.

Crow Dog, Mary, with Richard Erdoes. *Lakota Woman.* New York: Harper Collins, 1991.

Fortunate Eagle, Adam. *Alcatraz! Alcatraz! The Indian Occupation of 1969-1971.* Foreword by Vine Deloria, Jr. Photo essays by Ilka Hartmann. Berkeley: Heyday Books, 1992.

Jaimes, M. Annette. "The Pit River Indian Land Claim Dispute in Northern California." In *Critical Issues in Native North America,* Vol. 2. Ward Churchill, ed. International Work Group for Indigenous Affairs Document No. 68. Copenhagen: International Work Group for Indigenous Affairs, 1991.

Parlow, Anita. *Cry Sacred Ground: Big Mountain USA.* Washington, D.C: Christie Institute, 1988.

Voices from Wounded Knee, 1973: in the Words of the Participants. Rooseveltown. New York: Akwesasne Notes, 1975.

Community Resistance to Development

Alaska Beach Residents Association. "A Squatter Community and Its Problems of Land Ownership." *Carnets de l'enfance,* vol. 40 (1977), pp. 116-121.

Apter, David E. and Nagaya Sawa. *Against the State: Politics and Social Protest in Japan.* Cambridge: Harvard University Press, 1984.

Bahuguna, Sunderlal. "Women's Nonviolent Power in the Chipko Movement." In *In Search of Answers: Indian Women's Voices from Manushi.* Madhu Kishwar and Ruth Vanita, eds. London: Zed Books, 1985, pp. 129-133.

Fukushima Kikujiro. "Sanrizuka: 1966-1977." *Ampo,* vol. 9, no. 4 (1977), pp. 2-34.

Jain, Shobita. "Standing Up for the Trees: Women's Role in the Chipko Movement." In *Women and the Environment.* Sally Sontheimer, ed. London: Earthscan Publications, 1988, pp. 163-178.

Khoon, Chan Chee & Chin Wey Tze & Loh Kok Wah. *Thean Teik, the other side of development.* Penang: Aliran, 1983.

Scott, James C. *Weapons of the Weak: Everyday Forms of Peasant Resistance.* New Haven: Yale University Press, 1985.

Sharma, Kumud. "Women in Struggle: A Case Study of the Chipko Movement." *Samya Shakti: A Journal of Women's Studies,* vol. 1, no. 2 (1984), pp. 55-62.

Land Occupation

Alvarado, Elvia. *Don't Be Afraid Gringo,* Medea Benjamin, ed. and trans. San Francisco: Food First, 1989.

Blanco, Hugo. *Land or Death.* New York: Pathfinder Press, 1972.

Fox, Geoffrey, ed. *The Homeless Organize.* Special Issue. *NACLA Report on the Americas,* vol. 23, no. 4, Nov./Dec. 1989.

Julião, Francisco. *Cambão — The Yoke: The Hidden Face of Brazil.* John Butt, trans. Middlesex, England: Penguin Books, 1972.

Manimala. "Zameen Kenkar? Jote Onkar! The Story of Women's Participation in the Bodhgaya Struggle." *Manushi,* (Jan./Feb. 1983), pp. 2-16. Also in *In Search of Answers: Indian Women's Voices from Manushi.* Madhu Kishwar and Ruth Vanita, eds. London: Zed Books, 1985, pp. 149-176.

Menchú, Rigoberta. *I, Rigoberta Menchú: An Indian Woman in Guatemala.* Elisabeth Burgos-Debray, ed. Ann Wright, trans. London: Verso, 1992.

Montemayor, Jeremias U. *Ours to Share.* Manila, Philippines: R & X Book Store, 1966.

Paige, Jeffery M. *Agrarian Revolution: Social Movements and Export Agriculture in the Underdeveloped World.* New York: Free Press, 1975.

Rent Strikes and Tenant Struggles

Brill, Harry. *Why Organizers Fail: the Story of a Rent Strike.* Berkeley: University of California Press, 1971.

Brodsky, Barry. "Tenants First: FHA Tenants Organize in Massachusetts." *Radical America,* vol. 9, no. 2 (Mar. 1975), pp. 37-46.

Burghardt, Stephan. *Tenants and the Urban Housing Crisis.* Dexter, Michigan: New Press, 1972.

Chaskelson, Matthew, Karen Jochelson and Jeremy Seekings. "Rent Boycotts, the State, and the Transformation of the Urban Political Economy in South Africa." *Review of African Political Economy,* vol. 40 (Dec. 1987), pp. 47-64.

Hartman, Chester, Dennis Keating and Richard LeGates with Steve Turner. *Displacement: How to Fight It.* Berkeley: National Housing Law Project, 1982.

Lawson, Ronald, with the assistance of Reuben B. Johnson III. *The Tenant Movement in New York City, 1904-1984.* New Brunswick, NJ: Rutgers University Press, 1986.

Lawson, Ronald and Stephen E. Barton. "Sex Roles in Social Movements: A Case Study of the Tenant Movement in New York City." *Women and Social Protest.* Gwida West and Rhoda Lois Blumberg, eds. New York: Oxford University Press, 1990, pp. 41-56.

Lipsky, Michael. *Protest in City Politics: Rent Strikes, Housing and the Power of the Poor.* Chicago: Rand McNally, 1970.

Rider, Nick. "The Practice of Direct Action: The Barcelona Rent Strike of 1931." In *For Anarchism.* David Goodway, ed. London: Routledge, 1989, pp. 79-105.

Shelterforce, 439 Main St., Orange, NJ 07050, (973) 678-9060.

Sklair, Leslie. "The Struggle Against the Housing Finance Act." *Socialist Register* (1975), pp. 250-292.

Urban Squatting

Angel, Shlomo, et. al. *Land For Housing the Poor.* Singapore: Select Books, 1983.

Blondet, Cecilia. "Establishing an Identity: Women Settlers in a Poor Lima Neighborhood." *Women and Social Change in Latin America.* Elizabeth Jelin, ed. J.Ann Zammit and Marilyn Thomson, trans. London: Zed Books, 1990, pp. 12-46.

Cotto, Liliana. "The Rescate Movement: An Alternative Way of Doing Politics." In *Colonial Dilemma: Critical Perspectives on Contemporary Puerto Rico.* Edwin Meléndez and Edgardo Meléndez, ed. Boston: South End Press, 1993.

Jackson, Frank, ed. *Squatting in West Berlin.* London: Hooligan Press, 1987.

Lotta Continua. "Take Over the City." Ernest Dowson, trans. *Radical America,* vol. 7, no. 2 (1973), pp. 79-111.

Mayer, Margit. "The Career of Urban Social Movements in West Germany." In *Mobilizing the Community: Local Politics in the Era of the Global City.* Robert Fisher and Joseph Kling, eds. *Urban Affairs Annual Review,* vol. 41, (1993). London: Sage Publications, pp. 149-170.

Paris, Chris, and Gerry Popplestone. *Squatting: a bibliography.* London: Centre for Environmental Studies, 1978.

Pleskovic, Boris. "Squatter Housing in Yugoslavia." In *Spontaneous Shelter: International Perspectives and Prospects.* Carl V. Patton, ed. Philadelphia: Temple University Press, 1988, pp. 277-300.

Preston, Jon, et. al. *Ideal Home: Survival Edition.* London: Hooligan Press, 1986.

Schuurman, Frans, and Ton Van Naerssen. *Urban Social Movements in the Third World.* London: Routledge, 1989.

Shadow, POB 20298, New York, NY 10009, (212) 631-1181 message phone; (212) 330-8150, list of demonstrations and meetings.

Stokes, Susan C. "Politics and Latin America's Urban Poor: Reflections from a Lima Shantytown." In *Latin American Research Review,* vol. 26 (1991), pp. 75-101.

Wakefield, Stacy, and Grrrt. *Not For Rent: Conversations With Creative Activists in the U.K.* Amsterdam/Seattle: Evil Twin Publications, 1996.

Wates, Nick. *Squatting: The Real Story.* London: Bay Leaf Books, 1980.

Historical and Philosophical

Avila, Charles. *Ownership: Early Christian Teaching.* Maryknoll, NY: Orbis Books, 1983.

Avila, Charles. *Peasant Theology.* Thailand: World Student Christian Federation Asia Region, 1976.

Baird, Vanessa, ed. *Our Earth Our Home: Land Rights and Wrongs.* Special Issue. *New Internationalist* (Nov. 1987), No. 177.

Berens, Lewis Henry. *The Digger Movement in the Days of the Commonwealth.* London: Simpkin, Marshall, Hamilton, Kent, 1906.

Bhave, Vinoba. *From Bhoodan to Gramdan.* Tanjore: Sarvodaya Prachuralaya, 1957.

Christman, Henry. *Tin Horns and Calico.* New York: Henry Holt, 1945.

Devyr, Thomas Ainge. *The Odd Book of the Nineteenth Century: or Chivalry in Modern Days.* Greenpoint, NY: published by the author, 1882.

Emerson, Ralph Waldo. "Hamatreya." *The Norton Anthology of Poetry.* Alexander W. Allison, et. al, ed. New York: W.W. Norton, 1970.

Garland, Hamlin. "Under the Lion's Paw." In *Main-Travelled Roads.* New York: Harper, 1956.

George, Henry. *Progress and Poverty.* New York: Robert Schalkenbach Foundation: 1948

George, Henry. *The Land Question and Related Writings.* New York: Robert Schalkenbach Foundation, 1982.

Guatemalan Church in Exile. *Reflections: The Clamor for Land.* A collegial pastoral letter by the Guatemalan Bishops' Conference. May 1988. Managua, Nicaragua.

Hayes, Thomas Wilson. *Winstanley the Digger.* Cambridge: Harvard University Press, 1979.

Hirsch, Max. *Democracy Versus Socialism.* Third Edition. New York: Henry George School of Social Science, 1939.

Magón, Ricardo Flores. *Land and Liberty,* compiled by David Poole. Sanday, U.K.: Cienfuegos Press Ltd., 1977.

Midnight Notes Collective. *The New Enclosures.* (*Midnight Notes,* no. 10). Jamaica Plain, Massachussetts: Midnight Notes, 1990.

Mill, John Stuart. *Principles of Political Economy.* Toronto: Univeristy Press, 1965.

Neruda, Pablo. *Canto General.* Jack Schmitt, trans. Berkeley: University of California Press, 1991.

Ogilvie, William. *Birthright in Land: An Essay on the Right of Property in Land.* New York: Augustus M. Kelley, 1970 [1782].

Paine, Thomas. "Agrarian Justice," *Precursors of Henry George.* Max Beer, ed. London: G. Bell and Sons, 1920.

Proudhon, Pierre-Joseph. *What is Property?* Cambridge: Cambridge University Press, 1994 [1840].

Spence, Thomas. *The Political Works of Thomas Spence.* H.T. Dickinson, ed. Newcastle Upon Tyne: Avero 18th Century Publishers, 1982.

Spencer, Herbert. *Social Statics.* New York: Robert Schalkenbach Foundation, 1954.

Tennyson, Hallam. *Saint on the March, The Story of Vinoba.* London: Victor Gallancz, 1955.

Tolstoy, Leo. *A Great Iniquity.* New York: B.W. Huebsch, 1920.

Tolstoy, Leo. "How Much Land Does a Man Need?" *Twenty-Three Tales,* Louise and Aylmer Maude, trans. London: Oxford University Press, 1971.

Tolstoy, Leo. "Two Letters on Henry George," *The Novels and Other Works of Lyof N. Tolstoï,* Essays, Letters, Miscellanies. New York: Charles Scribner's Sons, 1899.

Tolstoy, Leo. *The Slavery of Our Times.* Aylmer Maude, trans. Great Britain: The Whitefriars Press Ltd.

Tolstoy, Leo. *What Then Must We Do?* Aylmer Maude, trans. London: Oxford University Press,.1960.

Wallace, Alfred Russel. *Land Nationalisation, Its Necessity and Its Aims.* London: Swan Sonnenschein & Co., 1906.

Wicksteed, Charles. *The Land for the People,* Second Edition. London: Swan Sonnenschein, 1894.

Winstanley, Gerrard. *The Law of Freedom and Other Writings.* Christopher Hill, ed. Cambridge University Press, 1983.

Index

Stewart B. McKinney Homeless Assistance
Act, 31-33, 34, 37, 80
Stokes, Susan, 129
Stoler, Laura Ann, 116
Stone, Aisha, 72
Strike Coordinating Committee, 175
Struggle for the Land (Churchill), 168-169
Student Non-violent Coordinating
Committee, 156
substance abuse. *See* drugs
Sumatra, 116, 179, 188
Sumo Indians, 111
Survey of Slum and Squatter Settlements
(UN), 136, 137, 188
sweat equity, 21-22, 32, 71
Switzerland, 129

T

Tacamiches, 64, 69, 104; eviction of, 3,
40-45, 48, 49-50; repression of, 99, 115.
See also Chiquita Brands International
Tanganyika. *See* Tanzania
Tangwena, 97-98
Tanjung Morawa (Sumatra), 116
Tanzania, 127, 131
Taos Pueblo, 132
Taquinaz, Venancio, 115
Teamsters union, 155
Tela Railroad Company, 44, 45, 46
tenant unions: Ann Arbor Tenants Union,
152, 178; Cambridge Tenants Organizing
Committee, 85, 161; East Orange Tenants
Association, 85, 145; in England, 112;
gender and, 82-83; National Tenants
Organization, 90, 94, 155; Newark Tenant
Organization, 123; New Jersey Tenants
Association, 85, 145; in New York City,
82-83, 86, 91-92, 140-142, 154-155, 175;
San Francisco Tenants Union, 10, 19,
22-23, 27; Vancouver Tenants Council,
152-153
Terio, Kuya, 51
terrorism, 129-130
Terrorism in Northern Ireland (Lee), 130
Thaxton, Ralph, 127
Third World, 7, 78-79, 84, 154, 187;
housing security in, 194-195; international
investment in, 104, 107-108, 142, 163;
labor in, 62, 73, 75; land distribution in,
55; land occupations in, 9, 11, 84;
repression of, 104-105; revolutionary

movements in, 126-130, 163; squatting in,
39, 72, 136, 188-190; urbanization in,
12-13, 189, 195. *See also specific
countries and continents*
Thomas, E.T., 24
Tierra y Libertad settlement, 128
title deeds, 18, 31, 62, 138, 149; adverse
possession and, 27-28, 68-70; Homes Not
Jails and, 20, 22, 35, 36, 37; in Honduras,
44, 45-47. *See also* expropriation
Tolstoy, Leo, 6, 7, 8, 53
Tompkins Square Park, 103, 117-118
trade unions. *See* labor movement
Transforming the Revolution (Amin, et al.),
163
Treaty of Ruby Valley, 169
Trony-Sunrise Associates, 178
Twain, Mark, 8
Tzeltal Indians, 126

U

UNICEF (UN International Children's
Emergency Fund), 146
Union de Campesinos de Queretaro, 80-81
United Brands, 40, 41, 45-46. *See also*
Chiquita Brands International
United Farm Workers, 156, 161
United Fruit, 40, 45-47, 104. *See also*
Chiquita Brands International
United Nations, 84-85, 151; Charter on
Social and Economic Human Rights, 52;
Committee on Economic, Social and
Cultural Human Rights, 50; Conference on
Human Settlements (Habitat), 136;
Conference on Human Settlements
(Habitat II), 84; Department of
Agriculture, 55; Development Program,
54, 189; Food and Agriculture
Organization (FAO), 15, 54, 145;
International Covenant on Economic,
Social, and Cultural Rights, 45; squatting
data from, 12-13, 188; on tenure security,
136, 137; women's land ownership data
from, 55. *See also* UNICEF
United Parcel Service (UPS), 186
United Press International, 174
United States, 39, 109, 187-188; housing
movements in, 11, 13, 186; land
ownership in, 55-56, 57; Native
Americans and, 12, 173; Third World and,
84, 104-105, 111

About the Author

Anders Corr's writing and photography on the subject of land and housing movements have been published in the *New York Times*, the *San Francisco Examiner*, the *Progressive*, *Z Magazine*, *San Francisco Bay Guardian*, *San Francisco Weekly*, the *Independent*, *Everybody's News* (Cincinnati), *Anarchy Magazine*, *Fifth Estate*, *Slingshot*, *Kick It Over*, *Land and Liberty*, *Squat Beautiful*, *Tenant Times*, *Street Spirit*, and *Spare Change*. A former squatter himself, he co-founded the Santa Cruz Union of the Homeless. He has been deported from Kenya and Mexico for refusal to carry a passport and has been charged or arrested 17 times and spent a cumulative of 4 months in jail for trespassing or trespass-related charges. He is currently studying political science at Yale. Anders maintains a squatting website at http://members.theglobe.com/hotsquat/. Readers may contact him at: anderscorr@yahoo.com.

About South End Press

South End Press is a nonprofit, collectively run book publisher with more than 200 titles in print. Since our founding in 1977, we have tried to meet the needs of readers who are exploring, or are already committed to, the politics of radical social change. Our goal is to publish books that encourage critical thinking and constructive action on the key political, cultural, social, economic, and ecological issues shaping life in the United States and in the world. In this way, we hope to give expression to a wide diversity of democratic social movements and to provide an alternative to the products of corporate publishing.

Through the Institute for Social and Cultural Change, South End Press works with other political media projects—*Z Magazine*; Speakout, a speakers' bureau; and Alternative Radio—to expand access to information and critical analysis. If you would like a free catalog of South End Press books, please write to us at: South End Press, 7 Brookline St., Cambridge MA 02139-4146. Visit our website at http://www.lbbs.org/sep/sep.htm.